HUNTING HISTORY

A WRITER'S ODYSSEY

HUNTING HISTORY

A WRITER'S ODYSSEY

ERNA PARIS

AT BAY press

Winnipeg

Hunting History
A Writer's Odyssey

Design and layout by Lucas c Pauls and M. C. Joudrey.

Published by At Bay Press October 2025.

Library and Archives Canada cataloguing in publication is available upon request.

ISBN 978-1-998779-88-8

Printed and bound in Canada.

This book is printed on acid free paper that is 100% recycled ancient forest friendly (100% post-consumer recycled).

First Edition

10 9 8 7 6 5 4 3 2 1

atbaypress.com

Canada Council for the Arts | Conseil des arts du Canada

We acknowledge the support of the Canada Council for the Arts.

Manitoba Arts Council | Conseil des arts du Manitoba

With the generous support of the Manitoba Arts Council.

Funded by the Government of Canada | Canada

CERTIFIED CANADIAN PUBLISHER

FSC www.fsc.org MIX Paper | Supporting responsible forestry FSC® C016245

CONTENTS

FOREWORD

ERNA PARIS WAS DETERMINED to complete this book in the months before her death from breast cancer in February 2022. Whenever her strength permitted, she returned to her writing desk—a clutter of handwritten scribbles on notepads, sticky notes, and even lipstick-blotted napkins—and resumed the task she had pursued, on and off, for a decade: making sense of her life as a writer.

Her understanding grew clearer as the prospect of her own death loomed. Although the subject of her writing had ranged across continents and centuries, she came to understand that her life's work had been driven by a compelling need to understand how mass crimes and historic injustices could occur even in seemingly peaceful and tolerant societies, and how these crimes have been remembered—and misremembered—by those directly involved, their compatriots, and subsequent generations. Driven to answer such questions, she wrote seven acclaimed works of literary non-fiction and won twelve national and international writing awards for her books, feature writing, and radio documentaries.

We know this about Erna because she was our mother. We know that her passion for justice was not simply a professional interest; we imbibed it at the dinner table and carry it with us still. The humanity that informed her writing—her ability to empathize with those she interviewed and to reveal the complexity of real people to her readers; her moral clarity about human rights and the restorative power of justice; and her belief in *tikkun olam*, a Hebrew expression referring to the capacity and responsibility of individuals to "repair the world"—not only shaped her work. It guided how she lived.

We therefore understood, long before she died, that this book would be far more than a literary memoir. Erna wanted to distill the lessons of a lifetime, grappling with questions that had haunted her since her youth. Our stepfather, Thomas M. Robinson, her husband of forty-one years and soulmate for even longer, understood this, too—so we were all relieved when she finished the manuscript in the weeks before she passed away. By completing her "quest," as she called it, she had, in her own way, defied death.

In doing so, she also revealed her tenacity—both to her calling as a writer and to her ideals. Discussing the possible title of this book, months before she died, one of us had jokingly suggested "There's Always Hope!" because, although Erna delved into some of the worst crimes humans can commit, she never succumbed to pessimism or its more corrosive cousin: cynicism. She recognized that she'd been born into, and lived through, a period of great hope—of recovery from the Second World War and of growing liberal optimism, which seemingly peaked at the end of the twentieth century. But as the world darkened in subsequent years, rather than dismissing these ideals as naïve (as many have recently done), she took a longer view, maintaining that human rights, the rule of law, accountability for wrongdoing, truth-telling, and reconciliation would always be the basis for any lasting peace, both within societies and between them.

She also understood that these values must be actively nurtured and sustained in the face of powerful counterforces, including the very human tendency to turn inwards, to treat others as "the other," and to evade the necessary but often painful task of facing difficult truths. In other words, she was a resolute optimist, but no utopian. She recognized that the work of promoting these values would never end, because it could never be fully achieved—including in her own homeland, Canada. As she warns in this book, "There is no guarantee of long-term success in diverse societies...." She saw herself and her writing, and ultimately her life, as part of this never-ending work.

When she died, Tom put everything aside to edit her manuscript, while working with literary agent Michael Levine to secure a publisher. A year later, when her family and friends gathered to celebrate Erna's life—belatedly, due to the pandemic—Tom announced the book was under contract.

Although he had formally retired from his position as a professor of classics and ancient Greek philosophy, Tom remained deeply engaged in scholarly writing and continued to travel to conferences around the world. Just days after Erna's celebration of life, he embarked on a multi-stop trip to deliver academic papers and visit friends in Europe. In Paris, his first stop, he suffered a grievous accident and was rushed to hospital in a coma. We flew to Paris the following day and were at his bedside when he passed away later that week.

It was a painful time, not least because our father, Jacques Paris ("Claude" in this book), had also recently died.[1] But it seemed somehow fitting that we were now in Paris, a city that both Tom and our mother had adored, and where Jacques and Erna had first met. She writes in this book about her formative experiences in the city, and how she loved returning throughout her life. One of her and Tom's favourite museums was the *Musée de Cluny* in the Latin Quarter, particularly for its sixteenth-century tapestries, still bursting with colour and fantastical images. A partial reproduction of one tapestry, "The Lady and the Unicorn," hung prominently on the wall of their Toronto home for decades.

---

1 The only names that Erna changed for this book were those of our father, his family in Bayonne, France, and his friend in nearby Guiche. Although all of these individuals are now deceased—the last of them, including our father, passed away after our mother but before the publication of this book—their pseudonyms remain in the text.

It took a few days for us to organize the return of Tom's body to Canada, where he would be buried with that of our mother, and we spent part of that time wandering around some of their—and our—favourite places. We, too, had a special attachment to Paris (not just because of our family name). One of us, Michelle, was born there, as you will read; and both of us had studied there and spent time living in the city as adults.

We also undertook the grim task of gathering Tom's personal belongings from the hotel room he had occupied, and there we found small but deeply touching surprise. On the desk lay a museum ticket stub, issued just one day before his accident. The image on the ticket was of "The Lady and the Unicorn." Tom, still in mourning for Erna, had visited the *Musée de Cluny*.

So we went there, too, and found a quiet spot on a bench facing "their" tapestry, thinking of our mother—as he surely had—and of him.

Back in Canada, the task of bringing this book to publication now fell to us. Working through the final edits brought us back into conversation with both our mother and stepfather—a remarkable, if poignant, gift. It also reminded us of our mother's extraordinary journey of discovery, her humour and compassion, her resilience and drive, and her rare ability to tell stories that are at once deeply personal and profound reflections on the best and worst of humanity. We take some solace in knowing that her words live on.

Roland and Michelle Paris
Ottawa and Toronto
July 2025

PRELUDE

HOW STRANGE IT IS to know, in retrospect, that the direction of my life was determined on a single day, from a single experience. The date was November 11, 1960—Remembrance Day, as it happens. I was twenty-two years old, a recent graduate of the University of Toronto, and I had just arrived in France for a year of further study.

At the time of the encounter, I was accompanying two new friends, both French, on a short trip to Alsace along the German borderlands—a region I had never seen, but closely imagined, having read Alphonse Daudet's *La dernière classe*, a short story about the painful loss of the territory during the Franco-Prussian War almost a century earlier.

The event itself was an unexpected visit to a Nazi death camp hidden in the forests of the Vosges Mountains. I could not know then that my adult life would be shaped in consequence. What I did understand, when I returned to Toronto a year later, was that I had been embroiled in experiences I could not have imagined as a protected Jewish child growing up in Canada in the 1950s. Almost all these happenings were connected to war. Or wars; they bled into one another. Just days before my visit to Alsace, the father of a new friend, a magistrate in the city of Nantes, had taken me to Oradour-sur-Glane, a town in the Limousin region that was destroyed by the occupying Nazis during the Second World War, and had cried as he recounted the story. On that same trip into Central France, I had attended a Catholic mass—my first—in a small village church where the priest invoked the ancient liturgy, calling my people "perfidious." During that year abroad I would encounter antisemitism for the first time. I would participate in student demonstrations against the Algerian War that was then raging in the colony, but also in the streets of Paris. By the time I returned to Canada in August 1961, I had been thoroughly, inadvertently politicized. What I didn't know was that I would spend my life exploring the psychological and cultural underpinnings that had produced the darkness with which I was confronted. Once I became a writer, that is. For writing has been key. How else would I know what I think?

This book is a reflection on that writing life—on my incremental efforts to tell the historical and political stories that reveal the best and the worst of what makes us human. For I concluded long ago that no behaviour lies beyond the boundaries of humanity, even at the far reaches of depravity. I have come to this understanding through reading and study, but primarily through meeting countless actors around the world: the perpetrators of major crimes, their victims, the hopeful activists, the historians (trustworthy or propagandists), and the political leaders who shape the way we view the past and the present.

For the most part, I have approached my work through physical travel to the places of study (almost always alone), observation, conversation, and reflection. It has been a personal odyssey, a lifelong adventure that has been, by turn, illuminating, thought-provoking, funny, occasionally dangerous, and inspiring, particularly in terms of the individuals I encountered and the intense, if transient connection that frequently emerged between us. I used to reject the idea that my compulsion to persist in this work might be described as an obsession, but I am now more accepting of the idea, for had I not embarked upon this voyage I don't know how I would have incorporated truths I could neither accept, forget, nor assimilate. There was a moment in 1979, when I first viewed the BBC series *The World at War* and saw the mountains of corpses in the just-liberated Nazi concentration camps, that I felt despair. I wrote to my husband, Tom, who was on sabbatical in England, that I couldn't live in a world where such things had happened and might happen again. But this lasted only a moment, because, on reflection, I believe it was my obsessive (yes, obsessive) curiosity that kept me on track—as well as an inherent optimism. I simply had to know how "such things" had happened, and under what circumstances. I have had to believe that prevention was possible, and that I might make even the tiniest contribution towards our collective understanding.

Although the Holocaust was the initial trigger for my explorations, I knew early on that I would extrapolate from that tragedy, for it became clear to me that what I was observing was universal, not particular. Gradually, incrementally, my investigations led me from an early examination of Canadian Jewish history and identity issues—where *did* I belong in this country?—to a larger sphere. This is the story of the slow emergence of awareness that led me from one piece of what seemed like a puzzle to the next, almost without my knowing. For example, I was half-way through writing my fifth book, *The End of Days*, a work about how and why the most open, pluralist country in medieval Europe became the most closed, with an inquisition and two ethnic expulsions, before it occurred to me that I had been writing a series on related themes.

In retrospect, I see the topics that have preoccupied me as topics generated by questions I have posed. How do we remember the past, and how is history exploited? How does the narrative of the past shape the future? Where is the best and the worst in human psychology likely to lead us politically? What are the origins of blood racism? Can we predict the consequences of a shift in the social consensus regarding minorities and majorities in multi-ethnic societies? What is the significance of justice and accountability for criminal acts? How can we protect ourselves from human frailty in world affairs?

I am aware as I articulate these questions of how presumptuous they may sound. In truth, I have never allowed myself, until now, to articulate the big picture in this way, possibly so as not to frighten myself into abandoning the work, possibly because I simply didn't have the vision while I was deeply immersed in things. I certainly don't claim to have succeeded in any of these thematic pursuits, or to have discovered definitive answers, only to have pushed myself relentlessly.

In preparing this narrative I have re-visited my work in search of surprising moments and experiences that propelled me forward—moments that triggered awareness. I have thought about what I might have learned since I wrote these books and may now view differently.

Since I am tracking the themes that have characterized my work, the structure of this book is largely chronological. I initially wondered what led a young, middle-class Jewish-Canadian woman to pursue this path. Today, I have a better understanding of the origins, but there was, in addition to the seminal experiences of my student year in France, the influence of my unusual family, especially my remarkable father, whose ideas of child raising—influenced by then-contemporary theories of behaviour-modification—were sometimes worthy of Barnum and Bailey. The liberal environment of mid-twentieth-century Canada, which will be familiar to many readers, also contributed to the choices I made as a young journalist starting out in the 1970s at the beginning of the feminist movement in Canada. I was lucky to work with superb editors, such as Doris Anderson of *Chatelaine* magazine, and Robert Fulford, then editor of *Saturday Night* magazine, both of whom mentored me. As I wrote about feminist issues, I learned about human rights. Because I spoke French fluently, I was assigned to conduct interviews with major Quebec activists during the tumultuous 1970s. The exposure to nationalism on my doorstep, so to speak, triggered memories of the Algerian liberation struggle I had briefly lived through with only limited comprehension. It also opened me to the nature of collective grievance and violence.

So, this is the story of a writing life—part journey through modern cultural history in Canada and the world at large; part personal story; part larger lessons about pluralism and its fault lines that I have learnt, absorbed, and tried to pass on. It is the fruit of a private space, for I have also lived as a friend, daughter, wife, mother, and now grandmother to three. As such, my life has had a reasonably conventional outer shape and rhythm; but my inner life has been driven by obsession and unwitting design.

Erna Paris
Toronto

CHAPTER ONE

NATZWEILER-STRUTHOF

THE ROAD STEEPENS SHARPLY as it climbs into the thick silence of the Vosges mountains. After a few kilometres a small sign indicates the proximity of a camp. A camp? I am twenty-two years old, and newly arrived in France to do graduate work at the *Sorbonne*. Today I'm travelling on a lark with two recent acquaintances, Jean and Christian, both students like myself.

We detour onto a side road and discover the entrance. We wait in silence. After what seems a long while, an elderly impassive-looking man materializes. He leads us into a small low-slung building of several rooms. In the first, a large black oven sits cold and silent. Once it burned corpses, he explains without expression. "A Jewish woman and her adolescent daughter were the first to die here." I grow taut with horror, overcome by the instant crush of my imagination. That mother is my mother; I am her terrified child.

I stumble after the others into an adjoining room, where there stands a large waist-high table with interior channels for run-off blood.

I hallucinate: It looks like an outsized version of my mother's silver well-and-tree serving platter.

Blithely, unknowingly, we had entered Natzweiler-Struthof: the only death camp created by the Nazis on occupied French soil. And like the source waters of a river whose tributaries snake across distant landscapes, my chance visit to this deserted site will shadow me forever.

IN RETROSPECT I WAS laughably ill-equipped for life "elsewhere" when I arrived in France in September 1960 for a year-course titled *Cours de civilisation française* at the *Sorbonne*. My parents had been in favour of adding this "finishing school" patina to my university career. They liked to think of themselves as Francophiles, because they had visited Europe just after the war and been awe-struck by France, where people drank wine and ate un-Canadian oddities such as stewed intestines, breaded pigs' feet, and garlicky frogs' legs, and where men frequented hair salons, not no-nonsense barber shops as they did in Toronto. To me, Paris was a place of magic. My childhood friend, David Lewis Stein, and I had talked incessantly about this earthly Shangri-La throughout the more boring of our university undergraduate classes. We fantasized about happy hours sipping absinthe in a Montparnasse café, where we might perhaps don little round eyeglasses à la Toulouse Lautrec; or sitting in the famous cafés of *Saint-Germain-des-Prés*, such as *Les Deux Magots* or the *Café de Flore*, where we were certain Simone de Beauvoir and Jean-Paul Sartre had scribbled their masterpieces on paper tablecloths while kindly receiving the sycophants who circulated about them hoping to borrow fame through proximity. Seated in the back row of our Philosophy of Mind classes, tuning out a professor who was droning on about "disembodied minds" (how ridiculous), we evoked the fragrance of the shiny brown chestnuts being roasted on Paris streets next to Metro stations whose steps, according to the pictures, rose steeply from subterranean depths into the sunlit air. We were certain we could sniff the Gitanes cigarettes whose musky fragrance perfumed the air, and the croissants and fresh baguettes being baked nearby. I pictured handsome Frenchmen sporting black berets tilted rakishly on their heads, and stylish women with wasp waists prancing along the sun-blotched pavements as though incarnating their city's proud glory.

France still dreamed of its former grandeur then, and the studies I had in mind at the *Sorbonne* were designed to instruct and impress young foreigners. I, however, needed no impressing, having proudly read Françoise Sagan's novel *Bonjour tristesse* about the soulful awakening of a teenage girl. And since I planned to spend innumerable hours at the cafés in *Saint-Germain-des-Prés*, I began to wonder whether I too might scribble an immortal work on a paper tablecloth while the waiters, accustomed as they were to young literary geniuses in their midst, smiled their encouragement.

French Civilization was without doubt a fine subject, but I had a different, though still inchoate, plan in mind. Since writing immortal prose in public places was unlikely to consume all my leisure time, my second project was to tackle the overdue business of losing my virginity, and putting a distance between myself and my parents was a prerequisite. Not surprisingly, I met my objective without delay—at *Le Relais Odéon* café on the *boulevard Saint-Germain*, a student hang-out a few minutes' walk from *Saint-Germain-des-Prés*. It was an early-autumn day, the light was golden-hued, and to my delight the air was indeed scented with roasting chestnuts being sold from street kiosks *and* the aroma of Gitanes. In the years to come, a mere hint of this tobacco would conjure up scenes from this first year abroad.

It was inside the smoky interior of *Le Relais Odéon* (where I also encountered that most awful of devices known as a Turkish toilet—a dirty hole in the floor of a cubbyhole—that I happened upon the presumptive candidate. Jean Riffaud was a sometime law student with an immediately endearing manner. It wasn't just the way he casually draped his scarf around his neck in the jaunty style of French students, or the sight of his longish hair curling sweetly over his shirt collar, or his way of looping the sleeves of his bulky sweater over his shoulders, or even his earnest anti-colonialist politics, which were natural enough, given that the brutal Algerian War was raging and he expected to be called up for military service (he was plotting an escape to Switzerland, he later confided)—it was the whole of him, the "Frenchness" of him. Almost immediately he invited me to tour the Left Bank in the used convertible his father had bought him, but what truly astounded me was his behaviour as we careened through the streets of Paris. At each intersection he stood upright on the car seat, pumped the air with his fist, and roared *"Vieux cons!"* at no one in particular. *Con* was, and is, a commonplace French obscenity, but with my imperfect grasp of the language I thought he was yelling at *vieux comptes*. Can this be true? I asked myself excitedly. Counts? Aristocrats? Of course! I decided. I'm in Europe, where there really are such people.

Jean and I arranged to meet the next day at my student residence.

I lived at the *Cité Universitaire* in the *Maison Néerlandaise* (Dutch House), where the concierge, a stout middle-aged woman, looked us girls up and down when we left for classes in the morning and returned in the evening. She was inordinately proud, because the previous year the Shah of Iran had visited Paris and fallen in love with a young Iranian student who happened to live in our residence. For the duration of my year-long stay at the residence, this custodian of our dress code and manners spoke incessantly of "our Farah Diba." The beautiful young empress-to-be, whose life later turned to tragedy when her husband was deposed and exiled, had seemingly bequeathed enduring fame upon us all. Sometimes I wondered whether the future empress had felt the same biting chill that I did in that penitential place. To save money, the managers turned on the heat during the day, when staff (but not students) were present, and off in the evening, when the former went home and we underlings returned from our classes. The Rhine River froze that winter, blocking shipments of coal destined for Paris. The police rounded up homeless vagabonds at night to warm them in prison cells. I had never encountered homeless people, and the sight of men and women sleeping on the streets clutching their bottles of cheap wine disturbed me. I was cold, but not like them. My father believed that incremental degrees of hardship bequeathed character, and my pitiful monthly allowance did not provide for a warm jacket.

Nonetheless, I felt lucky to reside at *La Maison Néerlandaise*, not least because my roommate Chantal did not speak English, and graciously corrected my stammering efforts to speak her language; and because I couldn't wrap my tongue around the four-syllable word *Néerlandaise*, which obliged me to practice constantly in case I got lost and had to tell a stranger where I lived. I was determined to learn the language well. I could put together a few phrases, thanks to my fine teachers at Forest Hill Collegiate in Toronto, but I couldn't understand anyone whose accent differed from my own, which included just about everyone, and for the first few weeks I lived in terror lest I be asked a question. I read dictionaries for pleasure, and practiced on whoever I could cajole into "conversing" with me.

I knew I was improving when, about six weeks into my stay, I woke one morning and found—miraculously, that I could pronounce all four syllables of the word *Néerlandaise* in proper sequence. About the same time, I realized excitedly that I had understood a class lecture in its entirety. In my astonishment, I rushed out into the courtyard of the *Sorbonne*, filled with joy. I was also reading superb literature. Jean Racine's *Andromaque*, the author's reinvention of the great drama by Euripides, in which the noble, now enslaved wife of Hector, heir to the destroyed kingdom of Troy, laments her tragic fate. (So moved was I that I later named a pet canary Astyanax, after Andromaque's murdered baby son.) I read Corneille's *Le Cid*, in which I encountered the wrenching conflict between romantic love and filial duty. Overcome with sympathy for Chimène and her young lover Rodrigo, I was certain I understood the demands of honour as Corneille depicted them. "Valour does not depend on age," he wrote. I understood. I, too, was young.

The ex-patriot experience was of a whole. I was falling in love with France and its heady culture, with the anything-goes street life of Paris, with the mellifluous cadences of the French language, and especially with the music of the day. In Canada, songs like "How Much Is That Doggy in the Window?" topped the charts. In France, in the autumn of 1960,

Jacques Brel sang his melancholic composition, "*Quand on n'a que l'amour*," and Edith Piaf defied her life's struggles with "*Non, je ne regrette rien*." Unexpectedly, I had encountered the brimming world of adult emotion: a bitter-sweet universe of love, regret, and sorrow, an inexhaustible realm of wished-for experience I wanted to devour whole.

But how? The chanson that affected me most was sung by Gilbert Bécaud, whom I imagined mysteriously arrayed in a trench coat à la Graham Greene, leaning pensively against a wall, smoking a cigarette. His lyrics spoke to my heart. "*Et maintenant, que vais-je faire/De tout ce temps que sera ma vie...?*" (What will I do now/With all the time that stretches before me...?)

I imbibed Bécaud's lyrics about the untrammelled life that opened endlessly before me, and I wondered anxiously how I might shape the limitless days.

ON OCTOBER 31, 1960, just days before the fateful trip to Alsace, Jean Riffaud drove me and my Toronto friend, Ruth Kellermann (we had travelled to France together), to his grandmother's home in the tiny village of Sauviat-sur-Vige in the region of the Massif Central. Jean's parents were visiting, and he wanted us to meet them.

For the sake of propriety, Ruth and I were housed in a small pension-style hotel next door to the Riffaud family home, where the only heat came from a ceramic bed-warmer the proprietor had kindly placed between our sheets; washing water was provided in a large pitcher accompanied by a basin. Outside the foggy window stretched the main street of the village, a mud track where oxen still pulled produce-laden carts and the locals still wore the mud-resistant wooden clogs known as *sabots*. The road was lined on both sides with ancient row-houses built of yellowish stone with red-tile roofs. A church steeple rose to the sky where the road ended, and the fields began. The woman who cleaned Jean's grandmother's home told me proudly she had never left the village. "Why would I want to go elsewhere when Sauviat is the most beautiful place on earth?" she asked, a puzzled expression creasing her brow.

Jean's parents were respectable middle-class burghers: his father was a magistrate in the coastal city of Nantes, his mother a housewife, full-bodied, perfume-scented, and seemingly benevolent. On a subsequent visit to their Nantes home, she invited me to bathe in her private bathtub. Her soap was divinely fragranced with almonds, and I have spent all my years looking unsuccessfully for its like, aware that the sensory memory has been transformed into something akin to Proust's cherished *madeleines*. At the grandmother's dinner table, to which Ruth and I were invited, Monsieur Riffaud the elder gently interrogated us. What a curious twosome we must have seemed. We were both Jewish, possibly the first of the genus our hosts had met. Furthermore, our parents had allowed us to travel unchaperoned across the sea. Madame Riffaud would never have permitted this, she later informed me; nice girls stayed at home until they were married. As dinner came to an end, Monsieur Riffaud announced his conclusions to the table: I was spirited and "volatile," he proclaimed. (I didn't know the latter word in either French or English, and quickly looked it up.)

On a darker note, two surprising events occurred during that visit to Sauviat-sur-Vige, both of which pointed bony fingers toward my future. The first transpired during a religious service to celebrate All Saints Day. Sauviat, with a population of a few hundred souls, was too small to maintain its own priest, so a designated cleric did the rounds on important holy days, and at 11 a.m. on November 1, 1960, he was saying mass in the village. It was my first visit to a Catholic church, and I was awed by the simple thirteenth-century stone edifice. As an untravelled Canadian, I could barely fathom such ancientness (which later helped me to understand one of my aunts who declared, while visiting me in Paris, that everything on the gorgeous eighteenth-century *Île-Saint-Louis* "would be seen as a slum in Toronto."). I didn't know the liturgy, and I had been enjoying the intriguing formalities of the service. Then came the sermon, when to my consternation I heard the priest excoriate the "perfidious Jews," following which the congregation, including Jean and his family, prayed for the conversion of my faithless people. I felt suddenly alone and visible; a pang of fear sucked the breath from my lungs. But the villagers, dressed in their worn Sunday best, showed no special emotion on their ruddy peasant faces. Neither Jean nor his parents glanced towards Ruth or me.

The following day Monsieur Riffaud took us to the nearby site of Oradour-sur-Glane, where, on June 10, 1944, the retreating Nazis had rounded up and massacred 642 civilians, then set their bodies on fire. The burned-out village had been left intact as a silent memorial. The standalone facades of stone houses displayed empty-socket window frames. Rubble had been piled against broken walls.

I had never seen a war site, nor had I met anyone who anguished over a tragic historical event as did Jean's father that day. I can still hear the tightness in his barely audible voice, still see the moisture in his eyes. Just sixteen years had passed since this atrocity was perpetrated. He wanted his son's friends—two Canadian innocents—to know.

I whispered my shock to him; he seemed grateful that I cared.

And so it was that my upcoming visit to Natzweiler-Struthof, just nine days later, had a double introduction of sorts in the remote French village of Sauviat-sur-Vige.

I'm not sure how I processed my visit to the Natzweiler-Struthof death camp in the days and weeks that followed. Perhaps I buried it deep inside so I could continue to live normally. Perhaps I spun a tight web around it the way a spider wraps objects for further use. But there was an immediate aftermath. November 11 was Remembrance Day in France as elsewhere, and not long after my friends and I exited the camp we came across a small knot of veterans who had gathered around a little war memorial—another thing I had never seen. The men were mostly old and bent survivors of the First World War, in which a paralyzing million-and-a-half French soldiers and ordinary citizens had perished. In my altered state, what struck me even more than the sight of the veterans was the monument itself—its sculpted figures of women and children grieving piteously. It was a second consecutive blow to my psyche: I was seized by a visceral hatred of war and violence that has never left me.

Back in Canada the following year, I submitted a short Remembrance Day article to the *Toronto Star* in which I criticized not just war, but the heroic language of glorification. I wrote that the suffering women and children that I'd seen on the monument in Alsace were the authentic face of conflict, truer than any depiction of victorious soldiers bearing arms. My piece was rebuffed by an angry editor who accused me of disrespecting those who had fought for our freedom. Undeterred, I resubmitted it as a letter-to-the-editor and the newspaper published it—my first appearance in print. I was thrilled.

What I now know is that the shock of the Natzweiler-Struthof experience fashioned my future. From that day I felt compelled to hunt down how it was possible for ordinary-seeming human beings to commit atrocities. I became ultra-sensitized to racism of all kinds. I felt fear when I passed hateful graffiti scrawled on the Paris city walls and in the Metro: "*A bas les juifs*" (Down with the Jews) was the most common of them during the postwar years. I felt fear when the woman I had thought was a friend raised her arm in a Nazi salute and shouted, "*Je suis fasciste*!" Protected child that I was, I had never encountered antisemitism before coming to France, although other young Jews growing up in Toronto were not so lucky.

My emerging political awareness was jolted into being by other psychic assaults. France was engaged in active conflict: the Algerian civil war had leaped across the Mediterranean and was being fought in the streets of Paris, especially in the student quarter around the *Sorbonne*.

There were few North American foreign correspondents in continental Europe at that time, meaning that the violence in France had barely registered in Canada. All the same, I find it retrospectively alarming that I knew so little about this bitter struggle, including the presence of shoot-outs in Paris cafés, and that I was naively unaware that the country had been in turmoil for more than half a century. I soon learned that from 1894, when antisemitic lies about Alfred Dreyfus, a Jewish-Alsatian military officer, triggered a long-lasting culture war over who was or was not "French," until September 24, 1960, the day Ruth Kellermann and I first stepped off the train at the *Saint-Lazare* station in Paris, there had been little respite. I also learned that the trauma of the First World War had not dissipated; that the Left versus Right politics of the interwar years (fascists versus communists versus socialists) had triggered something close to civil war; that the humiliation of defeat by the Nazis in June 1940, followed by the German Occupation and the Vichy Collaboration, was still an open wound, as was the loss of colonial French Indochina (including Vietnam) in May 1954. I learned most of this by reading the daily newspapers. Modern French history was still so raw and unprocessed that events of fifty years earlier still made news.

The war to decolonize Algeria had exploded in the immediate aftermath of the Indochina defeat, but in 1960 I knew as little about this conflagration as I did about what would soon be named the Holocaust. Later in my stay, I would learn more about the cultural context of the Algerian debacle. And what I discovered alongside history was the ferocious language of ideological passion.

In the autumn of 1960, the Left Bank student quarter, including the *Odéon*, the *Sorbonne*, the *Panthéon*, and the streets around the *boulevard Saint-Michel* was electric with tension. The earlier anti-colonial Indochina war had been fought with volunteers and local conscripts, but that policy had been converted to conscription when the liberation battle ignited in Algeria. The reasons were clear enough: Algeria was just across the Mediterranean, not half-way around the globe. More importantly, it was considered a part of Metropolitan France itself. (The puzzling myth that "France" teleports itself elsewhere in the world still applies to its remaining colonies—an idea worthy of the Mad Hatter. Geography is geography; call these places what you will, but they are not "France," which happens to be physically located somewhere else. There is one such place just a stone's throw from the coast of Newfoundland in Atlantic Canada, the two small islands of Saint-Pierre and Miquelon, where the approximately 6,000 residents proudly send an elected senator to the French National Assembly and import their wine and cheese and buttery delicacies from the French mainland.)

It was the idea of Algeria's being an indivisible part of France, and the violent rejection of this idea, that fueled the hatreds that made the Algerian War an all-encompassing conflict. During my student year, daily demonstrations took place in the streets of Paris. Battle-ready police wagons with blackened windows positioned themselves within the student quarter, one of them permanently blocking the entrance to the *Sorbonne*. For the first time I feared the police, whom I had been taught to respect. Someone I knew was beaten with a truncheon in plain daylight; other acquaintances disappeared into jail. "*Les flics! On se tire!*" (Cops! Run for it!) the students shouted when a police wagon appeared on the horizon.

Leftists who opposed the war as an exploitative fascist enterprise supported the Algerian National Liberation Front (FLN) largely through the filter of Stalinist propaganda (the Communist Party of France was one of the largest in Europe) and the emerging ideology of Maoism. Famous intellectuals, including Jean-Paul Sartre and Simone de Beauvoir, expressed their outrage at the racism and the violence that characterized France's colonial occupation of Algeria. Unbeknownst to me, Sartre, de Beauvoir, Marguerite Duras, François Truffaut, and the composer Pierre Boulez, among others, had published an open letter titled the "Manifesto of the 121" just days before my September 1960 arrival, in which they called on the government to recognize the Algerian uprising as an authentic struggle for self-determination. They denounced the use of torture by the French army—a fact both widely known and loudly denied—and demanded that the government respect the rights of conscientious objectors. Equally powerful propaganda on the Right invoked the indissoluble union of France and Algeria: to separate the two, they argued, would be to cleave asunder the parts of a united whole.

The war and the politicization of my French student friends, including Jean, amazed me. I was hardly a communist—I barely knew what a communist was—but I had recently graduated from the University of Toronto in Honours Philosophy and English, and considered myself a reasonably aware person. I had already considered (in the abstract) where

I might place myself along the spectrum of freedoms and human rights, were I ever to be put to the test. When I accidentally found myself engaged in a political cauldron I had no doubts about my allegiances.

To join my new friends in opposing the Algerian War was an easy choice for a young, liberally minded Canadian. It must also be said that I had little to fear, except the prospect of possible deportation should I do something rash. My French friends, on the other hand, risked prison. I understood this gamble better on February 13, 1961, when I joined a demonstration of some 500,000 anti-war protesters marching through the streets of Paris with signs, floating banners, shouts, and raised fists. Such scenes are now familiar to North Americans, but before the age of widespread television news, few among my inexperienced generation would have witnessed anything comparable.

The tightly packed demonstration collected people at every intersection, while mounted police in flanked formation arrayed themselves at the head of the march. The crowd surged, the line of horses held, people fell in the crush. I felt myself being pushed from behind. I feared I would fall. The singing, the shouting, the screams of people being trampled… increasingly fearful, I elbowed my way to the side, then rejoined the demonstration at the rear where escape was possible.

Eventually the human caravan stopped before a large building: the headquarters of the Communist Party of France, then led by Maurice Thorez.

"I'm Canadian," I whispered anxiously to a stranger standing next to me.

"Leave immediately," she warned. "Any foreigner caught here will be deported."

I didn't stay around to query the veracity of this important information. Ducking tightly packed bodies, I fled the chanting crowd. The thought of being unceremoniously shipped home to Toronto easily trumped my newborn commitments.

The rhythmic mantras of that war have remained engraved in my memory. The Algeria-is-France cohort would chant *"Algérie française!"* in a pulsing syllabized staccato. Our side would retort "*Le fascisme ne passera pas!*" (Fascism will not pass!) in similarly rhythmic cadences. On one cold winter day, students from both camps lined up on either side of the *boulevard Saint-Michel*. They shouted, chanted, hurled insults at one another. Before long they were pelting rocks across the road.

ON A MORE DISTANT battlefront, the war in Algeria also played a role in my virginity project. Although several months had passed, Jean and I had not "gone all the way," as people said then. As it turned out, he was also a virgin, and as nervous as I. We had a place, should we desire to use it: a room in the *Hôtel Danemark* on the *rue Vavin*. It was just large enough for a single bed and a wash basin, which (as far as I could determine) he used only to pee into. I refrained from commenting on this practice, but I did once ask him why he didn't wash. "My father never washes," he replied approvingly. That, apparently, explained everything.

We talked tentatively about the Maginot Line, then diffidently decided to move into action. At 5:00 pm on the appointed day, we climbed the stairs to his room, but as we began to warm to the idea, a loud chant, accompanied by persistent drumming, arose from the street below: *"Les Français dans la rue! Les Français dans la rue!"* (Frenchmen, into the street!). It was a call to an anti-war demonstration—and Jean was definitely anti-war. He hesitated, as did I, wondering where his patriotic allegiances would carry him. Happily, he chose me, though no Maginot Lines were crossed that day, after all.

Not long afterwards came my first visit to his parents in Nantes. To my surprise, Madame Riffaud—the same matron who would later introduce me to almond-scented soap—already viewed me as her prospective daughter-in-law. On the very afternoon of our arrival, she invited me on a shopping trip. Within minutes I found myself staring into the display window of a jewellery store.

"Which of the diamond engagement rings do you like, my dear Erna?"

I must have stammered something that sounded polite and unintentionally agreeable, because she charged ahead with the next item on her agenda.

"Would you consider converting to Catholicism?" she asked.

Taken aback, I replied flippantly: "If I were to convert it would be to practice my *own* religion!"

She seemed undeterred by the bold, not to mention rude, young woman standing beside her.

"My dear Erna," she persisted, "Monsieur Riffaud and I are so very fond of you, but we do have a question." She paused, and she peered at me closely.

"Why did the Jews kill Christ?"

Anger burned my cheeks. "I have no idea. I wasn't there," I said.

For decades—from the Dreyfus Affair at the end of the nineteenth century until the end of the Second World War—antisemitism had been a staple of French discourse. I was undoubtedly the first Jew Madame Riffaud had ever met. She must have believed all Jews knew the answer to this bedevilling question.

But my love affair with Jean soon came to an end. One evening, as we sat in the *Le Sélect* café on the *boulevard Montparnasse*, I tentatively wrote a short phrase on a piece of paper and shyly passed it to him. "*Je veux tout*," I confided. (I want everything.)

What I wanted to convey was my compelling desire for experience: my longing to explore, to travel, to learn; the urge to swallow, to incorporate, the world.

A triumphant smile spread across his lips.

"I knew it!" he cried. "You Canadians are all materialists!"

We didn't see much of one another after that moment of mutual incomprehension, although in retrospect I'm not sure why I expected him to divine my occult meaning.

Jean's absence merely made room for another encounter, also in a café, as it happened. On my roommate Chantal's 21st birthday, five of her friends descended upon *Le Lutèce* on the *boulevard Saint-Michel* to celebrate.

Sitting next to us was a handsome young man in sunglasses reading France's best daily, *Le Monde* (a point in his favour, in my estimation). As is the way in crowded French cafés, he had only to turn his head to join us. When we left to continue the party elsewhere, he came, too.

"I am a car," he told me in approximate English, indicating his mode of transportation.

We all set off for the Jardin des Plantes to visit the zoo. (Given that we were barely post-adolescent, this seemed a fitting thing to do.) Later, all six of us slept on the floor of Chantal's friend's attic-apartment, where I managed to finagle a place next to our guest.

His name, he said, was Claude. And I would marry him less than a year later.

CHAPTER TWO
BEGINNINGS

UNKNOWINGLY, I HAD PREPARED myself—and been prepared by others—for the later encounters that would shape my future, and for the questions about history that would envelop me. Reinforcing these influences was the postwar liberal ethos of Canada that first touched me as a young child. I remember the day in 1948 when the principal of Forest Hill Public School festooned the corridor walls with the pages of the newly minted United Nations Universal Declaration of Human Rights. I still see my child self standing on tiptoe in the hallway, straining to take in the document. "All human beings are born free and equal in dignity and rights," it declared.

"That must mean me," I thought with amazement, "and I'm not even ten years old!" I couldn't wait to inform my parents about my newly discovered rights, especially my authoritarian father. The excitement I felt that day may have heralded my future preoccupation with equality and civic respect. What I do know with greater certainty is that the pronouncement about individual freedom and rights in a document where adults promised protection made me feel secure and happy.

Liberal optimism was ubiquitous in Canada after the devastation of the Hitler era in ways even a child could comprehend. Outside of school, the notion that humankind (known then as mankind) was blazing a happy trail into the future was reinforced for me every Sunday morning at Holy Blossom Temple on Bathurst Street, where I attended "religious school." The Temple curriculum had little to do with religion then, focusing instead on the meaning of Jewish holidays as interpreted through a lens of social democracy, and in our classrooms we absorbed the contemporary *Zeitgeist* of hope. We sang lustily:

We'll soon be one world, one world, nations great and strong,
And with friendship to unite us, there'll be no one left to fight us.
We'll be all for one and one for all!

We also warbled a militaristic ditty about the heroic Palmach, the elite fighters of the underground army that had been founded to protect the Jews of Palestine before the creation of the State of Israel; and another that was sung by the equally heroic Zionist pioneers as they worked their newly planted fields. Human universality, not the particularism of Zionism, characterized Holy Blossom Temple in that era—a lesson I imbibed. Many immigrant families, including my own, were determined assimilationists who wanted nothing more than to be accepted as unhyphenated Canadians.

It was at Holy Blossom Sunday School that I first learned about what had happened to the Jews of Europe. Fourteen years old, half-asleep after a Saturday night party, I wink one eye open to see Heinz Warschauer, the principal of the religious school, enter our classroom.

I know little about Mr. Warschauer, except that he seems old and has a foreign accent. This makes him supremely uncool and tiresome. He seems to be carrying a small record player.

He says a pleasant hello, sets the player down on the desk, and places a record on the turntable. We fall quiet. What's he up to? Then a sound fills the room—a piercing screech, a continuous scream, punctuated by words in another language. I sit bolt upright, my breath catching in my throat. It is the voice of Adolf Hitler at one of his rallies, says Mr. Warschauer. The crooked smile he often displays is absent as he removes the record from the player. Then, with as much gentleness as possible, he tells us about Auschwitz, that people our age were murdered there, that girls my age chose death rather than be defiled.

In a 1972 memoir published in *Toronto Life* magazine, I recalled the moment:

> The day that knowledge burned through my head I wrote my first heroic adolescent poem about Jewish girls my age (of course) who had chosen to die rather than be "used" and I cried with shame and disbelief over my desk in my parents' mansion on Rosemary Lane (what a name) with the all-Canadian pennants (FHCI rah-rah) pinned up on the walls.

All the same, the knowledge in question remained superficial throughout my early years—and unwelcome. It did not prepare me for the Natzweiler-Struthof experience.

I may now have a better understanding of Heinz Warschauer. By suggesting to the impressionable youngsters seated before him that these doomed young women may have had a choice, he had perhaps hoped to soften the blow. Decades later, I came across him by chance in a shopping mall. He was sitting alone on a metal bench—solitary, and now truly old. I sat beside him, took his hand in mine, and thanked him for the kindness he had shown to us children, even as he revealed an unspeakable horror.

Before the day he played his record, I knew about the Second World War in the way of a small child. "Turn your back on the German submarine!" we urged one another in our schoolyard as we skipped rope. In a now-yellowed "First Grade Exercise and Workbook" preserved by my parents, in which I practiced printing inside the lines, I wrote: "There was an invasion in Europe ot-day (*sic*). We hope the war will soon be over." Scrawled above this entry was the date: Tuesday, June 6, 1944.

I soon absorbed more about the importance of these events. On May 8, 1945, just two days after my seventh birthday, I watched in amazement from the window of my father's downtown office at the corner of Yonge and Albert Streets as a jubilant victory parade careened wildly down the street. Strangers embraced, people sat precariously on the roofs of moving cars, others wrapped themselves in streamers and ribbons, and everyone cheered and waved Union Jack flags over their heads.

It was typical of my wily father to leave me alone to take in this remarkable sight. Although a chartered accountant by profession, Jules Newman was a born educator, and his ideas about learning almost always included direct experience, presumably because he was compulsively curious, himself. He would make a solo trip around the world in his early 1950s, long before many North Americans had discovered Western Europe.

Dad kept a shrunken head from South America on a shelf in his office, along with other curiosities. It had long straight hair, fine features, and a real expression—it seemed to me. I have no idea how, or where, he got it, although I subsequently learned there was a thriving black market for such heads in the 1940s—a demand that likely encouraged murderous head-hunting expeditions. There was no political correctness associated with amassing such trophies back then; in any case, my father was not one to worry about such things. His irrepressible inquisitiveness about the human condition, which he imparted to me, made him an aficionado of what used to be called "freak shows," and we often went together to the Canadian National Exhibition to view The Fat Man, The Snake Lady, performing midgets, smiling dwarfs, and a host of others who were paid to be stared at. It was at one of these shows that I first saw a human embryo bottled in brine, long before pictures of pre-natal development were available in puritanical Canada. Planning such encounters for my edification undoubtedly amused my father. He was high-spirited and whimsical.

Dad had an early dictating machine in his office, a strange contraption with a removable cylinder, which he encouraged me to explore on my frequent visits. The Dictaphone resided in a small room of its own, and when Dad shut the door, leaving me alone, I confided my childhood secrets to my dear friend, the moving cylinder. It never occurred to me that he might listen to what I had said afterwards—as I'm sure he did, laughing all the while.

My mother, Christine, was an artist, a pianist, and temperamentally ill-suited to both marriage and motherhood, as she once confessed to me in a sweet moment of candour. She and I were both compulsive readers, stopping on the street to decipher a scrap of detritus on the sidewalk, provided it was print. Anything with words on it—a flapping notice about a lost cat tacked to a lamp post, or a request for garbage removal—was worth a detour. We talked about world affairs and everything else, I the child and she the adult who had dreamed of a university education before being channelled into stenography for lack of money. It was she who taught me to read a daily newspaper.

One of her favourite books was *The Intellectual Life* by the British art critic Philip Gilbert Hamerton, which she shyly presented to me when I was about fifteen. First published in 1873, the work advised a fictional young gentleman about how to live the good life. Hamerton disputed the odd Victorian idea that a life dedicated to personal morality was incompatible with a life dedicated to the mind. He thought talented young gentlemen should "employ their time and talents to help the intellectual advancement of mankind," a credo my shy mother adopted in theory, but not in practice, since she once confided to me that she loved mankind but didn't really like people. Although British culture circa 1873 did not acknowledge female intellectual potential, Hamerton did generously suggest that some women might develop their minds in small ways, and Mother may have attached herself to this remote dream. Still, Philip Gilbert Hamerton must certainly have seemed old-fashioned even to her in 1925, the year she dated her copy of the book. It was the height of the Suffragette movement, and she was a blossoming nineteen-year-old.

My mother loved Alfred Lord Tennyson, Robert Browning, and the earlier Romantics. She read and re-read Byron, Keats, and Shelley, and especially Shakespeare's sonnets, as did her sister Beth, also a pianist, who had a tiny leather-bound volume of the poems always at hand until she was felled by dementia in her nineties.

Intelligent, reclusive, unworldly, almost certainly suffering from undiagnosed depression, Mother played Beethoven on her Steinway grand piano, a gift from my father, and gave piano lessons to the neighbourhood children. With the small amount of money she earned, she bought a small upright for my two children, which still sits (largely ignored) in our living room. She tried to appear interested in the boundless pursuits of my father, which included canoeing and fishing in Algonquin Park long before it became popular, along with riding incognito to his Toronto office on a motorcycle, whizzing by his unknowing clients who were stalled bumper to bumper in the morning rush-hour traffic. (Dad told me that his staid clients might disapprove of seeing the man who calculated their taxes zipping past them on a motorbike, but I suspect he simply enjoyed the twin freedoms of motorcycling and travelling in disguise.) Years later, he transported me daily in this fashion to my classes at the University of Toronto, where I disembarked in a private laneway near Varsity Stadium. We both wore large helmets and black cover-all capes, like Batman and Robin.

While Mother took refuge in Beethoven's sonatas, Father took over parenting with a vengeance. He read aloud at the dinner table, then orchestrated discussions in which everyone present was expected to have an opinion, including my younger siblings Peter and Jill, and any of my friends who happened to be present. My friends adored my father, who officially dubbed them honorary daughters and sons, although several among them later confessed that they'd been intimidated, if not scarred for life, by the conversational demands of our family dinner table.

Unsurprisingly, Dad's favourite book was *Life with Father.* He also read from *Cheaper by the Dozen*, a work that romanticized the paterfamilias of a large brood. The dad in that story was an efficiency expert who thought a household could be run like a factory; he blew a whistle when he wanted the family to assemble and generally cracked a benign whip. (I'm convinced my father would have gone the whistle route too, if he had thought he could get away with it.) My own dad was so efficient as a chartered accountant that he invented a systems approach to office organization that became widely in use in Toronto accounting firms.

He read aloud from George Orwell's *Animal Farm*, perhaps believing that a parable about talking animals would help us absorb the author's lessons about propaganda and the abuse of power. *Animal Farm* and the dinner-table conversations that followed each reading were my introduction to ideology and politics, and I still maintain a strong personal connection with "George." I love his wry irony, his respect for clear language as a vehicle for clear thinking, and his uncompromising truthfulness. His book *Nineteen Eighty-Four* cemented our already happy relationship. I imagined him in an ill-fitting English suit with dandruff flakes on his shoulders. I wanted to talk to him about cabbages and kings—about the meaning of life.

Oh, the things we discussed in my family. Politics. Ideas. Books. I used to joke wearily that we debated everything including "the price of wheat in China," which struck me then as the most remote subject imaginable. We kids were always "on," as was anyone else with the misfortune, or perhaps the fortune, to be invited to our table. On such occasions we would all be summoned to think about what books we might want to have with us were we to find ourselves, like Robinson Crusoe, stranded on a desert island, and to offer reasons for our choices.

Dad bribed his children with nickels and dimes to try unusual foods. On his daily peregrinations through Simpson's department store en route to the venerable Arcadian Court restaurant on the eighth floor, with its crystal chandeliers, wrought-iron railings, and arched windows, he would drop by the import section to survey what edible horror he might spring upon us next. One day he brought home a small tin of rattlesnake meat. Long before fresh shellfish was available in Toronto, he proffered oysters in a can. I ate most of the slimy offering just to show him that I could, and I spent the rest of the evening throwing up in the bathroom—but I had stood my ground. He was powerful, larger than life. Standing my ground was a daily exercise in survival.

My mind remained on hyper-alert long after the daily dinner-table years had passed. Someone, somewhere, might be about to challenge me—on any subject. I was in my thirties when a friend of my parents apologized to my mother for having engaged me in a controversial discussion about politics. Mother brushed off his qualms with a laugh. "Don't worry," she advised, "her father has been arguing with her since she learned how to talk."

Dad's lessons didn't end with talk. Between dinner courses my siblings and I were frequently commanded to stand and perform imagined emotional states. "Suppose you came home and found that your puppy had just been killed by a car," was one such assignment. As I explored the greater reaches of tragedy, feeling the pleasurable pain wash over me, I liked to steal surreptitious glances at myself in the mirror beside the dining table. Another day we might be asked to express what unexpectedly *receiving* a puppy might feel like. Then the mirror reflected unadulterated joy.

I was five years old when my brother Peter was born, which meant that throughout the entirety of my childhood I bore the brunt of my father's unrelenting educational initiatives. When I was seven or eight, he taught me to leap into the air—to trust that I would land safely on my feet. I stood on the toilet seat and jumped into his outstretched arms. With each successful leap he took a step backwards, until I was confidently launching myself across the room, arms spread wide like a soaring bird.

One childhood summer day he bought a shiny play-structure for our cottage lawn near Beaverton, Ontario, a red magnet that glinted in the sunshine. He encouraged me to hang upside down from the monkey bars and to master complex gymnastic turns; he'd be there to catch me if I fell. (I was well into my thirties before I could walk by a set of bars without succumbing to the urge to hang there for a blissful moment or two). We rode horses together, and if I was thrown from my horse, I was allowed approximately ninety seconds to remount, whether I'd been hurt or not. He promoted a putative career for me as a long-distance swimmer, once running his boat quietly beside me on Lake Simcoe as I completed a five-mile challenge. I still remember the way I paced my breathing that day, and the feeling that I could conquer any obstacle with him beside me. When

I was twelve, I desperately wanted to swim the English Channel, and was accepted into Gus Ryder's Lakeshore Swimming Club, but my dream came to an end the day Dad came to watch us train. He thought I looked exhausted—and that was the end of my swimming career.

He raised me as a tomboy, so I could accompany him on his fishing and cycling expeditions, and these too involved learning. For example, being allowed to fish was contingent upon my willingness to kill and gut my catch. The first time we did this together he showed me the still-beating fish heart and the intestines plump with crayfish. I was wide-eyed with amazement.

He could also be reckless: one day, to my horror, he angrily chased a black bear away from the deck of our summer cabin in Algonquin Park. And rebellious—a trait I inherited, to his supreme annoyance. Any Do Not Enter sign was a personal affront. On an outing in Algonquin Park, we once came across a wolf research centre marked Danger, Authorized Persons Only. Father saw red. How dare they? He took my hand, and we marched boldly through the gate. Once inside we found ourselves alone with a half dozen caged wolves who were watching us with undeniable interest.

There was little room for coddling in my father's world. No warm cuddling in his and my mother's bed after a terrifying nightmare. No rush to the Brownies meeting at Grace Church on-the-Hill in lower Forest Hill Village to rescue me the evening I fell and broke my brand-new front tooth in half, exposing the nerve. I remember the surprise on the Brownie leader's face when my father said over the phone that I should stay until the end of the session, as though nothing had happened. In agony, I returned to the group to find my fellow eight-year- olds on the floor searching for the missing half of my tooth. I was similarly allowed to take risks bordering on the irresponsible, such as fishing alone from an aluminum canoe at dawn. I put an end to that summer fun myself the day I hooked a huge bass and almost capsized the boat.

Importantly, he opened my eyes to the human aspect of the past, a thick layer of learning that would underscore my later writing life. On one languid summer day in my eighth year, we cycled to an old cemetery in the town of Beaverton, Ontario that contained the graves of early settlers. Many had died young from disease, or in childbirth. When he stopped before the tombstone of a young father his age—he was thirty-seven at the time—tears of identification streamed from his eyes. I stood before the nearby grave of a small girl like me, also in tears. These silent memorials to foreshortened pioneer lives conveyed first glimpses of the human condition that no school text could ever approximate.

Years later, on a family car trip that took us through Las Vegas, he quietly indicated an emaciated elderly woman playing a slot machine. Her eyes were glassy as she repetitively entered coins and pulled the lever. Dad drew my attention to a telling detail: the leather glove she wore on her right hand to protect it from the constant rubbing. I still see her in my mind's eye. In that one passing moment, I intuited the meaning of obsession.

He invented stories that unfolded over years, with the same cast of characters. Matilda Murgatroyd was a young girl, coincidentally my age, who was frequently chased by dragons whom she slayed with ease. When I learned to read, my favourite books built upon the imaginative foundation he had prepared for me.

Not too long ago, I was asked by a magazine editor to choose a children's story that had altered my life. I didn't hesitate. It was Hans Christian Andersen's *The Little Mermaid*, which I read when I was perhaps nine or ten. I can still conjure up three of the book's magnificent illustrations: the young mermaid visiting the witch's den at the bottom of the sea; the sight of her on the shore watching the prince dance with his bride on his ship; and her mermaid sisters calling to her from the foamy surface of the sea when it was time for her to die.

What the little mermaid wanted—the love of a human man—resonated with me even at that early age, but that's not central to this memory; rather, it was her courage in choosing an independent life despite being warned about the cost of failure. There was no Walt Disney in this telling; I remember accepting the sad fact of her death because she had understood and consented to this possibility from the start. She conveyed to me an early glimmering that a life of my own making was possible, an idea instilled in me by my father's indirect teachings.

We lived in an elegant house in Forest Hill Village on a street romantically named Rosemary Lane. (I once used it as a fabricated byline on a *Chatelaine* article.) Some of my friends called our house "the mansion on the hill," but since my thoughts were continually directed elsewhere, I never thought of it that way. Although we apparently had money enough, I was forbidden to become something my parents called a "clothes horse." With this and other minimalist attitudes in mind, they made certain my allowance was smaller than that of my friends, and that I had fewer possessions.

That my father and mother—the children of penurious immigrants—landed on Rosemary Lane was pure serendipity, and worth an explanation. During a short period in Canada's history that lasted from the end of the Second World War until the 1980s, the Canadian economy bloomed. Alberta discovered oil; returning Second World War veterans took advantage of free university education, then established themselves in business and the professions; an unprecedented baby boom increased demand for housing, giving birth to urban suburbs with large lots for children to play in; and a thriving manufacturing sector and investment in natural resources fuelled rising incomes, stimulating a demand for consumer goods and services.

Real incomes doubled, in some cases tripled. By 1960, two-thirds of Canadians owned a car, and 10 percent owned more than one—sleek, gas-devouring vehicles with "fins" protruding from their rear cruised the streets of Toronto. Women who had been pushed out of the postwar workplace, in a wave of propaganda designed to instill the belief that work outside the home was unfeminine, bought new household appliances by the millions. Washing machines made scrub boards obsolete; dryers replaced clothes pegs. The most influential new toy was television, which opened a window into America's emerging popular culture. We didn't have a set. My father disliked the passivity of television-watching, and when we finally cajoled him into buying one he placed it in the basement, where, as he correctly anticipated, we forgot about it.

Like thousands of other children of immigrant families, my parents lifted themselves from penury into the middle and upper middle classes by dint of hard work, disciplined savings, and sheer luck. In no other period of Canadian history would new arrivals move so quickly from the impoverished neighbourhoods of their childhoods to streets like Rosemary Lane. Forest Hill became an island of comfort in a city that was still covertly, often overtly, antisemitic: a poll in the mid-1940s indicated that the Japanese and the Jews were almost equally despised.

My parents moved to the Village after my Grade Two teacher at Hillcrest Public School made a poisonous remark that I relayed to them—and they were not alone. By 1951, 40 percent of Village families were Jewish, the densest proportion of any Canadian municipality. But being protected from the antisemitism that still characterized Toronto had its downside: Forest Hill was an inward-looking place that ill prepared its children for integration into society at large. In a 1972 *Toronto Life* article—my first look back at my childhood—I put it this way:

> Our lives in the '40s and '50s were insular and "unreal"—unconnected to the WASP reality of Toronto, unconnected to the rural reality of Canada. We knew almost nothing beyond the Village, the downtown department stores where we'd sometimes wander on Saturday afternoon and charge clothes to our fathers' accounts, and the bits of northern Ontario where we summered and wondered at the people who stayed there after Labour Day.

Forest Hill looked so unusual to the outside world that it became the subject of an early sociological study (euphemistically titled *Crestwood Heights)*, intended to examine our presumably exotic behaviour. Strangely dated now, the book sent mixed currents of pride and trepidation through the streets. Was it flattering to be noticed by eminent scholars, even if it made one feel like a species of butterfly pinned to a board? The level of detail requested by John Seeley, the lead author of the study, was remarkably intrusive: at Forest Hill Junior High School we children were asked to diarize all our activities, including what we ate for dinner each night. The study made people uncomfortable. The pogroms of the East European homeland felt close in those years, and to be noticed so publicly triggered an atavistic fear of danger, as did the still-unspoken knowledge of the Holocaust. Better to keep one's head down and live grouped together was the unstated message.

Crestwood Heights aside, the postwar good news increasingly influenced the Canadian social consensus. The ruling Liberals strategically pilfered popular policies from the Western-based Cooperative Commonwealth Federation (CCF), including family allowances, universal old-age pensions, and hospital insurance, among other welfare measures that promoted the public good. Years of anti-immigrant backlash, fuelled by the Depression and antisemitism, slowly morphed into a new accord about mutual acceptance. Liberal (and liberal) policies encouraged my parents and others to identify passionately as Canadians.

By pure chance I was raised during this happy period in Canadian history. It seemed natural to me that social change, underscored by economic prosperity, harmonized seamlessly with the values of my home. My lucky generation missed the battlefields of Canada's wars; and those Jewish youngsters who grew to adulthood in protected places like Forest Hill did not experience the bitter discrimination that still darkened our parents' memories.

And bitter it was. In 1903, at age eighteen, my paternal grandmother, Ethel Nussbaum immigrated alone to Toronto from Ternopol, Poland, then a region of the Austro-Hungarian Empire. Months after her arrival in the dilapidated Jewish quarter of the Ward, a few congested blocks bordered by Dundas Street on the north, Queen Street on the south, Yonge Street on the east and University Avenue on the west, she was married off to Benjamin Neiman (Newman), whom she had known in Ternopol as a child. In just a few years they had five children. The family lived in a shack on Chestnut Street, where Toronto's new city hall now stands. They had an outhouse, and no running water. My overwhelmed grandfather, whom I barely knew, abandoned his family and ran away to New York City. In old age he tried to make amends, but my father and most of his siblings did not forgive him.

Having been deserted as a child was a subject my father rarely talked about, but I know that his anger and pain never diminished. What he may have known, but cared nothing about, was that desertion was a common story in the immigrant Jewish communities of Canada and the United States. In her book, *Wives Without Husbands: Marriage, Desertion, and Welfare in New York, 1900–1935*, Anna Igra explores how the newspaper *The Jewish Forward* helped women seek out their delinquent spouses. Not only did the paper print their heartbreaking letters, it also created a column titled "The Gallery of Runaway Husbands" that featured shaming portraits of the miscreants. My grandmother, who spoke only Yiddish, would have been utterly penniless were it not for her neighbours, who made certain that she and her children ate and were clothed. She was resourceful, taking in other people's sewing. Eventually, she saved enough to move to Ulster Street, where she rented most of her house to boarders. To facilitate this, she and her children slept together in one room and spent their waking hours in the kitchen, warmed by a pot-bellied coal-stoked stove. Oscar, her eldest, would leave school to work as a tailor so his younger siblings could continue their studies. (Years later, my father and his siblings financed their brother's resumed education.)

The immigrant Jewish quarter of The Ward seethed with energy. In his book *The Jews of Toronto*, Stephen Speisman called it "a North American shtetl"—a Jewish village that recreated many familiar features of the old European homeland (to the consternation of old-stock Torontonians). "People gathered in restaurants, groceries, and confectionery shops. It all fostered a sense of security in a hostile environment, where these poverty-stricken immigrants evoked fear in the minds of the native Anglo-Saxon citizens, who passed through the Ward by streetcar on the way to the fashionable downtown stores," he wrote. Almost everyone was young and trying to make a living—as button-hole makers, collar- and cuff-sewers, fur-cutters, or machine operators who supplied the burgeoning clothing industry with an unlimited supply of cheap labour.

It was here that my mother's parents, too, began their life in Canada. Like so many others, Isaac Lipkin was a peddler. Sadly, he was an unmitigated failure as a businessman: all his small ventures collapsed. He was a musician (like his three daughters), a singer with no means of converting his talent into income. In the evenings, he and his socialist friends would gather at the Labour Lyceum building at the corner of Spadina Avenue and St. Andrew Street (it is now a Chinese restaurant) to sing and debate politics late into the night. My mother, sent by my grandmother to fetch him, would watch and listen unseen through the ice-fogged window, transfixed by his evident joy.

Isaac Lipkin was born around 1880 in Kiev, Ukraine, which was then part of the Russian Pale of Settlement. His wife, my maternal grandmother Anne Brusilovsky, was born in Moscow at the tail-end of a large family whose once-wealthy paterfamilias had worked for a noble family before Jews were expelled from the capital in 1891. (According to family lore, her older siblings had been bathed in milk.)

They met on a factory floor in Yekaterinburg, an industrial city in the Urals more than 1,000 miles east of Moscow—quite literally, as it happened, since the workers lived on the factory premises and there were no beds. Wages throughout Russia were the lowest in Europe, and industrial working conditions were abysmal, often entailing sixteen-hour days. My grandparents married, and when their first child was born, moved to St. Petersburg to find better work.

On the morning of January 22, 1905, Isaac Lipkin joined a massive demonstration of workers marching peacefully towards the famed Winter Palace of the Russian Tsars. They had in hand a petition for more humane working conditions that they wished to present to Tsar Nicolas II (a doomed pursuit, given the deadened sensibilities of the monarch), but panicked soldiers opened fire along the route and again in the Palace square, killing at least 200 men and women. My grandfather survived, but he was arrested and jailed in the Trubetskoy Bastion Prison which, like so many other former places of pain in the world, is now a tourist site.

In 2013, I went there to find him. My notes recall a sunny June day in St. Petersburg, and I am on a tourist bus listening to the recorded commentary. We are driving along a wide boulevard next to the Neva River. A magnificent eighteenth-century edifice built in green and white stone looms before us. "We are approaching the Winter Palace" announces the recorded voice. "This is where the failed revolution of 1905 began." The bus stops so we can gawk at the site. The palace is fronted by arched doorways and resplendent ionic columns. But it is the enormous Palace square that draws my eye; for it is there that my grandfather stood among thousands of hopeful others—a young man who dreamed that life for impoverished, powerless people like himself, for benighted Jews like himself, might become bearable in the empire of the Tsar. I imagine a mass of people colliding; soldiers in their winter caps and long coats, readying their rifles; a crush of bodies; the screams of the wounded. I imagine my grandfather—singer, socialist, romantic idealist—whose life in a distant country begat mine, and whom I hardly knew.

The next stop is the Peter and Paul Fortress, the site of the Trubetskoy Bastion Prison for political prisoners, a redolent space that tells of Russia's revolutionary past. I step through the prison doors with apprehension, following the traces of his life. The cell blocks have been swept clean for the legions of rubbernecking visitors like myself. Inside several of the tiny cells are life-sized mock-ups of individuals who once were held here—their beds, their wash basins. A plaque stating their name and date of imprisonment is affixed to iron-bar doors, sometimes with a picture. Many were mid-nineteenth-century revolutionaries whose hopes for land ownership and freedom of speech miscarried. There are many women. All are young intellectuals with intense faces; their unflinching determined eyes stare through round rimless glasses. Many have Jewish names. No surprise: this was an era of pogroms and anti-Jewish terror. (Later, in the great Hermitage Museum of the city, I will pause before a period painting of a suffering Jew on his knees before the lofty Tsar.) One of these cells once housed the writer Maxim Gorky, a Marxist activist. Others, like my grandfather's cells, were anonymous.

My grandfather wasn't in prison long. But enough was enough. After his release, he and my grandmother joined the two million Jewish refugees who fled Russia between 1881 and 1924.

How odd it is that the contours of their desperate story would eventually be popularized as a Broadway musical *Fiddler on the Roof.* Secular breakaways from traditional Orthodox families, young and disillusioned, all were fleeing pogroms and failed efforts to effect political change. Within this tidal wave of others, Isaac and Anne Lipkin and their baby daughter, Florence, crossed most of Europe by foot and by rail, eventually arriving at the German port of Hamburg, where they boarded ship and steamed up the River Thames to London, docking at Irongate Wharf by Tower Bridge, not far from the teeming East End ghettos of Spitalfields and Whitechapel that newly housed their impoverished countrymen. They were greeted by the "Guardians of the Jewish Poor," a small group of well-established English Jews. The welcome-language of the soup kitchens was Yiddish.

My mother was born here, in this London world of immigrant refugees, in November 1906. When she was two, the family emigrated once again, to Toronto.

During his final years (he died in 1998), my father penned a handwritten memoir describing his life in Toronto in the teens and twenties of the twentieth century. It's a finely written evocation of the city as seen through the eyes of a child who, unimpeded by anxious parents, roamed the streets with his friends. (They threw frozen horse-balls at one another, and fished for minnows in the Don River, which my grandmother would obligingly cook.) He writes of self-consciousness and performance anxiety so disabling that he switched between Harbord Collegiate and Jarvis Collegiate twice, because he was expected to make an oral presentation to the class. He tells of his mother taking him to the doctor for unspecified emotional problems, and that he subsequently spent much of his life in a deliberate attempt to overcome his fears. Had he had a father to guide him, perhaps he would have been stronger, he muses.

Stronger? I reflect on the formidable father he became. Did his daringness and domination of others result from his lifelong effort to overcome the vacuum of fatherlessness?

He had wanted to study medicine or biology, but knowing there was no money, he never bothered to raise the subject at home. Instead he apprenticed as a chartered accountant, graduating after five years with the highest marks in Ontario.

But the scourge of antisemitism marked his early life, as it marked the lives of most of his contemporaries. In language whose meaning has a familiar ring almost a century later, the anti-immigration lobby of the day accused non-British foreigners of being "unassimilable" (a favourite word), a "menace" (another favourite), and of belonging to "inferior racial stock." In the late 1920s, *Queen's Quarterly,* then as now a respected journal, published two articles, one titled "The Immigration Problem in Canada," by W.A. Carrothers, and the other "The Case for a Quota," by W. Burton Hurd. For these men, non-white immigration was written off as "impossible." "We cannot assimilate the yellow, black, or brown races..." opined Carrothers. Hurd was even more direct, worrying about "the high fertility of certain foreign stocks." In the 1930s, rental signs specifying "gentiles only" sprouted around Toronto as Hitlerian ideas crossed the Atlantic. Jews could only rent from Jews, my father writes in his memoir, but some established Jews who owned apartments also refused to rent to their co-religionists.

Although accounting was not his first career choice, it proved difficult to find an apprenticeship. No gentile firm would accept a Jewish student. (He never forgot the slight from the reputed Clarkson firm that declared that *they* did not discriminate but their clients might take offense.) Fortunately, the only Jewish firm in the city accepted him as a student. But even then, humiliation reigned: at the end of each week, the secretary threw the students' salaries on the floor.

My parents met as teenagers at a meeting of Jewish youth at a hall on Spadina Avenue. She later remembered a lively boy with wavy blond hair.

He remembered a slim, dark-haired girl who raised her hand to ask a question—about homosexuality, which was the purported topic of discussion. (She wanted to know what it was.) They married at the height of the Depression, and when my father finished his accountancy course and had saved a little money, they bought a motorcycle. True to later form, they set off to see the world, at least the reachable parts of it—starting with a seminal trip to Mexico, a country they would return to decades later to live in, and one that remains an integral part of our family life.

I FELL FROM PARADISE when I reached puberty. Like many men of his generation, my father held rigid opinions about the role of grown women—and to the apparent surprise of us both, I was unmistakably moving in that direction. His new prohibitions about ladylike behaviour (he thought women should be mysterious) seemed absurd to his twelve-year-old fishing companion. In any case, they came far too late. I was already too much like him, opinionated and strong-willed: his true daughter. His cycling partner and fearless gymnast protégée was not about to adopt feminine "mystery," whatever that was.

No longer was I willing to answer questions about books and desert islands, share thoughts about my friend George, or act out scenes of imagined happiness or sorrow. And the more controlling he became, the more I fought back. I argued boldly at the dinner table until he could bear my impudence no longer. Nightly he would chase me up the stairs, where I barely managed to lock myself in the bathroom before he reached the door. He never did catch me—probably deliberately.

At the same time, unbeknownst to me, my home and the interminable Sunday morning classes at Holy Blossom Temple were becoming places of moral learning. At sixteen, I had the good fortune to be taught by the German-Jewish philosopher and rabbi, Emil Fackenheim, an escapee from the Nazis. Mr. Fackenheim, like Mr. Warschauer, was impossibly old; his accent was often impenetrable, and his clothes stank of cigar smoke. But when he spoke, his eyes frequently brimming with mirth, I was intrigued. An expert on Hegel, he introduced us to the eighteenth-century German philosopher, Immanuel Kant, whose cosmopolitan worldview—that every person has intrinsic value simply by virtue of being human—reverberated in my mind and synthesized with the United Nations Declaration of Human Rights that I had discovered just a few years earlier.

On the annual religious holidays of Rosh Hashanah and Yom Kippur, our family would join the rest of the Holy Blossom congregation for services. The Union Prayer Book, copyrighted in 1940 by the Central Conference of American Rabbis, also reflected the liberal worldview of contemporary Reform Judaism. Yes, the high-minded poetic prose spoke of God and the historic Jewish people, but the text was unmistakeably universalist. As I write these words, the old book, which would later be revised to reflect the trauma of the Holocaust and more recent commitments to the state of Israel, lies open on my desk before me.

Sitting in the pews with my family, I loved reading lines like these:

> The generations of men come and go before Thee. Brief is their existence. Many are...the plans unfulfilled, the dreams unrealized when we are summoned to leave this earthly home...We recall [their] tender companionship...By love are they remembered and in memory they live.

The passage gently reinforced the inevitability of death and simultaneously provided comfort. In another section the text described the "noble purposes" that had inspired the departed, and their "high ideals" which we were urged to emulate. In responsive reading we collectively prayed that Canada "may ever be a stronghold of peace and advocate in the council of nations." Elsewhere we were reminded "only to do justice." In unison we asked to be granted the vision and courage that would enable us to pursue the "paths of truth and duty."

Although I was not then, nor am I now, a believer in God, the expressive moral texts of the Union Prayer Book connected me with the rootedness and continuity of family and people, including the grief that accompanies loss, and the high principles of duty and justice—and with the prophetic foundations of Judaism, all of which continued to inform my life.

Another place of unexpected learning was Camp Ogama, a children's summer colony situated on Fox Lake, a few kilometres north of Huntsville, Ontario. I was sixteen years old and a counsellor-in-training when I came under the influence of the young Alan Borovoy, who would go on to found the Canadian Civil Liberties Association and change the face of Canada. He was my camp section-head, responsible for activities for my age group. Fun beyond measure, energetic, wry, covertly intellectual, Alan loved to debate—with anyone, about anything. He later became a canny tactician who publicly embarrassed governments and institutions hoping to restrict civil rights. Among his many achievements, he publicized housing discrimination against minorities. His hectoring on behalf of equality terminated the tradition of teaching religion in public schools; and his badgering, always laced with humour, ended invasive strip-searches by police.

We campers were largely from *nouveaux riches* families that had moved north from the immigrant streets of downtown Toronto, but Alan still lived on Grace Street, where he had been raised. He went to Harbord Collegiate, then an incubator of the mind for bright immigrant kids—the same school my father had attended in the 1920s. He knew about worldly things we'd barely heard of, like the Spanish Civil War and communism.

Most Jewish summer camps held Friday evening services to mark the Sabbath, but Alan delighted in being different: he designed programmes to open our minds. We'd be pulled from our beds after dark and led to benches, hewed from a forested hillside, that overlooked a stage and the magical night-shrouded lake beyond. One starlit evening we watched in wonder as "Socrates," "Maimonides," and "Abraham Lincoln" asked probing questions about freedom, religion, and justice. On another occasion, Alan convinced David Lewis, then a labour lawyer (he would later head the federal New Democratic Party) to introduce us to social-democratic ideas. Under yet another night sky we witnessed an enactment of the Dresden trial, an event that had occurred less than a decade earlier, in which some of the doctors who had participated in the Nazi murders of mentally ill and disabled individuals were prosecuted.

Alan's pursuit of intellectual fun didn't end with language. He loved to sing, leaping into the air as he led us in rousing renditions of "Solidarity Forever," "The Banks Are Made of Marble," and songs from the Spanish Civil War and the Palmach ("Never say this present journey is your last…"). He roared with gusto, his right arm punching out the beat. Sometimes Jerry Gray of the folk group *The Travellers* arrived to serenade us. We campers belted out Pete Seeger's famous "If I Had a Hammer" at the tops of our voices. The lyrics were of a kind: they spoke of friendship and unity, of a just world governed by just leaders.

In late August 1955, as the camp bus pulled into the Toronto parking lot where our parents awaited our arrival, a hundred sun-tanned adolescents began to sing "Solidarity Forever"—with a twist.

We are communists forever.
We are communists forever.
We are communists forever,
Because Borovoy told us so.

My parents laughed, but others didn't. In the United States, Senator Joseph McCarthy was on the rampage. In Canada, the Igor Gouzenko scandal still resonated ominously. Gouzenko had fled the Soviet Embassy in Ottawa taking with him Russian-language documents proving the existence of a Soviet spy ring in Canada. Because the Jewish communist movement was still strong in 1955 (not until the following year would Nikita Khrushchev's famous revelations about the crimes of Stalin precipitate an exodus from the Party), the Jewish community was apprehensive.

We kids were only vaguely aware of these developments—aware enough to enjoy shocking our families by making up the song on the trip home. Regardless, Alan Borovoy was a democratic socialist in those days and never a communist, and his disdain for communism only grew in virulence in later years. (I never did ask him whether enrolment in Camp Ogama decreased the year after we belted out that song to our assembled parents.)

Privately, Alan was kind and consoling. The following summer, my first as a junior counsellor, he assigned me to a cabin of thirteen-year-old girls. A day or two later I began writing a letter to my parents in which I described my new charges using the flinty observational techniques my father had taught me. I left the unfinished letter lying on my bed for a few moments, and when I returned, the girls had read it. An uproar ensued.

Alan took me for a walk along the balsam-lined dirt path that led from the camp and talked to me quietly. I was distraught. I apologized for my carelessness. He offered solace.

Our friendship endured for sixty years until his death in May 2015. It was threaded with constant laughter and fraught with debate, particularly over absolute freedom of expression, which he believed in, and I did not. On the day he was buried, hundreds of friends attended a graveside memorial, and as his coffin was lowered into the ground we sang in his honour a song of Rosh Hashanah, the Jewish New Year, a song beloved by the militant secularist who had remained loyal to his roots, a song beloved by the atheist warrior who had led the struggle in Canada for equality, democracy, and civil rights.

My interest in books and ideas led me to study English literature and philosophy when I reached university age, but whatever on-campus profile I acquired was not for studiousness. I danced in musical productions and practiced gymnastics as a cheerleader (*Tronna, Tronna, Tronna Varsity/ We shout and fight for the Blue and White/and the honour of U of T*). It was heady stuff for an eighteen-year-old. I had a "fan club" led by the University College boys' residence, Hutton House, that rhythmically shouted my name from the stands at football games—although when it came to understanding the rules of the game, I was a frank failure. Under my leadership, our cheerleading squad once chanted "Hold That Line" to the opposing team.

Gradually, privately, I grew more interested in my studies. I read Plato's *Republic* with the startled surprise of someone peering through a hidden window. Stepping, like Alice, into that undiscovered world, I encountered Socrates' challenging questions about the nature of justice. In retrospect, it was in these texts that the ancient Greek thinkers and the imperative of the ancient Israelites to pursue justice first converged and synthesized in my mind.

I took my first steps into the intriguing landscape of philosophy in an introductory class taught by the legendary—and frequently inebriated—Professor Marcus Long. More than a hundred students were crowded into the amphitheatre classroom on that day, and since I was chronically late, I found myself perched in the top row at the back of the large hall. I can still visualize Professor Long as he drew a circle on the blackboard, then randomly placed an x within its circumference. "That circle is your environment," he said. "The x is you. Every action you take, or hesitate to take, will change your environment and yourself too. You will become what you do." It was basic existentialism: the Sartrean idea that "man is condemned to be free" because the personal choices we make will determine our character and, in direct consequence, our future.

Another philosophy class delivered a second piece of learning. The professor, whose name I have forgotten, happened to be talking about the different ways those events we call history can be shaped by selection or manipulation. Since I had unthinkingly looked upon the known past as a collection of facts dutifully recorded by a tribe of faithful scribes, the idea that "history" might be open to interpretation—perhaps *malevolent* interpretation—stirred my imagination.

I was the first person in my extended historical family ever to graduate from university. After the ceremony in the University of Toronto's Convocation Hall, I saw my family at the back of the, by then, almost empty room: my parents, my siblings, and my paternal grandmother, Ethel. They were the last to leave, since the adults were holding one another and crying. Almost sixty years had passed since Ethel Nussbaum had reached Canada to inhabit the teeming immigrant slum of The Ward. Neither of my parents had been able to pursue the education they longed for. With my graduation, a new era had opened in our Canadian family.

But even then, I knew I had to leave the stifling confines of Forest Hill Village. I knew intuitively that a dimmer light awaited me if I stayed in Toronto, including the possibility of marriage to someone who might want me to live in the soul-destroying suburbs that were then the residence-of-no-return for some of my friends. The stultifying conventions of adult Temple membership and suburban life terrified me.

In my 1972 memoir for *Toronto Life*, I put my fears about being emotionally crushed this way:

> ...Parachute into the vortex of that circle and erase all the outer lines so that even the memory of escape becomes a vague, once-held notion. Harden, darken, become brittle there, a tiny dot at the centre of forgotten thoughts...No, I would escape—to Paris...

It was the morning of my adult life; I was a furled leaf waiting for the right angle of the sun to open me to the world.

Like my father, I was primed for adventure. I would spend a year studying abroad—in France.

CHAPTER THREE

MY MARRIAGE—AND FRANCE'S HIDDEN HISTORY

HE WAS A TWENTY-FIVE-YEAR-OLD engineer from south-western France and the son of a conservative Catholic family—attentive, artistic, and fun to be with. He was also my exit visa from Forest Hill. On my first night home in Toronto in August 1961, I broke the news of my engagement to my father, who promptly disappeared into his bedroom. Since he had always thought of himself as a citizen of the world, and since the ethos of our home was what one might call "Jewish-Universalist-Humanist," there wasn't much he could reasonably say to dissuade me. The most he could muster on exiting his room several hours later was, "I don't want my grandchildren to speak with a French accent." I ache for him, in retrospect: He and mother were going to lose me, something I understand better now than I did then. France might have been China in those days, so far away did it seem.

I met Claude at the Toronto airport around Christmas time. I was as nervous and excited as a child, a fluttery state I confided to a stranger while applying lipstick in the airport washroom. I noted that my husband-to-be was as handsome as I remembered him, and when we walked in the front door of the Rosemary Lane house, I wondered what my parents and my then-teenaged brother and sister, all of them stiff-looking with wonder and anxiety, would think. Claude put them at ease. His English might have been approximate, but he smiled a lot.

Within hours curious friends and family members had descended upon us. "A handsome Frenchman!" "And she met him in a Paris café!" My hyper-inquisitive aunts and uncles demanded to know whether he would convert to Judaism. He politely declined, although he did agree to remove one of his given names—the ultra-Catholic "Marie"—from the wedding invitation, which brought them a degree of solace. Since the groom had not converted, Gunther Plaut, the newly arrived young rabbi of Holy Blossom Temple, had attempted to banish the wedding ceremony from the main sanctuary of the Temple to a small side-chapel in order to avoid criticism, but I had wept copiously and he had relented (to his later chagrin). And so it was that on December 28, 1961, Claude and I walked down the aisle in full view of the community.

Our Rosemary Lane home had never looked more beautiful than it did the day of our wedding reception, although an omen of the future—had I believed in such things—did reveal itself. As we entered the house, our family cat laid a gift at our feet: a dead mouse.

Claude was slated to read a few words of thanks in English, which unfortunately hadn't progressed much beyond his introductory "I am a car." (We spoke only French together.) When the moment arrived, he bravely shaped his lips around the strange syllables, the strain showing on his face. My aunts, uncles, cousins, and friends held their collective breath and leaned in to listen, all of us reflected in the large dining room mirror that had once witnessed my childhood theatrical sallies. Who *was* this handsome man who had entranced their Erna and was going to take her away?

On New Year's Eve, Claude and I flew back to Paris to begin our life together. Apart from just one other honeymooning couple, we were the only people on the transatlantic flight. Ominously, I became aware that the other two were snuggled together in close conversation, while Claude and I seemed to have little to say to each other.

He had rented a tiny studio in a small housing complex on the *rue Stephenson* in the 18th *arrondissement* of Paris, a working-class neighbourhood so close to the tracks of the Gare du Nord that the walls and floor of the room rattled whenever trains passed by. There was a bed, a table for eating, a bathroom, and a "kitchen" with a refrigerator and stove. (The latter loomed large in my mind because I didn't know how to cook.) A young woman my age lived in the attached studio, and although we hardly spoke beyond the formalities of "*Bonjour Madame*," I assumed she must be pregnant since she spent her days knitting baskets full of baby booties and jackets. Perhaps she was as lonely as I, but such was the etiquette of the day that we did not communicate.

The transition from my heady student days in Toronto and Paris to the isolation of housewifery was proving difficult; I was, as I was quickly discovering, a lot less urbane and cosmopolitan than I had imagined with the misplaced cockiness of adolescence. To make things worse, there were strong societal pressures, even laws, militating against independence for married women. I learned that I was no longer able to open a bank account without my husband's written permission, although I had had one when I was a student. And there were humiliations. The rough-speaking baker across the road where I lined up to buy our baguettes took malicious pleasure in calling attention to my youth and foreignness. "Did your husband mess up your hair last night?" she laughed coarsely, stabbing a finger in my direction. The other customers turned to look at me and smirked. I burned crimson.

I was becoming increasingly apprehensive about marriage. The couple that lived across the courtyard engaged in nightly screaming matches, waking their two children and everyone else in the complex. Once at midnight, a male neighbour roared *"Ta gueule!"* (Shut your mouth!), which quieted them for an hour or so. I had never heard people speak in tones of such hatred, and the idea that marriage could harbour such pain frightened me. Ironically, the woman in this couple did try to befriend me, and I gratefully accepted her overtures—until the day I returned from a doctor's appointment and mentioned the name of the doctor.

"But he's a Jew!" she shouted; her face creased with scorn.

"*I'm* a Jew!" I retorted, my heart pounding in my chest.

We had only one conversation after that exchange. I cannot recall the subject, but it was then that she raised her arm in a Hitler salute and proclaimed, *"Je suis fasciste!"*

Because Claude wanted me to meet his family, we set out for the ancient city of Bayonne, in the Basque country near the Spanish border. The train ride was a long eight hours through beautiful countryside, such as the forested Landes, which I was seeing for the first time, but the trip became even longer after Claude recognized a family friend on board. He introduced me as his wife. "Oh, I remember you," she gushed, "I was at your wedding!"

I knew that Claude had been previously married, but since that alliance was a youthful misstep that had lasted less than a year, I had barely given it a thought. Now I found myself confronted with a talkative woman who thought I was someone else. To my dismay, Claude did not correct her; and since his former wife was French, meaning that she spoke without an accent, I spent the rest of the voyage smiling mutely lest the truth of my embarrassing identity become apparent.

Claude's family lived in a large corner house on a leafy street not far from the local bull-fighting arena. (Bayonne was included in the Spanish fighting circuit.) The house, like most residences in the region, was white stucco with red shutters and a red-tiled roof; purple bougainvillea vines embraced the façade. It even had a name: *Lur Ona*, a Basque phrase that translates roughly as "a good place."

It was sizeable—three-stories high, with a dark-wooded interior that looked intimidatingly sombre. A study containing an impressive-looking desk piled high with papers led off a central hallway. Across the corridor, a door opened into a formal dining room reserved for special occasions. The large kitchen was visible through yet another door that opened into an adjacent room occupied by an oversized dining table. It was here that the family socialized and ate most of their meals—and where I was introduced to my husband's family.

Claude was the youngest child of parents who were now in their seventies. He had a much older brother, Christian, and a sister, Odile. There had been a third brother who had died in a car accident some years earlier. One by one I was presented to each of the adults; we shook hands, nodded, and smiled. Then Christian's five young children, who had been lined up in the formal dining room next door, were ushered into the room in single file. They each shook my hand shyly, then vanished. Soon the men also disappeared, including Claude, leaving me alone with my mother-in-law and Christian's wife, Claire.

I sat primly on a straight-backed chair against the wall waiting for...I didn't quite know what; but the two older women simply carried on an earlier conversation. I felt crushed. Why were they excluding me? Were they not interested in knowing anything about me?

After several moments of extreme self-consciousness, I burst into tears and fled the room.

There was general consternation. What had happened? In truth, even I didn't know. What had appeared to me as indifference hinted at cultural differences I couldn't fathom. That night, there was still further commotion: When Claude and I discovered to our surprise that we had been assigned separate bedrooms, we noisily rearranged the furniture with childish bombast and moved in together. In the morning we learned the reason: Claude was divorced, so his devout mother did not recognize our marriage.

Odile intervened. "*Maman*, they are just as married as Christian and Claire!"

Reluctantly, *Maman* relented.

Despite its inauspicious beginnings, my relationship with the family grew increasingly warm. Notwithstanding their religious conservatism and my alien origins, they were open-minded. My mother-in-law accepted my Jewish origins, even urging me to attend services at the local synagogue. Given her faith-oriented world view, she was unable to understand how I might be an ethical person without attending to religion.

Odile purposefully introduced me to the pomp and liturgy of the Catholic Church at Sunday mass in the little church just up the street. I enjoyed the music, the incense, the entire spectacle, but my commitments ended there. Undeterred, my new sister-in-law prayed nightly for my conversion.

Like an anthropologist who unknowingly stumbles into unfamiliar terrain, I found that my growing familiarity with the rituals of Catholicism, together with my later visits to the great cathedrals of France, stretched my horizons far beyond the parochial Jewish world of my childhood. More than two decades after this early exposure, I would write *The End of Days,* a book about the politics and power of the Catholic Church in medieval Spain, including the operations of the Spanish Inquisition against the insufficiently orthodox, and the expulsion of the Jews and later the Muslims. Writing that book, I felt gratitude for my early exposure to the layers and texture of Catholic culture, which later helped render what was at first ancient and strange almost familiar to me.

My parents visited Bayonne from Toronto, and despite the language barrier were welcomed by the family. My father had an unlimited capacity for charm, and before long Claude's father was showing him his private wine cellar. François had hundreds of bottles maturing in his basement, including a Poire William *eau de vie* that he produced by first attaching bottles to the pear blossoms that flowered every spring from a tree in his back yard, allowing the fruit to grow inside. To be invited into the intimacy of a French family was a privilege, and my parents knew it.

The family came from the Lorraine region of France near the German border, an industrial area that, like neighbouring Alsace, had been seized and re-seized by Germany since the Franco-Prussian war of 1870-71. My mother-in-law and her sister had lived through the First World War with German soldiers billeted in their home (they would come downstairs every morning to eat a cooked breakfast in the kitchen). German would have been their language outside the house, although they never allowed that they knew a syllable of it—a little like my own parents who had been raised in Yiddish, but pretended it was a foreign tongue. My father-in-law, an engineer who specialized in blowing up bridges, had fought the Germans in that war. One of his hands had been hit by a shell and was permanently deformed, but remarkably, he had found the very shell that wounded him and kept it as a cherished souvenir of battles and close calls.

When the Great War ended, François and Jeanne, her sister Adèle ("Marraine"), and their elderly parents crossed the entirety of France in hopes of moving as far from Germany as possible. They settled in Bayonne, where François bought an existing chemical factory. Little did they know that two decades later, Bayonne and its surrounding region, so far from Lorraine, would be incorporated into the Occupied Zone from the moment Marshal Philippe Pétain signed his infamous armistice with the Nazis in June 1940. Little did I know during my early visits what I would later learn about the chemical factory, and how this knowledge would lodge in my psyche.

My father-in-law died of lung cancer in the early 1960s, his aged, gnarled fingers yellowed by nicotine, his faith in God seemingly intact. His parting from his son remains seared in my memory, for Claude and I were about to move permanently to Canada.

"I'll never see you again, *mon fils.*" He looked at Claude with deep sadness.

Odile, who was kneeling at his bedside, intervened: "*Papa,* you know we will all meet again in heaven."

"Yes, but.... " said the father, after a silence.

I wondered then, as I wonder now, whether, when faced with the pain of final separation, he might have reached the limits of his faith.

My mother-in-law died in the late 1970s, after Claude and I had divorced. I visited her just before her death, and on that last, intense journey of good-bye, I experienced France with unexpected vividness. In Paris, the rich aroma of espresso coffee, the familiar fragrance of Gitanes, the taste of Camembert cheese—all made me smile with happy recognition, for I had been away for six years, and such offerings were not yet available in Toronto. I felt joy at the sight of the narrow medieval streets. When I arrived at *Lur Ona* in Bayonne, Odile was waiting for me at the front door. She was the same: vivacious, warm, funny, angry, caustic, lonely, resilient—my loyal life-long friend, if no longer my sister-in-law. The house was also as I remembered it: cold, uncarpeted, and uncomfortable among the red roofs, the bougainvillaea, and the sea almost close enough to inhale. Random domestic phrases I thought I had forgotten washed over me: a flat tire; a cup of flour; leeks *béchamel*; to jack up a car. And the songs of my youth—Brel, Aznavour—took up unshakeable residence in my mind. I wrote in my diary that theirs was a family à la François Mauriac, unhappy solitudes, for the most part. I found myself thinking about the connections between language and culture, about how the ordinary phrases of French daily life so often referenced Catholicism while the English language did no such thing.

I visited the ancient unmarried aunt we called "Marraine." She was in a home for the elderly; we were happy to see one another. It was she who once confided to me that she had lived a life *"sans aucune joie"* (without any joy), having cared for her elderly parents after the First World War, then lived in her sister's home, where she did menial tasks in return for room and board. I took her hand with love. When I left, she gave me a transparent green vase. It looked like jade.

Maman looked smaller and whiter, but she didn't look to me like a dying person; I remembered that I had never seen a dying person. She seemed happy that I had come. She took my hand in hers and whispered, "Now I have seen everyone I love."

For the rest of my life, the family, in its different generations, held me close to them. As they explained, I was the mother of Claude's children, and their aunt. Family mattered to them, and to me. Besides, we liked one another. Perhaps loved is the better word.

I may have been uncertain about being a wife. Most definitely I was distressed by the label "housewife," a designation that carried fearful overtones of the curtailed life I had left behind in Forest Hill Village. I was, however, already sure about one identity—that of "writer"—although I had no idea about how to become one. I was, I therefore decided, an *unpublished* writer. Yes, I had written a little for the University of Toronto student newspaper *The Varsity,* but otherwise my literary opus consisted of teenage diary entries, several adolescent poems, and a few short stories. Sadly, I hadn't managed to scratch out my masterpiece on the paper tablecloth of a *Saint-Germain* café during my previous student year, but the dream persisted. In those days, French hotels demanded to know your occupation on check-in, and to be a housewife was simply not to have one. The authorities, whoever they were, suggested that we nonentities write *aucune*—*no* occupation—in the space provided. I found this humiliating. When we travelled, I always wrote "*journaliste,*" in the expectation of magically becoming one.

Realizing at last that writers did occasionally write, I worked up my courage and applied for a job with the venerable news agency *Agence France-Presse*. I had a university degree. I knew English. I now knew French reasonably well. What more could they want? A person like me who could translate important dispatches from one language into the other would certainly be in demand. So, I climbed an outside staircase to the minimal offices of AFP and explained my plan to the editor.

He looked weary and bored, but he was curious enough to give me a try, handing me an English-language dispatch for translation before ushering me into a small room with a desk and a typewriter.

There was one small problem I hadn't considered: I didn't know how to type. Cheeks blazing with shame, I stared at the copy in front of me, then at the stalwart black creature sitting mockingly on the desk. I was Rumpelstiltskin's daughter, commanded to spin straw into gold. I tried pecking out a few words with my index finger.

Half an hour later I had produced only a handful of misspelled sentences, which I showed to the editor. He gave me a withering look. Don't call us, he advised me dryly.

Fighting disappointment, I decided to become a book translator. Although I didn't often think about my visit to the Natzweiler-Struthof concentration camp in those days, that lingering shadow, in concert with the antisemitism I continued to encounter, was leading me to ruminate uncomfortably on what it meant to be a Jew. So, I settled down to translate Jean-Paul Sartre's *Reflections on the Jewish Question* for the international

English-language market. It didn't occur to me to inquire whether the book had already been translated. When you're young, you think you're inventing the world.

I was about ten pages into my magnificent *oeuvre* when I received a letter from my parents. They had found a translation of the book on a remainders table in New York City. Crushed, I dropped the project *and* the translation career. The great Jean-Paul Sartre may have noted that "man is condemned to be free" to make choices, many of them presumably bad, but unbeknownst to him *he* had chosen badly with his first translator, and therefore missed encountering me.

The walls of several Paris metro stations were disfigured with antisemitic graffiti, which upset me. Since this was before the influx of Sephardic Jews from the former French colonies of North Africa, the extant Jewish community of France would have mostly been direct or indirect survivors of the Holocaust, making these markings especially odious. I didn't know any French Jews, but I did have one memorable encounter. It happened that Claude and I were buying bread in a bakery on the *rue des Rosiers* in the Jewish quarter of the city when it emerged somehow that I was a Canadian Jew.

"How is it for *us* there?" the shopkeeper asked me in a half-whisper, his forehead creased with intensity. "Fine," I answered hesitantly, as surprised by the "us" in his question as I was by the suggestion that "things" might be bad or good. Thinking communally was foreign to me then.

On the other hand, the ongoing Algerian War was helping me to understand the idea of a collectivity as I absorbed the foundational tropes of colonialization, including the racist, proprietary assumptions of the colonizer and the easy-to-see desperation of the colonized. The street battles in Paris were heating up again, although as a housewife in the 18th *arrondissement* I had less access to the roiling student quarter, and Claude did not share my emerging interest in politics. Fortunately, my habit of reading a daily newspaper persisted.

I learned, for example, that on October 17, 1961, while I was in Toronto, the Paris police under the command of Maurice Papon had ordered a violent crackdown on a pro-Algerian liberation demonstration. More than two hundred Algerians were killed that day, many of them tossed into the River Seine, where they drowned. Others were reportedly lynched, Southern-U.S. style, and hung from trees in the *Bois de Vincennes*, Paris's largest public park.

The same Papon had been a collaborationist Vichy official in Bordeaux during the Second World War. Much later, in 1998, he would be convicted of complicity in crimes against humanity for organizing the deportation of French regional Jews to a holding camp at Drancy, near Paris, from which they were transferred to Auschwitz.

Then, in February 1962, just weeks after my return to Paris as a married woman, nine demonstrators had been killed by police at the Charonne metro station in the 11th *arrondissement*.

Since none of these events were reported in the French media with outrage, and occasionally were not reported at all, the French public went about their business reasonably unperturbed, although perhaps less safely than they assumed.

One evening, as Claude and I pulled up to an intersection, the rattle of gun shots punctured the air. We screeched to a stop, jumped out of the car, and took refuge in a street café, along with the frightened passengers of other vehicles. The crossfire persisted for many minutes. We had just missed driving through it.

Only later would I understand that much of the credit for ending the guerilla-intensive internecine Algerian War belonged to Charles de Gaulle. His accession to the presidency of France in 1958 did not immediately change the course of the conflict, for it would continue to deteriorate. But as Jonathan Fenby makes clear in his illuminating work *The General: Charles de Gaulle and the France He Saved* (a book which I read much later), de Gaulle came to realize that "there was no long-term alternative to a federal system within which France's colonial territories would have the right to vote for independence." This was a radical view at a time when the colonies of European empires were wakening to rebellion.

De Gaulle survived multiple attempts on his life, as well as a failed putsch in April 1961 by a gaggle of pro-*Algérie Française* generals. Columns of citizens carrying shovels and pitch forks marched toward Orly airport, where they planned to confront the arriving generals as though the year were 1789. As the unlikely scene was broadcast by the international media, I fended off frantic calls from my parents urging me to take refuge with my aunt Beth, who was living in London.

When the loyal patriots arrived at Orly, they found themselves alone on the tarmac. The reason was de Gaulle. He had used his genius for high rhetoric to broadcast a stinging attack on the would-be "putschists" that made them look like amateurish fools in the eyes of all, including the French army in Algeria, which refused to join the coup. Charles de Gaulle was a remote, aloof man, but he knew how to talk directly to his constituency. To see him via television as he raised his long arms in the familiar "V" for Victory while exhorting every French citizen to help him bring peace was an unforgettable sight. *"Françaises, Français, aidez-moi!"* rang out as his hallmark call to action, his voice swelling with emotion.

Behind the politics, street warfare and heated rhetoric, there was also diplomacy—and on July 1, 1962, some six million Algerians cast their votes for independence, approving the negotiated Evian Agreements to end the war. The costs had been horrific. The death count for Algerians over the eight years of the conflict range from 300,000 to more than a million. Among the French military, including student conscripts like my boyfriend Jean Riffaud, who had failed to escape to Switzerland before he was called up, there were approximately 18,000 combat deaths and 65,000 wounded. Tens of thousands of "Harkis"—Algerians who fought alongside the French—also perished. Shamefully, the Harkis remained pariahs in both Algeria and France: in Algeria because they were seen as traitors, in France because their status as Muslim collaborators with the French army made people uncomfortable. The continuing low-class status of Algerians and their descendants in France and their failure to integrate originates, in part, from the unfinished business of the war, but few make that historical connection today.

What I understood then were only the bare glimmerings of complexity, as though what was observable on the surface of things was the tip of an opaque iceberg with a dense, impenetrable interior. I knew little about the wartime French Resistance, nor did I understand the psychology of the Vichy government and its willing collaboration with the Nazis. My efforts to comprehend what lay congealed in this dark ice were stymied by my youth and ignorance—by my inability to understand the historical context of what I had seen at Natzweiler-Struthof, for example, and by the impossibility of speaking about it to anyone, including the man I had married. Why did no one whisper even a word about what had happened to France's Jews—or to France itself—during the German occupation? The war had ended just sixteen years earlier. Was there a relationship between that recent trauma and the bloody Algerian conflict, really a civil war, that had followed in its wake? Because at the core of both these events lay the twin realities of occupation and liberation in which France had been both occupied *and* a colonial occupier.

I was beginning to ask the questions that would underscore my future writing life, but they were, so far, only partially coherent.

In truth, it was too soon to talk about the Jews of France, just as it was too soon to talk about the Holocaust and too soon to talk about what was happening *now* with the Algerians. Which is why I sustained a further jolt on one of our trips south to visit Claude's family.

The village of Guiche, populated by a few hundred souls, perches at the summit of a winding mountain road that climbs from the city of Bayonne into the Pyrenees mountains. It was once an important military stronghold, which is its continuing claim to fame. An eleventh-century castle belonging to the Dukes of Guiche, members of the noble Gramont family who still own the property, once loomed over the serfs below. At the time of Claude's and my visit, a lesser family had assumed the mantle of local fame: they were the Montands, who owned one of south-western France's best *charcuteries*, and were reputed to produce the best Bayonne hams in the country. Victor Montand was a boyhood friend of Claude's, and while they were catching up on each other's news, René Montand, the father of Victor and mayor of the village, invited me to join him in his small house close by. After a few moments of pleasant conversation, his expression changed. He looked at me intently and said: "There is something you ought to know. Your father-in-law was tried after the war for economic collaboration with the Nazis. His chemicals factory was in great demand, as you can imagine."

I stared at him, too dumbfounded to reply, too surprised to ask for clarification. I turned and walked briskly out the door.

Years passed, and I said nothing. It was the mid-1970s, and years after my marriage to Claude had ended, before I spoke to his sister Odile about what René Montand had said. Her response was flustered. She assured me that her late father had had to comply *and* that he had also risked his life by ferrying refugees across the Spanish border in a false trunk he had built into his car. She said I didn't understand. She was probably right; apart from René's account, I had no proof that he had been formally tried after the war, although many prominent industrialists had been detained and questioned. In the 1970s, however, no one really understood much about what had happened in those days, including, I suspect, Odile herself. The truth had been deliberately occulted, I would later learn.

Because I had broached the taboo subject of the Collaboration, she wanted me to know that her family had *helped* the hunted Jews of their immediate neighbourhood.

According to the 2012 Jewish Virtual Library, the official police census of March 15, 1942, registered 308 Jewish families in Bayonne, including refugees from Belgium and Luxembourg who had been unable to find transportation across the Spanish border into Portugal. In April 1943, almost all of them were deported.

Among the tiny number of survivors were members of a family who had lived across the street from Claude's family. The parents did not return from the Auschwitz death camp, but remarkably their two daughters did. Odile was not insensitive to their suffering, but her true pride in the sisters was that they had both become Catholics on their return, and that one of them was now a semi-cloistered nun. She wanted me to meet the sister who was still at home.

I feel a wave of dread washes over me as we mount the rickety exterior staircase to the second-floor apartment. The atmosphere inside is gloomy and airless. A woman of indefinite age sits hunched in a chair in an otherwise empty room, waiting to receive us. I remember nothing about the conversation, or even whether there is one; I only want to escape her obvious misery.

On our way out, Odile explains that her parents—my ex-husband's parents—had hidden the possessions of these neighbours, knowing that catastrophe loomed. This information, which is meant to reassure me, frightens me even further. My thoughts dwell on the terror of the police arrests right here on the street where my in-law family lives, right opposite the house I have slept in so many times, and where my Jewish children have spent their holidays. My thoughts dwell on the horror of the Auschwitz camp these Jews were deported to; on my own visit to Natzweiler-Struthof, no longer a shadow, but suddenly raw and vivid; on the awful *raison d'être* of those post-Holocaust conversions to Catholicism; on the destroyed woman hunched motionless in the chair on the second floor.

Odile is speaking to me of the presumed happiness of the sisters, both of whom are now exultant congregants under the kind and watchful eye of Jesus. Might I one day embark upon the same splendid path? she inquires with a sideways glance.

I HAD SOMETHING ELSE on my mind during our visit to Guiche in 1962. I was due to give birth in December of that year. Since Claude and I had no relations in Paris, a nurse of our acquaintance referred me to one Dr. Holler, a physician she had once worked for. The doctor was a short roundish man in his fifties whose office was located just steps from the famous Place de la Bastille of French Revolution fame. I imagine that

Dr. Holler had contempt for revolutions of any kind. He was a traditionalist, whose views on women and childbirth dated back decades or more—and the thing he disliked most about me, he did not hesitate to say, was my irritating habit of asking questions about my pregnancy and the impending birth. On one occasion I apparently went too far: I had read that natural childbirth, which was in fashion in North America, consisted of breathing and relaxation exercises to control pain and minimize the need for medical intervention. I asked Dr. Holler whether we might explore that method.

He drew a deep breath and glared at me: "The mother of all of us, Eve, had her children 'naturally,' and so will you!" When my own mother arrived in Paris just before my due date, he tried to co-opt her. "Madame," he said, "Your daughter asks too many questions." My reserved mother barely spoke French, but I saw the anger rise in her cheeks as she drew herself up to her full height of 5 feet 3 inches and spluttered: "*Monsieur*, her father and I have *raised* our children to ask questions!" I was never prouder of her than at that moment.

The French had a strange regulation: you could be delivered by your own doctor, but only in a clinic. If you wanted the added safety of a hospital, you had to entrust your delivery to whatever resident happened to be on duty that day.

I chose the clinic, and when the auspicious day arrived, I found myself in a small room with Dr. Holler and two midwives. The latter were kneading my abdomen as though they were preparing pie dough. Claude and my mother were also present, although Claude, who was prone to fainting, quickly excused himself from the unfolding drama. My mother may have expressed surprise at the kneading because she, too, was unceremoniously escorted out the door. "Who's having this baby, your mother or you?" snarled one of the midwives.

I heard Dr. Holler mutter something about the umbilical cord being around the baby's neck, and maybe we should all move to a hospital. Then I, too, fainted. Through a fog I heard one of the midwives ask the other about my condition. *"Elle est partie,"* the colleague informed her.

(She's gone.) Through my dimmed awareness, I thought she meant that I had died.

When I came to, Dr. Holler seemed to have straightened things out, since we didn't seem to be going anywhere. "Push!" he cried. I did. *"Madame, vous êtes formidable!"* My years of gymnastics seemed to have paid off. Then she was there, my daughter, Michelle.

Michelle almost didn't make it through her first night. Following the popular behaviourist ideas of the day (the same theories that had influenced my father a generation earlier), French newborns were fed every three hours, whether they were hungry or not, but only from 6 a.m. until 6 p.m. The babies were swaddled and placed on their sides in cribs beside their mothers. Strict instructions about not feeding during the night were repeated often and ominously.

Up and down the corridor, in every room, newborns screamed with hunger, but my baby's cry sounded different, like strangulation. I rang the bell. No one came. I rang again. A nurse sauntered in, looked, then shook Michelle upside down. She had rolled over on her back and was choking. When the nurse left and the hunger cries began again, I guiltily lifted her out of her bassinet and put her to my breast. I shall never forget that first powerful tug—the urge to live, incarnate, and the gift of silence that followed as she slept in peace. In retrospect, I should probably have thanked my father. In his world view, nonsensical rules and prohibitions were meant to be broken. Back home (Claude and I had moved to a larger apartment near the *Bois de Vincennes*), I held my newborn in my arms and played Beethoven's Seventh Symphony for her edification: the pro-culture values of my Rosemary Lane home had kicked in immediately. And I waited for Dr. Holler's first visit.

He was not impressed with my fumbling attempts at motherhood. A Toronto friend had sent me Dr. Benjamin Spock's revolutionary book *The Common Sense Book of Baby and Child Care*, which eventually sold more than fifty million copies in dozens of countries. Spock's message was a lifeline for me in a country where I had few supports. He said that infants were individuals, and needed to eat when they were hungry, including at night. He said that it was good to hug a baby, and that parents should follow their instincts.

Michelle was happily sucking on a pacifier when Dr. Holler approached her crib. He yanked it out of her mouth and threw it across the room. I picked it up and put it in my pocket. "Canadian women can't nurse," he announced after I told him I was having minor difficulties. He told me to stop nursing immediately. Cow's milk would do.

Within days my baby was sick, and even I realized it was time to drop the doctor. Not knowing where to turn, I corralled a woman in our apartment complex who had three sets of twins under the age of six. (When she opened her door, they escaped down the hall in all directions.)

The patrician-looking paediatrician to whom she referred me worked out of his home, and when I stepped through the door I was swarmed by eight small children. Extricating myself, I entered his examining room and placed Michelle on the table. "You have a very pretty daughter," he remarked. I took the chance to compliment him on his family. "The children must be a lot of work for your wife," I unwisely added. His smile faded. He straightened his shoulders and raised his chin. Eyeing me coolly from atop the bridge of his nose he sniffed: "She accepts that with a great deal of joy." Had I offended him, possibly on religious grounds, by appearing to suggest that he had produced too many children? I fled as soon as it was seemly to do so, clutching a prescription for life-saving infant formula in my hand.

As before, my loneliness grew extreme, and as before, neighbours did not speak to one another. There was one other apartment unit on our landing, but the woman and I merely exchanged greetings—*"Bonjour Madame"*—when we crossed paths. One morning there was an urgent knock on my door. She said she was having a breakdown and begged me to take her to the hospital. Following that crisis, we occasionally had tea, which is how I learned about birth control and abortion rights in France. Since there was no formal access to either, she and her sister performed abortions on one another with knitting needles almost every month. She was concerned, but the danger wasn't going to stop her. One day she confided her experience of what she called sex hunger. She'd been a virgin before marriage, she told me, and was now enthralled by sexual passion. She and her husband made love at least three times a day, corresponding with breakfast, lunch, and dinner, with at least one nightcap before sleep. Her choice to abort differed from that of a religiously devout young couple of Claude's acquaintance whom we had befriended. Married for six years, they already had five children. Still in their twenties, they had decided that celibacy was the only option, and slept in separate bedrooms.

Whether it was loneliness, anxiety, homesickness, or postpartum depression I shall never know. I doubt that there was a ready diagnosis in 1963 for the sort of emotional distress I began to suffer, but if there was, neither Claude nor I would have known what steps to take. My parents telephoned infrequently—calls were expensive—and at the first sound of their familiar voices I would cry inconsolably. I couldn't sleep. I had palpitations, and I developed a lump in my throat (after a test for thyroid disease, it was diagnosed as a plain old "lump of sadness"), but I continued to subscribe to the harsh platitudes of the era. "Pull up your socks and get on with it." "You made your bed, now lie on it." Claude was away at work all day, and our poor communication had worsened. My friends and I had looked to the day when we would marry and have children without suffering so isolated a life. Where was I? Where were the familiar words of my maternal language? Where were the student crowds I'd happily (though ill-advisedly) joined to confirm my social commitments? Where were the friends I had left behind—those few I trusted and who knew me well? Where was the stimulation of conversation and books and study? Where were the young men who had cheered me on the football field? I, so cocky and certain I was a "citizen of the world," as my father had taught me, was an immediate failure at the very job I had yearned for even as I studied Plato and Shakespeare—a job I had not imagined beyond the romance of my wedding day.

The baby and I were alone together—she thriving, I floundering. One day I recognized that I was experiencing something beyond the blues. I looked out the window to the street below and saw people scurrying by, caught up in the pressing business of their lives. "They are alive, and I am dead," I heard myself say aloud.

A caring physician came to see me. He smiled and spoke gently. I cried at his kindness. He told Claude that I was too young to be so far from my family. He told me to take Michelle and return to Canada for a visit. So, I bundled up my six-week-old daughter and we flew home—to the house on Rosemary Lane.

To speak English was a relief; to re-experience familial love warmed me; to visit my friends with my beautiful baby made me happy. But my body told me I didn't want to return to France: the morning I was slated to leave I couldn't move my neck on awakening. My friend Simmy, a physiotherapist, was summoned. She kneaded, stretched, and rotated my neck. Finally, I was ready, at least physically. But nothing was the same after my return to Paris. In fact, it became increasingly clear to us both that I couldn't stay much longer. We set a departure date: November 1963, then travelled south to Bayonne to say goodbye.

Claude's father was dying. It was his and Claude's mother's turn to feel, as my parents had felt, the pain of losing a child to a distant world. By chance alone, my family had won that fateful lottery—something I only came to understand when I watched one of my own children disappear into another country after schooling there, and I wondered whether I might have lost the intimacies of family life forever.

On November 22, 1963, our little family shipped from the port of Le Havre on the new ocean liner *Le France*—the same day President J. F. Kennedy was murdered. The shocking news was announced as we docked at the British port of Southampton to take on passengers. The rest of the journey across a November-wild North Atlantic passed in seasickness and collective mourning.

I arrived home in Canada still largely innocent of the world, but with growing intimations of complexity. That and the growing realization that I was too-firmly married to a man with whom I could not share my thoughts.

CHAPTER FOUR

BECOMING A WRITER

DURING THE DECADE OF the 1960s the questions about history, war, and remembrance that had haunted me throughout my time in France took residence inside a deliberately willed fog that lifted only sporadically. I was conventionally busy. I gave birth to a second child, my son, Roland. Claude was doing a master's degree in urban planning at the University of Toronto, and I had promised to transform his mangled written English into something more readable. I was encircled by family and friends.

Occasionally, the French spectres poked unbidden through the mist, disturbing my routine. The trigger might have been a news item on continued tumult in France, although there was still little reporting. It might have happened during one of our visits to Bayonne to visit Claude's family, where a memory from my recent past in that country overcame the fortress of my defenses. It might have been the slightly later broadcast of the BBC documentary series *The World at War*.

It was during one of these unexpected moments that I made my first written attempt to capture the essence of my visit to the Natzweiler-Struthof camp. Words and imagery overcame me as I wrote, at last, of the walled-off moment. I mailed my opus to Joe Rosenblatt, who was then the editor of *Jewish Dialogue*. He brushed it off. "No one wants to think about those things," he replied bluntly, and correctly. I filed my piece away. Almost a decade would pass before I brought it out again.

Since Claude was a student, one of us had to work, and my private identity as a writer (unpublished) would not put food on the table. Teaching was what women did. I was accredited quickly; English, French, and (amazingly) Latin were my subjects, and in the fall of 1964 I found myself standing before a class at David and Mary Thomson Collegiate in Scarborough: a teacher of English Literature. I loved teaching (except for the then-current rule that obliged hulking sixteen-year-old boys to ask my permission to use the toilet) but it was in conversing with my colleagues that I began to extrapolate from the French experience. As we talked during coffee breaks and lunch hour in the staff lounge, I encountered, for the first time, an anti-liberal stance in my own country.

Bruce Evoy, head of the English department and an early aficionado of the writer Ayn Rand, was determined that we underlings teach her work to our classes. I hadn't heard of Rand before being obliged to teach her novel *The Fountainhead*—a polemical tract I resented wasting time on with students who might never read another book once they left school. Rand's larger-than-life cardboard characters, their self-assigned superiority, their disdain for "lesser" beings and their powerful sense of entitlement appalled me. I was still largely ignorant of Second World War history, but I knew I had encountered this proto-fascist thinking in the ubiquitous noise of postwar France.

Bruce and I debated over sandwiches in the teacher's lounge every lunch hour, to the amusement of our colleagues, who crowded around to cheer and boo. I knew I'd never win anything more than an argument (a rare outcome): Bruce was the department head, and his course choices weren't going to change. But I did succeed in privately subverting his curriculum. I taught *The Fountainhead* as mandated, but as a springboard for a critical discussion of the ideas it contained, and as an example of truly bad writing.

Another teacher on the staff was a proponent of eugenics: he thought that unmarried women who had more than one child should be forcibly sterilized so that society wouldn't be burdened by their culpable stupidity. Together, both he and Bruce led me to early thoughts about law and human rights as cardinal protections for the despised, and to the certainty that they either applied to all or to none. Looking for commonality, I joined Alan Borovoy's Canadian Civil Liberties Association. The CCLA printed and mailed to its members a now-familiar statement by the German pastor Martin Niemoeller, who had been imprisoned in a Nazi camp. Niemoeller's message about the incremental nature of persecution, and the denials of bystanders, resonated with me.

> First, they came for the Socialists, and I did not speak out—
> Because I was not a Socialist.
> Then they came for the Trade Unionists, and I did not speak out—
> Because I was not a Trade Unionist.
> Then they came for the Jews, and I did not speak out—
> Because I was not a Jew.
> Then they came for me—and there was no one left to speak
> for me.

I remembered the day Professor Marcus Long drew a circle on the blackboard at the front of the classroom with an "x" along its circumference, and I heard his admonishing voice warn about the long-term implications of everyday choices. For years, that piece of yellow paper scripted in black greeted me from its home on my refrigerator door, where it shared space with pictures of family and friends. Later, it migrated elsewhere while remaining within sight. As I write these words, it is pinned to a bulletin board beside my desk, looking ragged with age but still speaking truth.

Niemoeller's personal statement suggested to me that multi-ethnic societies require hawk-eyed vigilance in order to prevent themselves from fracturing along dangerous lines of "us" versus "them," as had happened in Germany. His words also triggered other thoughts: the memory of our family dinner-table, where I had been introduced to George Orwell and his canny, power-hungry pigs; the universal "one-world" values of Holy Blossom Temple interwoven with the imperative to pursue justice; the philosophy classes where I had read Plato on what "justice" might possibly mean, and where I had learned, to my utter surprise, that history can be shaped through propaganda; and my appreciation as a student of the ways in which Shakespeare revealed the commonality of human emotion and behaviour...all foundational pieces from my early life, some of them now beginning to converge.

AS THE 1960S ENDED, two chance happenings brought me nose-to-nose with my unanswered questions. The first of these made me a *published* writer—at last. The second brutally reconnected me with France. Both, as it happened, were related to the unequal status of women.

I had not forgotten the humiliation of being a married woman in France: the legal dependency, the deprivation of adult rights, and the cruelty of anti-contraception and anti-abortion laws. Women's issues were just beginning to enter the Canadian mainstream in the late 1960s, but I, as a mother of two young children, and living in a failing marriage, was preoccupied with other things—until one day in 1968 when a notice of jury duty arrived at my door by registered mail. Men were legally required to serve, but women were allowed to excuse themselves—possibly so they wouldn't have to hear raw evidence that might offend their delicate sensibilities, or perhaps because beliefs about the irrational female brain were still in circulation then. It didn't occur to me to excuse myself. I was excited at the prospect.

The case concerned a twenty-three-year-old woman who had accused a man she had dated of bodily assault and rape. To my great surprise, I was one of twelve people chosen from a panel of more than one hundred, and as the only woman on the jury, I could only guess at why. Did the defense team expect I would be fair? I had been a high school teacher, for what that was worth, and adjudicating difficult situations clearly came with that territory.

On the appointed day, eleven men and I perched high in the jury box in a quiet teak-panelled courtroom in downtown Toronto. Slightly below us to our right sat the judge. Facing the judge were the lawyers for the prosecution and the defense. And opposite us hunched the thin, expressionless defendant, a man in his late twenties.

From the first moments of testimony, I found myself in uncharted territory. The prosecution asked the complainant to relate the putative sexual assault in graphic detail. An emergency room nurse testified that the woman had suffered injuries. A man from the forensic crime laboratory reported his findings. There were questions about the woman's previous sexual history, but none about that of the man. She seemed to be as much on trial, I thought, as he was.

When the testimony was finished, the judge leaned down from the bench and spoke to us. "Peggy," he said, "is not a virtuous woman."

Pardon? What was the point of *that* remark? It was unclear to me whether we were supposed to consider this pointed information in relation to whether she had consented to intercourse. What the judge did say was that we were to think about whether we believed her story in general. Then he read aloud the current law against rape.

The doors to the jury room were bolted behind us. We elected a foreman, then took a preliminary vote: nine guilty, one unsure, two not guilty. I voted guilty. We began to debate the evidence and the law as it had been explained, but to my astonishment the conversation turned almost immediately to the subject of female sexuality, where—as the only woman in the room—I was suddenly an unwilling expert. Peggy had submitted at the end of a physical struggle. Wasn't that consent? the men wanted to know. Wasn't refusing sex more important than being beaten up?

The very question implied that women were all the same, and that moral "purity" trumped everything else, including assault. Hours later, exhausted and emotionally drained, we took a vote; we were 11:1. The hold-out, who was now obliged to explain himself, admitted to everyone's surprise that he didn't believe in the existence of rape. "That's what I've always told my son," he said, by way of putative explanation, his voice breaking.

So, we returned to the courtroom, a hung jury. The judge re-read the relevant section of the Criminal Code, slowly and deliberately, looking intently at each one of us in turn. I knew he was saying we had to find consensus.

Back in our stuffy deliberation room, the man who didn't believe in rape asked another juror to accompany him to the washroom, where he could speak privately. The two men remained there a long time, and when they returned to the table, the doubter's eyes were red and swollen. We voted again. We were now unanimous.

Back in the courtroom, each of us stood up and spoke our verdict aloud. The ordeal was over. As we readied to leave, a guard pulled us aside. "I've been dying to tell you this all day," he said conspiratorially. "This guy's already served time for rape. The defense couldn't put him on the witness stand, the Crown would have torn him to bits!"

I remember the heady sense of altered reality I experienced as I left the courthouse and walked up University Avenue that day. I felt a compulsive need to capture this event, which had forced me to think hard about the lives of two strangers, both of whom deserved justice. The thought that I was a "writer" flitted across my mind. Had the moment to cross the publishing Rubicon arrived? I telephoned my friend David Lewis Stein, who was already a working journalist. Would he help? "Yes," he said without hesitation. "Get something down and I'll look at it."

David and I had been friends since our days at Forest Hill Collegiate. We had shared four years of philosophy and English classes at the University of Toronto. He had, for a brief while, lived in my parents' home after suffering a breakdown in our third year and having nowhere to turn. We had talked and talked, all day and into the night—and had both stood at the bottom of our class that year. Now he edited my tentative words and helped me to assemble the structure of a magazine piece.

Hal Tenant, a staff editor, stepped forward to meet me in the waiting room of *The Canadian* magazine. He lifted the manuscript pages from my hand and smiled benignly. I must surely have looked like the ingénue I was. The next day he called me back and handed me a cheque for $100. I lovingly photocopied the miraculous piece of paper. I taped it to my bedroom wall. I would be published. Erna Paris, published writer.

When the article, theatrically headlined "The Drama Behind the Jury Door," appeared in August 1968, I was told that every defense lawyer in Canada read it. Why? Because it was illegal to publish the deliberations of a jury. Who knew? Not me. I waited in trepidation for the arrest warrant. None came.

The second seminal event took place in my own home. In 1969, the Canadian Broadcasting Corporation aired Marcel Ophuls' landmark documentary *The Sorrow and the Pity*, about France's collaboration with the occupying Nazis. No one in France had yet seen this explosive film; another two years would pass before it opened in two select Paris cinemas, where it caused a sensation. State-controlled television also refused to broadcast the documentary. Much later, in a 2012 interview on *Télérama,* Ophuls revealed that the head of the state-controlled French network had asked Charles de Gaulle what he should do with this hot-potato film, which evoked what the network executive called "disagreeable truths." "France doesn't need truths; France needs hope," de Gaulle replied.

Not until 1981 was *The Sorrow and the Pity* televised in France, and only then because it had become impossible to sustain the myth of universal resistance to the occupying Nazis. The Second World War had ended a quarter of a century earlier, and the younger generation had been schooled to believe that, except for a few certifiable monsters, everyone had either fought with, or tacitly supported, the French Resistance. But in 1972, the American historian Robert Paxton had published *Vichy France: Old Guard and New Order, 1940–45*—a bombshell that had set off an unending quarrel about who did what to whom during the war that can still be heard today.

Paxton followed up with a second explosive work, *Vichy France and the Jews*, co-authored with the Canadian historian Michael Marrus. In retrospect, it is no surprise that foreign historians were the first to instruct the French about their own suppressed history. No local scholar would have dared to do so in those years.

I remember my encounter with *The Sorrow and the Pity* in striking detail. Our small television set occupied a corner of the living room, and I watched from just a few feet away. On the screen unfolded black and white archival footage from the era of the Nazi Occupation, along with bold interviews about the wartime fate of France and France's Jews. I held my breath as Marcel Ophuls articulated the questions that had lain buried in me for so many years, toxic inchoate questions, questions without sequence—until now. With each scene and each masterful interview, the dense fog within me began to thin and part. Here was footage of Marshal Philippe Pétain, the hero of the First World War battle at Verdun and now the leader of the collaborationist Vichy regime, offering "the gift of himself" to his compatriots by agreeing to partner with the Nazi conquerors. Here was Prime Minister Pierre Laval publicly hoping that, to defeat bolshevism, Germany would win the war—the same Pierre Laval who had worked tirelessly with the Nazis to deport as many Jews as possible, including children, to "the East" —a euphemism for the death camps. Here were close-up conversations with upper and lower-class *résistants* alongside conversations with upper-class bourgeois collaborators, whose Catholicism underscored their hatred of godless bolsheviks, thus propelling them into the orbit of the Nazis. Bolshevism was identified with the Jews—hence the antisemitism of these upper-class collaborators. Bolshevism was also identified with the Resistance—hence their anti-Republicanism. I learned that day that this collaborationist stance was shared by most of the French, who saw Pétain as a rescuing hero and *Pétainisme* as a rescuing creed.

Here was a Jewish scientist who was arrested as a teenager, tortured, and imprisoned; when his voice broke over having been betrayed by the country of his birth, my eyes stung at the injustice. Here were archival pictures of the roundups of innocents. And unforgettable pictures.

When it was over, I sat immobile. I thought hard about Claude's family, who had been so kind to me. And I thought again about the seminal hour I had spent at the Natzweiler-Struthof camp. What would I do with my new knowledge? The way was unclear.

Claude didn't see *The Sorrow and the Pity*, and we never spoke about my private grief. Fifteen years later, when we were long divorced and he had moved to Montreal, I was in that city promoting *Unhealed Wounds: France and the Klaus Barbie Affair*, the book that was born from the beginnings of illumination which I had experienced on seeing *The Sorrow and the Pity*. He came to hear me speak. He sat in the front row, in my direct line of vison. Afterwards, we had dinner together. We talked of many things that evening, but neither of us said a word about the lecture I had just given, or the subject we had never confronted.

THERE WAS LITTLE I could do in the immediate moment after I learned about life in wartime France and the memory of the era; that time had not yet arrived in my life. But the women's movement was a different story, especially now that I was a "real" writer, the author of a magazine article that some people had read. There was more: aside from having been made aware of my subordinate status as a wife in France, I had been privately introduced to emerging feminism several years earlier, the evening I first opened the pages of Betty Friedan's *The Feminine Mystique*.

It was 1963, just after Claude and I returned to Toronto with Michelle. Since we hadn't yet found a place to live, we were occupying the small apartment above the garage in my parents' home. Claude was comfortably asleep beside me in the darkened room as I, flashlight in hand, opened the book everyone was talking about. Within moments, the words on the page seemed to grow darker and bolder. Friedan had called something unspoken and seemingly ineffable "the problem that has no name."

I sat bolt upright. I immediately understood the white-bone truth of what I was reading: that the social mores that imposed Marriage and

Motherhood on women to the exclusion of any other identity might rightly be called repressive—and that it might, just might, be possible to distinguish oneself as a female individual if one were brave enough to counter convention. My father had seemed to encourage this when I was a child. There was little Mathilda Murgatroyd who slayed dragons, and the Little Mermaid, too. Yet, when I became adolescent, Dad had forgotten his own teachings. Like all my friends, I had been directed towards a solely domestic life, despite my education.

Betty Friedan wrote that the constraints my friends and I privately chafed at had not been present a generation or so earlier, when women were allowed to pursue careers, especially during the war years, when men went overseas, and their wives replaced them in the work force. The white stream from my flashlight illuminated ideas I had never encountered before. When Freidan suggested that the frilly-aproned housewives who flashed their white teeth across hundreds of advertisements for laundry soap and vacuum cleaners did *not* have to be the models for our future lives, as my generation had been led to believe—we women whose fresh university degrees had purportedly equipped us for nothing more than baking tuna casseroles and changing diapers—I knew that I wouldn't sleep that night.

But what good was this awakening if it merely exposed the walls that contained us? What could be done when even my given name was usurped on a place card at a University of Toronto function for the wives of graduate students, where we were identified only by the names of our husbands? Feeling trapped, I spoke about my unhappiness for the first time—to my mother. Quiet and wise, she said there were moments in life when it was normal to seek counsel. So, I made an appointment with a psychiatrist who had a home office at the end of Rosemary Lane. On the appointed day, I entered by a side door and was ushered into a book-lined study. The space was still, the books looked inviting. His face was professionally impassive, and I poured out my heart.

When I had finished speaking, he turned on me. "You understand nothing!" he said angrily. I was, he spat out, an inadequate wife, an inadequate woman. "You have penis envy!" he hissed as I cringed. I saw the bubbles of white spittle collect at the corners of his mouth as he ushered me out the door.

I crept home in disgrace. To my knowledge there hadn't been a concerted campaign to destroy independently-minded women since the burnings of the Inquisition and varying policies of shaming for putative adultery and other supposed sins against the patriarchal structures of society, but the rape trial and the Freudian I had just encountered had opened my eyes to the systemic discrimination against women that seemed to be woven into the fabric of Western culture.

Justice and Injustice. These were becoming subjects of profound interest. As was the possibility of personal transformation. As my marriage imploded, I was gripped by the possibility of beginning life anew—and by the inherent dangers. This may be why I volunteered to talk on the telephone to desperate people at the Toronto Distress Centre, run by the Reverend Gordon Winch, who later was awarded the Order of Canada for his caring work. Perhaps I thought that if I could help others, I might also learn to help myself. The desire for personal transformation may also explain why I wanted to write a magazine article on priests and nuns who were leaving the Church, as many were doing in the early 1970s. Like me, they were summoning the strength to leave a failed "marriage"—to navigate the void that loomed on the other side of safety.

My first published magazine article had occurred by happenstance: I had been thrust onto a jury, an experience I thought I might be able to process by writing. I had been published once, and my longing to write now revived. I didn't know Robert Fulford, the famous editor of *Saturday Night* magazine, but I mustered the courage to telephone him cold. To my surprise, he took my call. To my further surprise, he was intrigued by the priests and nuns story and agreed to meet me. When I arrived at his downtown Toronto office, I found him talking on the telephone with his girlfriend, Geraldine Sherman, a CBC radio producer whom he would later marry. My presence seemed not to matter. The billing and cooing, as my parents' generation might have called it, went on for a good ten minutes while I sat straight-backed and red-faced on a wooden chair immediately adjacent to Bob's desk, wondering how I might back out the door without being noticed.

Bob encouraged me to proceed. Across the decade of the 1970s, he would generously mentor my professional development.

One of the many people I interviewed for the story of nuns and priests leaving the Church was a Jewish woman who had converted to Catholicism, then became a nun. Another was a young man who had fallen in love with one of his parishioners and wanted to marry. Both spoke to me with passion and openness. These were my first interviews, and I immediately loved the intimacy that came from close listening. (Soon afterwards I received memorable advice from my friend Barbara Greene, a successful radio documentarist. "Move in close with your microphone, but keep it low," she counselled, "and always make strong eye contact.")

The resultant article was a high point of my nascent writing life, for I had never experienced the sense of elation that seized me as I wrote. It was summertime. I was seated in my garden, working with a pencil and a lined note pad, almost observer-like as words formed in my mind and spilled into existence of their own accord. I felt transported by language and emotion that magical afternoon. What I didn't know then was that such moments arrive only rarely in a writer's life.

At home, communication between Claude and me continued to falter, despite couples therapy and valium, the easy prescription-of-the-day for depressed women. I tried to ignore the hollowness; I had two young children who loved their father. One day I asked a friend who had experienced divorce at what point a person might decide to leave a marriage. (I remember distancing the subject by phrasing the question in the neutral third person.) "When you feel you have no other choice," was her reply. I understood. "Choose life," she was saying, quoting Deuteronomy.

Had Claude not been offered an important job in another city, I might not have had the courage. As things stood, I simply could not move there with him.

The day we told our children we were separating remains one of my most painful memories.

I was immediately preoccupied with problems, not least how to support my children. I lost my desire to write. Then, one day in 1972, the telephone rang. It was Bob Fulford. "You've just won a gold medal from the Media Club of Canada," he said excitedly. I had won this award for the piece on priests and nuns—the second article I had written, and a work I had more or less forgotten in my changed circumstances.

"Thank you!" was all I could muster. I felt the blood rush to my head. After a few speechless moments, I turned to a friend who was visiting. "I'm going to be the best woman writer in Canada!" I proclaimed, in a burst of pre-feminist optimism.

Thrilled at having unexpectedly won this prize, I weighed my options. A return to teaching would be practical. Forging a freelancing career would be risky. Yet I never seriously considered anything else. In that era, feature journalism offered a possibly sustainable career. There were dozens of magazines in Canada; the CBC was commissioning freelance documentaries; TV Ontario was also hiring; the burgeoning Canadian cultural scene was thriving. So, I chose the life I had always wanted—the life I had once pretended to inhabit. I knew it would never be a big life in monetary terms, even if I were successful (my daughter jokingly called me "Ern-a-living"), but it was enough. Before the era of "me and my money," it was enough.

Chatelaine under the editorship of Doris McCubbin Anderson had been quietly revolutionizing the lives of Canadian women since the 1960s. Doris was jettisoning traditional 1950s content (how to cook tuna casseroles and starch men's shirt collars) in favour of an issue-driven publication that was sabotaging the "rules" governing women's place in society.

Too shy to call her directly, I summoned up the nerve to telephone another famous person I didn't know. I admired June Callwood's magazine work, and I knew she was Doris Anderson's friend. I stood stiffly in my kitchen as I dialed her number on the wall phone just over the breakfast table. But what should I call her? She was then married to journalist David Frayne. "Is this Mrs. Frayne?" I stammered at the woman who answered the phone.

At least, she didn't sound annoyed. Heart pounding, I told her I had won an award and that I wanted to be a writer, and did she think Doris Anderson might speak to me?

"Yes, she would," replied June without hesitation. In our thirty-five years of subsequent friendship, I was often reminded of her kindness. Publicly, she was one of Canada's most influential social activists; in her private life, she was unfailingly generous.

Doris Anderson answered her own phone. Again, I stammered that I had just won a prize, and I would like to be a writer and, uh, could we perhaps meet? I strained to decipher her tone, expecting a cool rejection. But no; with the largesse I would come to cherish, she invited me to her office that same week.

The *Chatelaine* workplace occupied part of an entire floor of the Maclean-Hunter building in Toronto, at the northeast corner of Dundas Street and University Avenue. One walked through large doors into a circular open space flanked by private offices. Someone directed me to Breda Harding, the editor's receptionist, whose desk fronted the large corner room that belonged, I presumed, to Herself. I was ushered inside. Sitting behind a huge desk, busily painting her fingernails scarlet red, sat an attractive, broad-faced woman with dark hair that curled around her face. "Hellooo," she said in a flat drawl I did not recognize. (I had never travelled west of Ontario, and she was raised in Saskatchewan.) She smiled. "Please sit down."

I don't remember the details of our conversation, except that I'd been too naïve to know that I'd been expected to bring a few ideas to the meeting. Nonetheless, I walked out with an assignment: *Chatelaine* was sending me to Calgary—on expense account, no less—to research a piece on "new volunteer work for women." The story was pure Doris: Take an established women's activity—volunteer work—and stand it on its head. The "new" volunteer work I was sent to investigate involved neither fundraising, hospital auxiliaries, nor symphony committees, but resettling teenaged runaways and child prostitutes.

I boarded the airplane for Calgary, hardly believing my luck. The flat Canadian prairies looked endless as we streaked across a blue sky the likes of which I'd never seen. Finally, there in the distance rose the Rockies—a jagged wall of mountains, capped with snow.

Everything was new—the environment and the kind of people I met. I'd never known anyone who volunteered their time to help the lost and the failing. They were delighted that *Chatelaine* was interested in them, and I was filled with admiration in return. They and the children they were helping opened my eyes to social problems I had never adverted to. Perhaps in a small way I identified with the girls' attempts to re-start their failed lives.

Among the young women I met was fifteen-year-old Charmaine, whose story intrigued me. I sensed that she would open up to me privately, and that her life would be of interest to the public. Would Bob Fulford be interested in a profile? I called him collect from a local payphone. Yes, he said, he was.

I invited her to a restaurant for tea, and I chose a corner table where we could speak quietly. She was wary at first, her young thin face already lined with worry. Then she softened. Her parents had named her Charmaine because the year she was born a popular song by that name had topped the charts. However, naming her was the last piece of attention they paid her. She'd been beaten at home, failed at school, then ran away at age thirteen. Since then, she had lived on the street, supporting herself through prostitution and living hand to mouth.

She had wanted to change her life, to become a better person, so she had decided to change her name to Angela. From street person to "angel." At fifteen, she hoped a change in nomenclature might suffice.

We kept in touch. One Christmas she called me. She was in Toronto. I invited her to the house to share the holiday with me and my children. She joined us. She said she was well.

The next time she called she was a patient in the Wellesley Hospital. I visited. She had had a baby and the baby had died. I believed she had been charged, but she wouldn't say. Shocked, I asked her to keep me informed. She didn't. We lost touch.

I often think about her and ask myself why I didn't do more to help.

During the 1970s, before I turned to book writing, Doris was my mentor and educator by virtue of the meaty research articles she assigned me. I researched and wrote a three-part series on women and business that included two articles on dead-end jobs for women in retail, supermarkets, the banks, Bell Canada, and Air Canada (low-paid and dead-end were then the only jobs available in those sectors); and a piece on clerical workers called "Why Secretaries Get Mad" that elicited a barrage of mail. I also researched a series on family law reform, focusing on what needed to change if divorced women were to win equal property rights and adequate child support. I was learning about the real world of women's work, such as it was, and about human rights in the process. My own mother hadn't worked for pay except to teach piano, and even then, her students came to her. My generation of young women was beginning to enter the professions—but I didn't know anyone who was a secretary, clerk, or telephone operator, or who stood on her feet all day selling purses in Simpson's.

In 1972 Doris sent me to Ottawa to interview party leaders, cabinet ministers, and their opposition critics on their attitudes towards abortion rights, equal pay for equal work, and other issues pertaining to equality. The published piece infuriated the Robert Stanfield Conservatives (the day the article appeared, the journalist Larry Zolf called to say they were holding a caucus meeting to discuss their national exposure as reactionaries).

One of the leaders I interviewed was David Lewis, who then headed the federal New Democratic Party (NDP). I knew David only slightly—I had canvassed for him in his riding of York South—but I knew his son Stephen well. Stephen would become the leader of the Ontario NDP, Canada's ambassador to the United Nations, and the UN Secretary General's Special Envoy for HIV/AIDS in Africa, among other high-profile posts, but I knew him from my teenage summers at Camp Ogama and we had remained friends.

I liked David (everyone called him by his first name), but he seemed to believe that as a friend of the family I would treat him with deference. I, on the other hand, was proudly independent. David didn't come off very well in my piece. He was a fine person, but a man of his generation who held ineradicably sexist attitudes towards women.

The morning the article appeared I was awakened by the ring of the telephone next to my bed. "Erna, how could you do this to me?" a wounded voice said in my ear.

I was still half-asleep, but I defended myself. I told him I tried to be honest and fair. He was silent. I'm sure he understood. He was a principled man.

Stephen was delighted. "Now *that's* what I call investigative reporting!" he said laughing.

From the start, Doris's unfailing expectation that the articles she published would be well-researched and strong, but always fair, struck a responsive chord in me and helped shape my approach to the discipline of research and writing. She nurtured me, and in doing so launched my writing career. When we met in 1971, I was a divorced single parent with financial worries. She knew this, and "kept [me] busy," as she wrote in her memoir *Rebel Daughter: An Autobiography*. I once needed $1000 to send one of my children to summer camp, and the deadline for payment was fast approaching. I proposed a profile on a monetarily successful Canadian author who was ignored by her snobbish peers because she wrote so-called "pot boilers." It wasn't really a Doris story, but she understood my situation. She accepted without hesitation, and I knew it was a gift.

The parties in her Rosedale house were legion and the amount of alcohol consumed legendary. All her authors were invited, having been transformed into personal friends. Doris also enjoyed lunchtime drinking (as she acknowledged in her memoir), and whenever she invited me to a restaurant (frequently at the now defunct *Le Provençal* on St. Thomas Street) to discuss a story idea, I worried in advance. I was a notorious failure as a drinker, having fluffed two attempts to match the drinking habits of my mostly male journalist friends (I would spend the rest of the day comatose). I had tried refusing the waiter's offer while Doris ordered a pre-lunch cocktail, and I felt her disapproving look. Was I trying to make her look bad? Eventually, I took to ordering a "Virgin Mary," spicy tomato juice in a cocktail glass. My drinking from a glass with something red in it seemed to satisfy her.

In the 1970s, Doris also divorced and became a single parent, as her mother had been before her. We leaned on each another, she by inviting me and my children to swim in the outdoor pool at her Rosedale home, I by listening sympathetically to her problems. She was increasingly famous, but lonely. And breathtakingly honest. One summer evening, as we sat in my darkening garden, she told me, "I'm an institution. I have no one to call when I can't sleep at three o'clock in the morning."

It would be hard to overstate the role Doris Anderson played in the lives of younger women who today may be ignorant of what she achieved on their behalf. Doris relentlessly pried open the tightly bolted gates of the male fraternity, making it possible for the next generation of women to step into the world of business and the professions. She tackled tough subjects, including abortion, the need for day care, and the inequality of women in the workplace. Although the Canadian social revolution she stoked through *Chatelaine* remains unfinished—the emergence of the "Me Too" movement simultaneously exemplifies both that truth *and* how far women have come—Doris incrementally changed social attitudes. In the wake of her activism, millions of women and their daughters have pulled down the walls first described by Betty Friedan.

I will not forget that she took a chance on the diffident young woman who telephoned her so long ago. Before she died in March 2007, I thanked her for believing in me.

IN THE WINTER OF 1975, designated by the United Nations as "International Women's Year," I negotiated a series of eight one-hour radio documentaries with Geraldine Sherman, then the executive producer of the CBC radio programme *Ideas*. The series' title would be *Sex and Civilization*. What I proposed was an exploration of attitudes towards women and female sexuality throughout the entirety of Western history—a history project, in other words. And, as I now see in retrospect, a preposterously huge subject.

I wonder today at my *chutzpah*. My experience in the documentary genre was practically nil. I had prepared a few short radio pieces, most of them for a CBC programme about Canadian diversity called *Identities*, a subject matter that piqued my interest as a member of a minority. What drove me may have been the realization of my ignorance. I had been writing for *Chatelaine* about different aspects of the women's movement, but I knew nothing about the origins of women's inequality.

What I wanted to understand was the underlying reason for the imbalance of power. Yet when I think back, I believe that my true subject, though still foggy, was even larger. What I sought to grasp were the origins of otherness—a looming question whose roots trailed back to France, where I had first encountered racism. Where did inequality begin? How was it practiced? What were the consequences?

My attempt to understand patriarchy, misogyny, and how contemporary society might possibly confront these ancient practices was my first large-scale (albeit oblique) glance back at my still-hidden unease.

My documentary subjects were huge—each could have been a book, a series, an entire library, a life's work. They were:

- the influence of sexuality on the structures of Western society
- how the institution of patriarchy has shaped the lives of both men and women
- the ancient myths and archetypes of sexuality in Western literature and their effects
- the origins of the sexual attitudes that so profoundly influenced the Catholic Church, and the consequences of these attitudes across the centuries

- the modern dilemma of sex and love, and why we often have trouble putting the two together
- the twentieth-century technology of sex, as pioneered by Masters and Johnson
- the social consequences of pornography, and
- current research about the nature of male and female

Fortunately, there was no shortage of money at the CBC in those halcyon days—a boon, since I had only six months to map out the programmes, conduct my interviews, edit the shows, and write the scripts. I could travel anywhere I chose and talk to anyone who agreed to meet me. I interviewed Margaret Mead, a woman of notable importance and curmudgeonly manner. When I questioned her about her research in Samoa, she wrongly accused me of prurience and threatened to walk out of the New York studio. We finally did manage to talk about women and "otherness" as translated into myth and ritual in what were then called "primitive" societies.

I also interviewed Susan Sontag about her essay, "The Pornographic Imagination," in which she defended literary pornography as a narrative of "extreme states of human...consciousness, those so peremptory that they exclude the mundane flux of feeling...." Her interests were remarkably expansive, her reading astonishingly broad. I loved that she had written, "The most interesting ideas are heresies."

We met in her modest Riverside apartment in New York City. She wore jeans and no make-up, and her long straight hair was streaked with grey. It felt entirely natural to be talking with America's famed icon of culture about the nitty gritty of extreme sexual expression as we sat at her kitchen table, two women drinking coffee from chipped mugs, while her young son, David Reiff (who would also become a writer) darted in and out of the room. The 1970s were an era of liberation and breakthrough. The taboos of our mothers' and grandmothers' generations were dissolving—and pornography was inherently about taboo. As I wrote in my introduction to the programme, "If the social taboo is obscene language, that's what pornography will offer the reader. If the taboo is nudity, then nudity becomes pornography. And if the taboo is the actual portrayal of sexual intercourse, then we'll begin to see films showing just that."

Sontag described erotic literature as being ahistorical, a timeless world in a closed space, removed from society, often of a fantasy nature—castles or chateaux or secret basements, for example—and the pornographic imagination as an "asocial, or antisocial place identified with the private, which has nothing to do with the community, and which, when carried very far, means defiance of the community." We talked about violence—the power-submission equation underscoring pornographic writing—and its social context, which reduced the passive female to a plaything. It seemed to me that much of 1970s culture incarnated what Sontag called "defiance of the community"—or perhaps it was the making of a new community as mores loosened and reconfigured themselves, while still objectifying women.

I also met the psychologist Rollo May, the author of *Love and Will*, a compelling book on relationships, along with John Money, a sexologist from Johns Hopkins University who was conducting groundbreaking research on sexual identity and the biology of gender, a subject that would not become mainstream until much later.

At the time I met him, Money was as odd as was his subject. After the formal part of our interview, which was conducted at his gender identity clinic—during which I was fascinated to learn that for obvious reasons of species reproduction "female" is the basic state of nature; males, by contrast, must be created *in utero* and are more fragile throughout the life cycle—he invited me to continue our conversation over tea at his home later in the day. At the appointed hour I entered a large space filled with outsized pieces of African and Asian statuary, where the *pièce de résistance*—a ceiling-high penis—loomed just inside the front door. I saw him observe my startled reaction with barely disguised mirth as I carefully circumvented the entrance-blocking impediment. (An expert on hermaphroditism, Money counselled sex reassignment. In the 1990s, publicity surrounding an unsuccessful case led to a controversy that permanently clouded his legacy.)

Unsurprisingly, some people found some of the *avant garde* subject matter of *Sex and Civilization* disturbing. Unfortunately, they included my producer, Angela M., a devout Catholic who, in keeping with her name, pasted stickers of smiling winged angels on her office door. She and I clashed at every step of the way over her desire to soft-pedal, and my determination to be direct. Another was Lorne Tulk, the CBC technician who recorded my shows. One day he informed me that, after long consideration, he understood why I was interested in these topics: it was, he had concluded, because I was a lesbian. On yet another occasion, as I gave a talk previewing the radio series, a man in the front row stood, turned to the audience, raised his index finger, then let it slowly droop. The men in the room laughed uproariously.

I didn't yet know where I was headed, but in retrospect I recognize these eight radio shows as my first attempts to probe the underbelly of racism by studying the history of shifting social attitudes. The religious and social construction of female otherness seemed no different from the religious and social construction of other discriminatory thinking.

In 1975—International Women's Year, and the year *Sex and Civilization* was broadcast—more than 2000 women rose from their seats at a rally in Toronto's Massey Hall. We linked arms and belted out Helen Reddy's famous tribute to the times:

I am woman, hear me roar
In numbers too big to ignore,
And I know too much to go back and pretend…

We were young, bold, and optimistic. We were tasting unprecedented freedoms. And yes, in case anyone asked, we intended to change the world. And we *did* change the world. Among the social revolutions of the 1960s and 1970s, only the women's movement was transformative.

Many of the older women in our lives took note. From behind the closed door of her lonely life, my own mother encouraged me with a quiet intensity.

CHAPTER FIVE
THE EMERGING THEMES THAT WOULD DEFINE ME

I HAVE OFTEN THOUGHT THAT plain luck carried me through. I had the luck to be born to immigrant parents whose fortunes rose in just one generation, in step with the roaring postwar economy of Canada. Out of that new prosperity, I attended university and travelled to France, where I was seized by the subject that would later define me. With that education, I could pursue my dream of becoming a writer, and even more fortuitously, at a moment in Canadian history when an unprecedented explosion of cultural nationalism was reshaping public life and the arts.

I proposed articles and CBC documentaries which I hoped might help me understand Canada's shifting political culture. Quebec's Quiet Revolution of the 1960s, for example, had followed on the heels of the very Catholic Maurice Duplessis regime (known as the "Great Darkness")—the most repressive government on the North American continent. Before long, "quiet" turned violent: in October 1970, the *Front de Libération du Québec* kidnapped James Cross, a British diplomat, and Pierre Laporte, a prominent Quebec politician. As is common at such dire moments, most Canadians, very frightened, firmly supported the draconian War Measures Act, invoked by then-Prime Minister Pierre Elliott Trudeau on October 16, which suspended *habeas corpus* and curtailed civil liberties, among other things. More than 12,000 troops were deployed in Quebec, including 7,500 in Montreal. Four hundred and ninety-seven people were arrested. Army tanks patrolled the streets of Montreal looking for terrorists; the Canadian media operated under a climate of fear; and indiscriminate roundups threw hundreds of innocent people into Quebec jails where they were held without charge, without bail, and without legal assistance. Canada was—for a short, frightening time—a police state.

The killing of Laporte on October 17, 1970, ensured that there were very few vocal critics of the War Measures Act, including in my circle of acquaintance. Notable exceptions were Bob Fulford and the broadcaster Barbara Frum. Other public figures, including the literary scholar Northrop Frye and the pianist Anton Kuerti, also signed a petition of protest.

I, too, was opposed—and surprised to find myself outside the mainstream within liberal circles, including my close friend David Stein, who was already a journalist of moderate influence. Although my voice was too small to be noticed, I protested. I agreed with NDP leader Tommy Douglas, who said, "The government, I submit, is using a sledgehammer to crack a peanut." There were ways to track down killers by using traditional police work that did not require trampling civil liberties. Pierre Trudeau claimed that he was protecting Canadian democracy, but the ease with which basic rights were suspended at his will was far from reassuring.

My observations of the Algerian War playing out in Paris may have shaped my response to nationalist violence. I had seen escalating brutality in the streets of that city, a virtual civil war that included the armed presence of police and military. I thought that state-sponsored violence might be warranted on a battlefield, but government-sanctioned violence on civilian streets was a frightening demonstration of how easily democratic rights can be overturned.

I was beginning to grasp that the theoretical underpinnings of violence in Quebec derived from a charismatic leadership able to articulate the anger, marginalization, and sorrow of their aggrieved followers. The archetype of this genre was Franz Fanon, a physician, psychiatrist, Marxist, and anti-colonialist born in the French colony of Martinique in 1925. A descendant of slaves, Fanon became the most influential revolutionary intellectual of his and successive generations. In his 1961 book *Les damnés de la terre* (*The Wretched of the Earth*), he argued that, because colonized peoples were wrongly and deliberately dehumanized by their oppressors, their demeaned status allowed them to overlook the humanist principles that prohibit violence in the pursuit of liberation. Fanon's ideas were especially resonant in France: at the height of the Algerian War, the French philosopher Jean-Paul Sartre wrote a sympathetic preface to Fanon's book, in which he, too, condoned violence. For Fanon, violence against the colonial oppressor opened a way to psychological catharsis, and to the transformation, then liberation, of the individual and society.

I had read Fanon's newly published book when I lived in France as a student and found it remarkable. Although I rejected his central argument for violence, I heard the anguish in his voice as he described the grief of personal humiliation and social marginalization. I believe that my life-long interest in the psychology of those who trigger radical political change, and of the followers who are susceptible to the words of charismatic leaders, may have been sparked by his work.

The *Front de Libération du Québec*—Marxist-Leninist, separatist, and paramilitary—had its own intellectual guru, Pierre Vallières, whose book, *Nègres blancs d'Amérique* (*White Niggers of America*), was directly inspired by Frantz Fanon. For Vallières, the Québécois were the oppressed "natives" and English Canada the colonial oppressor. The "humiliation" of the Québécois (another concept picked up from Fanon) made violence a necessary tool of revolt and revolution.

Who *were* the protagonists of this national drama? What underscored their anger? Beyond the intellectual leadership of Fanon and Vallières, was there a connection between what was happening in Quebec and the civil war that recently raged in Algeria and France? And did any of this relate to the other history of violence that haunted me? In 1971, hoping my ability to speak French might open doors in Quebec, I proposed a profile of Robert Lemieux, the radical lawyer for Pierre Vallières and Charles Gagnon, to *Maclean's* magazine, then edited by Peter C. Newman. Newman was enthusiastic. He even provided me with an expense account for my travels to Montreal—a further indication in my eyes that I could truly call myself a writer.

Lemieux was publicly trumpeting his support for the FLQ, arguing that the death of Laporte was due to Pierre Trudeau's War Measures Act. He had been imprisoned for four months during the October Crisis for associating with the FLQ. The stay behind bars that had radicalized him even further.

I had Peter's wife, Christina (née McCall), to thank for this assignment (she was also on the editorial board of *Macleans*.) A formidable writer on Canadian politics, Christina had published a superb piece in *Chatelaine* in January 1971 tracking the evolution of Quebec's Quiet Revolution from its origins to the "apprehended insurrection" of October 1970.

The interior of the Montreal courthouse felt electric with emotion. The families of members and associates of the FLQ who were on trial anxiously paced the halls, presumably taking a break from proceedings taking place behind closed doors. Lawyers in black gowns strode purposefully to their encounters with clients and judges. Cigarette smoke thickened the air.

I knock on what I think is the correct door. A jaunty-looking man in his late twenties invites me inside. He sits down opposite me, on the other side of a large desk. A cigarette dangles rakishly from a corner of his mouth; his curly dark hair is long in the style of the day, and a small brush mustache oversees his upper lip. He looks at me warily. He had previously interrogated me about my motives before accepting my request for an interview—to which I had replied truthfully that I wanted readers in English Canada to understand him better. This had no doubt pleased him; he clearly craved publicity.

It's hard to imagine, in retrospect, the heady atmosphere of those Quebec days—the excitement, the idealism, the rebellion against the old ways, including the heavy hand of the Catholic Church, the potent scent of danger, the thrill of trespassing boundaries. I already knew a few things about the man sitting across from me. I knew that, as a student at McGill Law School in the mid-1960s, he had studied under the venerable Frank Scott; that he had been influenced by Scott's powerful defense of civil liberties; and that this belief in the protections of civil liberties would metamorphose into a justification of violent insurrection à la Frantz Fanon and Pierre Vallières. I already knew that he had turned to radicalism in 1966 after his Montreal law firm assigned him to defend Robert Lévesque, an early FLQ member who faced six charges of robbing and bombing an armoury; and that his overt identification with this client had ruffled the law firm, which fired him in 1968. Now out on the street, Lemieux had undertaken the independent defense of Pierre Vallières and Charles Gagnon, as well as that of the brothers Paul and Jacques Rose, both of whom were charged with the kidnapping and murder of Pierre Laporte.

"Never before in Canada had there been such trials," he boasts, fixing me with appraising eyes. "The judge thought I would advise them to plead guilty, that I would cry that my clients were sorry. I refused to do that. It was embarrassing for the court to have defendants who challenged society as a whole. The judge was furious that his name would be forever associated with this event. Even the police in the courtroom threatened me."

"They threatened you?"

He declines to explain—although he does manage to bristle with anger at remembered injustice and at the same time to look pleased with himself. "The FLQ is a legitimate defense against the violence of a capitalist system, where food is destroyed when people die of hunger, where in this city of Montreal infant mortality is two or three times higher among francophones than anglophones...!" Whatever theatrical role he is playing in the drama of revolutionary Quebec, there is, at least, a solid underpinning to his ire, I think.

When the interview ends, we leave his office together. Admirers besiege him in the courthouse foyer. He signs autographs. I note that he has a special eye for his female acolytes. Someone presses into his hands a copy of a Jules Verne novel (*Familles-sans-nom*) about the Lower Canada rebellion of 1837. History and politics have merged into a single narrative that he seeks to personify.

He drives me back to my lodgings, where we take our leave. Hours later, at 2 a.m., I am awakened by a feathery tapping on my door.

"Who's there?" I call out apprehensively.

"Robert," comes the whispered reply.

"*Vas t'en!*" (Get out of here!)

Such risky behaviour. Didn't he know I might have exposed him in *Macleans*? Showman that he was, he thought his notoriety and good looks would buy him favours—that was certain. What the tapping on my door also suggested to me was the then-common assumption that women were usurpers in the realm of serious journalism, and that seduction would put them in their proper place.

Like countless other self-involved revolutionaries, Robert Lemieux was a theatrical romantic. His ideas—slogans, really—were of the cookie-cutter variety, which meant that when the political tumult subsided in the 1980s, he lost his allure. Eventually he moved to the remote community of Sept-Îles, where he continued to defend unpopular cases. He also became impoverished and was reduced to pumping gas for a living. He died in 2008, in virtual obscurity.

All the same, Robert Lemieux and his radical cohorts fronted a social upheaval that left an indelible mark. The Quebec that emerged from the era of FLQ violence had divorced itself from its repressive past, just as the end of the Algerian War ended France's colonial domination of that country. One of the connecting threads between the FLQ, the Algerian conflict, and the earlier Nazi era was the glorification of violence to achieve an idealized end, and the presence in each instance of ambitious charismatic thinker-leaders who presented themselves as trustworthy guides to that better life.

Robert Lemieux was also an early "judicial guerrilla," a breed of radical lawyer better known in Europe than in North America. A decade later

I would meet the acknowledged prince of the genre: Jacques Verges, the French lawyer who defended the Nazi war criminal Klaus Barbie.

A FEW MONTHS AFTER "The Radicalization of Robert Lemieux" appeared in the June 1971 issue of *Maclean's*, I began work on another political profile. Keith Spicer was the swashbuckling new Commissioner of Official Languages. In 1969, just over a year into his first term as prime minister, Pierre Trudeau introduced the Official Languages Act as a means of promoting national unity and addressing Quebec's growing nationalist movement. It was a form of soft diplomacy—in contrast to the hardline stance he would take during the October Crisis a year later.

The Act promised bilingual services from federal government agencies across the country. It was not popular legislation: civil servants with high school French feared for their futures; immigrant Canadians couldn't understand why French should be preferred as a second language over, say, Ukrainian or Italian; and others blustered that if French Canadians wanted to speak French, they should move somewhere else—possibly to a remote Pacific Island. In Quebec, members of the political class initially scoffed at the idea: Parti Québécois leader René Levesque argued that separation would happen by 1976, regardless of tinkering by Ottawa.

Into this charged atmosphere sprinted thirty-six-year-old Keith Spicer, a prime ministerial appointee. His job was to investigate complaints from the public and civil servants in 150 federal departments, agencies, and crown corporations. For example, an anglophone in Rimouski might object that no one at Air Canada there could speak to him in English, or a francophone in Thunder Bay might complain that his job interview had been conducted in English only, to his disadvantage. Spicer had the legal authority to summon witnesses and compel them to testify—a controversial power in an inherently contentious job. When we met in early 1972 in his large, mandarin-style Ottawa office, even he described his job as "impossible." This was not a surprise, since his charge was to foster understanding between extremes ranging from the militant Protestant Orange Lodge to the Parti Québécois. When he travelled to Moose Jaw in November 1971 to "meet the public" after the city council had voted twice to keep him out but then relented, a woman called out loudly, "There's that SOB Spicer who's trying to push French down our throats."

I liked Spicer. He was bold, but diplomatic—and a recognizable Canadian liberal. His disarming response to his critics was to emphasize mutual respect, a seemingly straight-forward stance, but far from obvious in the wary days of FLQ radicalism and René Levesque separatism. When he gave his first report to Parliament in late 1971, Spicer said that it was his intent "to consider justice in state bilingualism simply as an ideal of human dignity and [a] long-term bridge to understanding among Canadians." That such motherhood thoughts were controversial is an indication of the tenseness of the times.

I concluded in my article that "stormy was perhaps the most optimistic forecast possible for the future of bilingualism in Canada." But I was wrong. Polls since the 1970s suggest that both anglophone and francophone Canadians have backed bilingual federal government services and the right of official-language minorities to be educated in their maternal language, even though the failure of the Meech Lake Accord and the Charlottetown Accord in the early 1990s, and the nail-biting 1995 referendum on Quebec independence, temporarily lowered support for these ideas among anglophones.

In 1990-91, long after his term as Commissioner had ended, Keith Spicer headed the six-person *Citizens' Forum on Canada's Future*, which also was initiated by the federal government. This time his mandate was to engage in "a dialogue and discussion with and among Canadians...to discuss the values and characteristics fundamental to the well-being of Canada." His report reinforced the pollsters' findings that most Canadians favoured the idea of bilingualism, although they had concerns about the way the policy operated. But the most telling evidence can be found in statistics compiled by the Treasury Board of Canada Secretariat and the

Public Service Commission of Canada, where a comparison of the status of English and French in the federal public service between 1974 and 2012 demonstrated the country's gradual move towards linguistic equality. In 1974, only 19 percent of positions requiring knowledge of both official languages were filled by functionally bilingual employees; in 2012, the percentage was 42.5 percent—still not ideal, but better. And in 1978 only 64 percent of supervisors met the language requirements, while in 2012 a full 95.2 percent made the grade.

"When you look at the failures of language policy in many other countries, especially Belgium, Cyprus, and even the United States, the transformation of Canada's linguistic reality during this short period is close to miraculous," Spicer told me in the spring of 2015. "It's a triumph for the common sense of Canadians. What they often resisted in 1960, they later declared a fundamental value."

The Official Languages Act itself was a markedly Canadian response to violence. Negotiation and compromise, the trademarks of our approach to nation building from the time of Confederation, led to legislation whose underlying ethos of pluralism subsequently shaped our thinking and institutions. Spicer received the Order of Canada in 1978 as recognition of the seminal role he played in pioneering this social transformation.

Something in my interview with Spicer suggested another magazine piece—specifically, an exploration of how English-speaking civil servants with only high-school French might be coping under the new legislation. I approached Bob Fulford, who thought it an excellent idea for *Saturday Night*. I researched and wrote the article, "Guilt, Anxiety and Bilingualism in The Civil Service," quickly. In it, I gave voice to the people Spicer had mentioned: those worried public servants who now fretted over their promotions and resented francophones they thought could ruin their careers. I wrote that procedures during this fraught transitional time needed to be more transparent.

The article appeared in March 1972, the same month as my piece on Spicer, and it took public-service Ottawa by storm—a controversy that was abetted by *Saturday Night*'s provocative cover illustration of a large frog. I was appalled by this gratuitous insult that did not reflect what I'd written. I hadn't penned an attack on francophones; on the contrary, I'd purposely investigated more than one side of the official bilingualism issue. Learning French was a survival issue for anglophones in the public service, but the ability to learn a new language, perhaps at an advanced age, differed from person to person, particularly in an atmosphere of—for many—fear and perceived pressure. On the other hand, a functionally bilingual public service was deemed important for Canada itself.

The day the *Saturday Night* article appeared I received a telephone call from a producer at Radio-Canada in Montreal. How marvellous that I'd written two articles about bilingualism, he purred; the host of their evening current affairs programme would like to interview me that very day. The show was live and broadcast nationally. He was certain their listeners would like to hear from me.

Unsuspecting, I agreed on the spot.

The show was already live on air when I answered the phone in my Toronto home that evening. The host introduced me as someone who had simultaneously written a laudatory piece on bilingualism for one publication and an attack on bilingualism for another. My eyes widened. He wasted no time. "So where *do* you stand, Erna Paris?"

Had I been more experienced, I might have made a suave, reasoned reply, such as: "Good evening, it's a pleasure to join you. In answer to your question, I profiled the Commissioner of Official Languages, after which I subsequently explored the less happy side of the new language programme. I believe that together they paint a true and complete picture of reality."

Instead, I froze—on live radio. The host crowed triumphantly as he thanked me for my important contribution to his programme. It was my first experience with ambush journalism.

I loved writing feature stories from Ottawa. The monthly magazines didn't pay well, but one had time to research and to think about the writing. And certain experiences were memorable. One afternoon, as I waited in the antechamber of the Treasury Board before interviewing the minister, Bud

Drury, his assistant suddenly materialized before me. He looked incredulous. "Are *you Maclean's*?" he blurted out. I saw anger rise in his face. How could a prestigious national magazine send this slip of a young woman to interview *his important boss*? (Had he known how inexperienced I was, he might have been justifiably miffed; as it was, he was merely sexist.) To cover his bases, he quickly arranged for several aides to tape my interview with the Minister. Never was an interview so carefully covered on the receiving side.

Meeting Bud Drury and other high-placed ministers gave me an inkling of the confidence I would need as I later travelled the world hunting down the way leaders control their national historical narratives.

IN THE FALL OF 1972, I received a telephone call from Christina Newman. I didn't know her or Peter C. personally; they were remote stars in a distant galaxy. So, when Christina invited me to visit their home, I was delighted. They did not say why I was invited. I thought it must be a social occasion, although I didn't know why such celebrities would want to befriend me.

They lived in a spacious stone-fronted house in Rosedale, an affluent Toronto community that resembled my childhood neighbourhood of Forest Hill. When I was ushered through the door, I was surprised to find myself the only guest. Tea was served. We all smiled at one another, and I admired the antics of their little daughter. Then came a job offer. Would I like to become an assistant editor at *Maclean's*, the person responsible for the back-of-the-book columns? I was speechless. A job with a paycheck? In my innocence it hadn't occurred to me that the invitation might involve an offer of employment.

I leaped at the opportunity without much understanding of specifics. My high school guidance counsellor had once told me I could do whatever I set my mind to—and that was enough for me. My annual salary would be $12,000. Not as much as the men in the office, I later learned, but a fortune to me and a security net for my children.

The tension in the air was palpable the moment I stepped off the elevator on the *Maclean's* floor in the old Maclean-Hunter building, and it didn't come from a high-frequency hum of happy productivity. The open reception space felt too quiet when one considered that an unknown number of congenitally loud journalists were squirreled away in nearby rooms. A receptionist sat at a table facing the elevator doors, keeping an unfriendly eye on all comings and goings. As she marched me towards Peter C. Newman's private space, I observed my future colleagues at work in their small offices. No one looked up, which struck me as odd; most writers are preternaturally curious.

Peter was enveloped in a cloud of pipe smoke and listening to the big band-music of Stan Kenton on earphones; this, I later learned, was his preferred way to work. He must have intuited my nervousness, because he smiled welcomingly and tried to put me at ease. After a few introductory comments about pension plans and tax deductions, none of which I understood, he led me to my new office. It was furnished with a desk, a telephone, and a typewriter. On the desk was a stack of papers, unsolicited articles submitted by the public known in the trade as the "slush pile." My job would include reading these in search of a publishable nugget.

That part looked easy; the rest did not. I had never been an editor, and some of the columnists I was supposed to deal with were high-profile writers such as Heather Robertson, author of a famous book, *Reservations Are For Indians* (an indictment of Canada's policies with regard to native peoples, and the first of its kind), and John Gray, the magazine`s Ottawa correspondent, whom I had known casually at the University of Toronto, and who was already an established professional. I was certain that whatever he wrote each month would be *perfectly* fine with me. As for copyediting, I suspected I was below par—a distinct danger for me and, not incidentally, for the reputation of the magazine. Having taught the rules of English grammar as part of the high school English curriculum (cramming the night before my classes), I was reasonably confident that I understood why gerunds, participles, and their syntactical colleagues performed as they did, and that I'd be able to make necessary corrections. Spelling might be another story.

For the remainder of my first day I sat behind my desk, waiting for someone to appear at the door to teach me my new job, but with the exception of a welcome visit from Joan Weatherseed, the upright and proper staff copyeditor (had she noticed errors when editing my freelance pieces?), no one passed the portal. I didn't dare approach any of my new colleagues. One was the formidable Walter Stewart, whose outspokenness I knew by reputation. In his memoir, *Here Be Dragons,* Peter C. Newman called him "a professional shit disturber." Walter was a staunch social democrat, an NDP supporter, the son of militant atheists, a prolific book author, and an experienced newspaperman. The very thought of him made me tremble.

In the office next to mine, Tom Hedley held court. He was a young Torontonian who had already hit the big time, having worked at *Esquire* magazine during its glory days in the 1960s, when the likes of Tom Wolfe, Hunter S. Thompson, Gay Talese, and Joan Didion were inventing the New Journalism, a revolutionary approach to non-fiction feature writing which discarded the dispassionate reportorial voice while borrowing from the tool kit of fiction—dialogue, scene-setting, description, metaphor, and varying points of view, including the subjective first person—without losing the story's factual underpinning. There were plenty of critics, including those who claimed that the authors of the new genre were writing more like sociologists or psychoanalysts than journalists. There was truth to this, but I still loved the new genre. I thought that far more could be communicated by employing these new techniques than conventional journalism had allowed.

Tom also intimidated me. During all my time in that office, he barely acknowledged my presence, much as I would have liked to talk to him about the New Journalism. All the young writers I knew were trying to emulate the famed New York writer, Tom Wolfe, especially his witheringly funny 1970 piece, "These Radical Chic Evenings," about a gathering Leonard Bernstein had held in his Manhattan apartment for the

Black Panther Party. Joan Didion was also a favoured master of the genre, although she discomfited me. In her collection of essays, *Slouching Towards Bethlehem*, she had written: "People think the writer is their friend; the writer is never their friend." I thought a lot about that observation, and I decided early on that I agreed with her. To be friendly with the subject of an interview is not to be "a friend," that is, someone whose subsequent portrayal may be seen as a betrayal of confidence. Years later a writer of my acquaintance asked me a related question about writerly "betrayal" while I was speaking from a public stage. I said that if I ever thought I had betrayed a subject, I would stop writing. I said that people who agree to be interviewed on the record have implicitly agreed to a joint contract.

As befitting his celebrity status, Hedley wore a permanent scowl as he swanned about the office, and before long he disappeared to edit *Toronto Life* magazine before leaving Canada once again for the United States. His greatest claim to fame, the creation of the movie *Flashdance* (inspired by a Toronto bar girl and produced with its Canadian references expunged) came later.

I tried hard, but some of the columns I was supposed to edit defeated me. One of these, on nuclear heavy water, sent me to the research library—to no avail. Study as I might, I had no idea what the author, a scholar in the field, was talking about. Checking his gerunds and participles was the most I could do, after which I timorously submitted the piece to Peter C. for publication. Heather Robertson was another story altogether; I was bowled over by her fearless writing. She was a Canadian nationalist—a *Western* Canadian nationalist—which endeared her to Peter and Christina. In one memorable column she wrote that she would *never* leave the West. We became friends a year later, after she moved East. She had met her future husband Andrew Marshall and that was that.

Heather died prematurely of cancer in 2014. She was an outstanding writer, a woman of intelligence and high principle. Her books deserve to be better known.

I also worked with Myrna Kostash, who, like Heather, would become a life-long friend. Myrna was an emerging feminist in those heady transitional days of women's liberation, a social warrior, and a skilled writer whose finely crafted prose I studied carefully as I tried to hone my own. Her staunch pro-feminist pieces drew unfavourable attention from Peter and Christina, particularly when I praised them in editorial meetings. One morning I arrived at my desk to find an anonymous scrawled note that read, "You and Myrna Kostash think you've invented feminism...."

Peter's criticisms of me intensified as the weeks passed. Never proffered in person, they were delivered as little bombs planted on my desk just before my day began. A short piece I wrote for the magazine was returned to me with the word JUVENILE scrawled across it in large black letters. Peter's criticisms of others on his staff thickened the tension. Walter Stewart, whom I came to know and like, once vowed to me in anger that he would write a book about the dismal treatment he received. He quit *Maclean's*, but never did write the book.

John Gray and I had lunch together whenever he came to the Toronto office, and, like all *Macleans* staff lunches, the subject—the only subject—was everyone's frustration with Peter C. After one of these noontime sorties, Peter called me into his office. He looked uncomfortable. "I wish I'd been a fly on the wall during your lunch," he said remorsefully. He knew the effect he had on others. I felt uncomfortable, and sorry for him.

He may have been hoping I would leave on my own accord, but, hard as it was to take that elevator to the office each day, I couldn't. I had just begun. I needed the money.

But then I made a truly reprehensible error.

Roy MacGregor, then a young writer in his twenties, had been hired by Peter and Christina to write a music column; and the subject of the article in question was the rock group *The Who*. I had no idea who *The Who* were, as I had lost interest in North American popular music after having encountered the wondrous work of Jacques Brel and Edith Piaf during my years in France. I had, however, heard of *The Guess Who*. So, I decided that Roy MacGregor had erred, and with my thick-nibbed editorial marker I interjected the word "Guess" into the name of the group every time it appeared in the story. No one caught the blunder before publication, and it appeared in print.

The stack of outraged letters to the editor grew higher by the day. "Pack up," said Peter C. in so many words.

I was devastated. I had failed at my first job in the business. I walked past the receptionist, took the elevator, and left the Maclean-Hunter building. A red pay phone stood on the south side of Dundas Street. I called David Stein. "Come right over," he said.

The next week I went to the unemployment insurance office and sat forlornly among a dozen other cast-offs waiting for my name to be called. When I reached the service desk, the woman taking my application found my status as a former magazine editor so amusing that she invited her colleagues over to titter. Later, when I began to earn money from my freelance work, I wrote to cancel the monthly payments. Within a week I received a letter from an astonished bureaucrat who said she had never heard of anyone doing such a thing. Honesty was both noteworthy and humiliating, I came to understand.

Flying home from Mexico after visiting with my parents during Christmas week, I gingerly picked up the latest issue of *Maclean's*. A large correction box stared at me just inside the cover. It reported that an over-zealous editor had changed the name of *The Who* to *The Guess Who*. Peter C. Newman, editor-in-chief, offered his readers his most sincere apologies.

Many years later, I received a surprise telephone call from Christina. "I'm sorry for the way you were treated," she said bluntly. She and Peter had separated, she told me. I wasn't surprised. Christina was an excellent political writer, and she had once confided that Peter wasn't pleased. Perhaps he put it best himself in a 2011 interview with John Robert Colombo, published in the *Literary Review of Canada*. "We divorced over religious differences," he quipped. "I thought I was God, and she didn't."

I NEEDED AN EXPERT on dualism for one of my *Sex and Civilization* programmes, dualism being the ancient theory of the separation of mind and body which entered the early Catholic Church, with enduring consequences for women. The belief was simple enough: women were considered the "lower," bodily element of the human; men were the rational mind and therefore superior. Marjorie Harris, a young freelancer like me, thought she knew just the person to interview. He was Tom Robinson, a professor of classics and ancient Greek philosophy at the University of Toronto. She said he spoke without "ums" and didn't need editing. That sold me. In those days audio tape was edited manually, so anyone who might spare me tedious hours was a find. I phoned Professor Robinson, and we arranged to meet at his office.

He was seated behind his desk, a handsome young man wearing an amused half-smile. I probably did look a sight—like a skinny waif, he later told me. Five years after my separation solo parenting, tight deadlines, and money worries were taking a toll on my health.

And so it happened that our very first conversation was about Greek philosophy, a connection that took me back to my own formative years at the same university. It was the start of many conversations, for at this writing Tom and I have been partnered for more than forty years.

Some weeks later, after we had recorded a formal interview at the CBC on mind-body dualism and its long-term influence on male views about women, Tom invited me to dinner. We walked to a restaurant on Yorkville Avenue, which was still the hippie capital of Canada, although beginning to gentrify. Over pasta he proffered an invitation entirely consonant with the era and, I would learn, with his interests.

"How would you like to come with me to Ethiopia to see the flora and the fauna?" he purred.

I thought I had never heard a "come up and see my etchings" line quite so interesting. I peered at him closely. He was smiling, but he meant it.

"Yes, I would!" I immediately replied.

We never did get there—a war broke out, and travel in the region became impossible. But Tom was a traveller; an amateur ornithologist and biologist; a lover of astronomy and classical music; a man who would spend much of his life tramping through the Amazon jungle and other remote parts; a multilinguist who lectured in universities around the world; a sometime poet, translator, and later in life, a playwright. He too wanted to "swallow the world." We recognized one another.

A good man, I told my family.

Of his innumerable intangible gifts to me over the decades, including becoming a caring stepfather to my two children, the first was the most transformative. The monthly deadlines for feature magazine pieces were wearing; I wanted more—but what? Our bank accounts were still separate in those early days. He contributed to the household, but I remained responsible for the children. So he offered me a deal: six months full support while I explored the possibility of different work.

I had three options in mind. The first was law school (a career I still yearn for in my weaker moments). I would take the LSAT admission test. The second was a proposal I was chafing to make to the Law Reform Commission of Canada, based in Ottawa. If they put me on a small retainer, I would publicize their interesting work, which was unknown to the public. The third idea was to write a book.

I passed the LSAT exam but put that possibility on a back burner. The Law Commission said they were interested in my proposal but had no money. As for the third option—the one that felt the most exciting—I outlined a book proposal and applied for an Explorations grant from the Canada Council.

The book idea was about identity in a multicultural, immigrant-based society like Canada, an idea that emerged from my incipient wonderings about how exactly apparently successful plural cultures came into being, musings that would later expand to questions about whether such cultures could endure.

The book I had in mind invited me to explore my longstanding, largely unspoken apprehensions about my own identity as a Canadian. I had been born, raised, and educated in Toronto. And I belonged, of course—didn't I? The answer was, yes, sort of. I spoke without a foreign accent, I was not a member of a visible minority, but I grew uneasy when people adverted to my Jewish origins. A residue of the anxieties my parents and other first-generation Jewish immigrants had experienced still lived inside me. Like them, I feared antisemitism; on the other hand, I was adamantly not going to live in a ghetto.

Looking back, the impulse to write a book about Canadian Jews was not unlike the impulse that had led me to the *Sex and Civilization* radio documentaries. I wanted—needed—to understand the history and context of social identities. Where *did* I come from? My parents were both uncertain of their ancestry: in their fraught desire to assimilate as Canadians, they had remained deliberately ignorant about their East European past, beset as it was with pogroms, then genocide. I initially thought that a book about the process of arrival over three generations—my grandparents, my parents, and myself—might help me feel more comfortable in my skin. Because there was something palpably missing in my understanding, something only vaguely apprehended, something only inchoate and to be avoided as I went about my life as a Canadian-born woman. I wondered whether that "something" might be my Eastern European ghetto past and the associated trappings of Orthodox Judaism that were my legacy but entirely foreign to me. I had received a strong communal message, perhaps subliminally, that I and other young Canadian Jews must leave all of that behind. To look forward and never backward was the imperative. Not to do so would be to remain uncomfortably distinct, and perhaps affect one's future in this country.

The historical continuum intrigued me. How did one move from the station of my grandparents, who had arrived in Canada at the beginning of the twentieth century without skills or education, to my (would-be) assimilated parents, then to me with my distinctly modern dilemmas? I wondered about the process of assimilation—of belonging; and about how people adapted the values and attitudes of their old-world origins to what was then a thoroughly Anglo-Saxon land.

My first thought was to write a book about three generations of two or three Jewish families, with a focus on the women: how daughters had resisted their mothers and their mothers' world, and how granddaughters had moved into a new sphere altogether. But that plan seemed narrow. Hadn't sons also rejected their family's dreams? What really interested me, I decided, was what immigrants and their descendants had chosen to cherish from all the baggage they had brought with them from centuries of life in Europe. It was the process of adaptation that piqued my curiosity—the long passage to becoming Canadian.

I was getting there, but the idea still didn't feel right. Because when I started to research the topic, I saw that it was the larger events against which individual life dramas were played that had effectively shaped people's lives. The past had shaped immigrant Jewish culture, but new events, new history would redirect lives. Before long, the generations-of-families story was taking a back seat to the happenings of their times.

I was well into this work when the telephone rang one morning. The news was not good; my grant application to the Canada Council had failed. Crestfallen, I asked the woman at the other end of the line to return my supporting material.

"Why?" she asked. "Just leave it here, and I'll submit it in the next competition. There'll be a new jury." Surprised at this suggestion, I agreed.

During this second waiting period, my brother Peter and his then-wife Lisa mailed me a cheque for $5000—the precise amount of the elusive Explorations grant. In case I missed the cut again, they wanted me to write the book, regardless. Peter and Lisa were in their early thirties, new parents, and barely established financially. Their generosity was unforgettable.

I did get the grant the second time around, and I returned the money, with interest.

All very well, but I had no idea about how to structure my expanding book idea. The Canadian Jewish experience did have a unity, but it had also been geographically defined in different parts of the country. How would I incorporate that? Eventually, I decided to focus on historical themes. I would study the early history of the Canadian Jewish experience in Quebec, where the community had its origins and had battled against discrimination, then follow the saga in that province to the turbulent 1970s, when the rise of Québécois nationalism made staying in Quebec an uncomfortable enterprise for many Jews and anglophones.

In Toronto, home to the second largest Jewish community, I'd study the ideologies that characterized the immigrant community, for the Jews from Eastern Europe had themselves been obsessed with identity issues since their emancipation, over the course of the nineteenth and early twentieth centuries, into the larger societies where they had lived apart for hundreds of years. The new arrivals had brought their internecine debates to Canada, where their passionate quarrels had continued to roil the community. In this section of the book, I would recount the vibrant story of the Jewish socialists and their breakaway cousins, the communists, as well as their considerable impact on the emerging twentieth century Canadian labour movement.

In Western Canada, I would explore the history of the pioneer Jewish farmers, most of whom had never interacted with a cow or a tractor, let alone milk or drive one, before reaching the stony, land-grant farmlands of Manitoba and Saskatchewan.

In each of these places I wanted to explore the process of adaptation, shift, and cultural change. History, in other words: the sometimes chance events along the way that determined the future. I'd find the people, ferret out their stories, and recount their experience in what I hoped would be a compelling narrative.

It was an ambitious project, and once again, if I had permitted myself to question its viability, I suspect I might have been too intimidated to continue. What motivated me was my intense interest in the subject. What daunted me was the prospect of writing a book-length work. I confided my fears to my friend David Stein. He helpfully suggested that books were just magazine articles on the same subject linked together. "It's easy!" he said. I wasn't convinced.

Today, I ask myself which of my chosen themes has continued resonance almost forty years after the publication of *Jews: An Account of their Experience in Canada*.

First, the dramatic story of Canada's early difficulties with majority-minority relations in Quebec remains endemic to the Canadian experience of immigration and integration, and especially to the continuing identity issues that plague Quebec society. Quebec has never ceased to grapple with the question of who is a Québécois and who is not. First it was the Jews whose right to belong was challenged, then it was the Anglos. Now it is Muslim women who are consider a "danger" to society if they cover their heads while carrying out public duties. Quebec's unbending commitment to secularism, copied from France, and itself a religion of sorts, has contributed to xenophobia.

My description of the world of the Jewish communists in Canada also remains relevant to our twenty-first-century lives, in my view, as a vivid example of how difficult the transition from one culture to another can be for the first generation of immigrants. There are always choices to be made about what to hold on to from the past and what to abandon, about what will hinder one's ability to sink roots in the unfamiliar place of arrival and what is more likely to promote successful integration.

CHAPTER SIX

THE JEWISH EXPERIENCE IN CANADA—WHAT I LEARNED ABOUT WRITING AND CANADIAN HISTORY

IT WAS MY FIRST visit to Library and Archives Canada—my first visit to any archive, as it happened. The venerable building on Ottawa's Wellington Street, built in symbolic proximity to the Canadian Parliament and Supreme Court, felt to me like the physical incarnation of Canada's history, including its Jewish history. I took my seat at a table in the reading room and sniffed the musty air. Seated around me were other silent readers examining portfolios of original documents. I hoped my inexperience in this inner sanctum didn't show.

As I waited for the librarian to bring me the requested papers about early Quebec—more specifically about the century of the remarkable Hart family, 1760-1860, whose encounters with Catholic Quebec have been mirrored, tangentially or directly, throughout the history of the province—I thought about two other Jews who participated in Canada's defining moment: the battle of the Plains of Abraham on September 13, 1759.

Abraham Gradis, a Jewish Frenchman from Bordeaux, had never set foot in New France, since according to the 1685 Revocation of the Edict of Nantes, King Louis XIV had prohibited both Jews and Huguenots from settling in the new colonies. Nonetheless, the ship-owning Gradis family became the most important link between France and the new continent. Directed by Abraham, they supplied General Louis-Joseph de Montcalm and his troops with food, supplies, and munitions, while also carrying messages across the sea, including Montcalm's letters to his wife.

On the other side of that battle, an Englishman, Alexander Schomberg, well-educated, cultured, and a high-ranking member of General James Wolfe's staff, was born into a similarly celebrated Jewish family that had distinguished themselves in the Royal Navy. As the British fleet travelled up the St. Lawrence River towards the steep cliffs of the Quebec settlement looming ahead, Schomberg was distressed to observe that the English in their ships were vastly outnumbered by the French on land. His response was to pen a few prescient lines in French, the language of the enemy, but also the recognized language of culture: Were we here to practice diplomacy, he wrote, our numbers would suffice. To wage battle, we are too few.

Si nous venions en ambassade
Nous étions beaucoup
Mais si c'était pour combattre
Nous étions bien peu.

Yes, in the eighteenth century some high-ranking officers wrote poetry as they approached the battlefield, a quaint anachronism three hundred years later when complexity of thought may be eschewed for 280 Twitter characters. I have quoted these lines for their understated insight into dire reality, but also because many years later I happened to see General Wolfe's own handwritten encounter with the same forbidding moment in the Thomas Fisher Rare Books Library at the University of Toronto. As his fleet sailed toward what looked to be certain doom the man who would soon redirect the course of Canada's history also turned to poetry, quoting Thomas Gray's mournful "Elegy Written in a Country Churchyard."

... The boast of heraldry, the pomp of pow'r,
And all that beauty, all that wealth e'er gave,
Awaits alike th' inevitable hour.
The paths of glory lead but to the grave...

Wolfe died on the Plains of Abraham, as he expected he would do. So did Montcalm. But the British won the battle, and in 1760, just one year later, the British general Sir Jeffrey Amherst marched into Montreal, captured the city, and ended the last remnants of French rule.

Amherst's staff member, Aaron Hart, a Jewish lieutenant in the British army, was the first Jew to settle in the colony, He developed the seminal fur trade in the central region of Trois-Rivières, eventually becoming one of the wealthiest landowners in the Empire outside Britain, a condition which warranted a visit from Edward, Duke of Kent, and a request for a loan from the United States president, Andrew Jackson. (It was granted.)

Aaron Hart was both generous and politically astute (the objects of his philanthropy included the Catholic Church in Trois-Rivières), but his son, Ezekiel, who also made Canadian history, was less fortunate. In 1807 Ezekiel was elected to the Assembly of Lower Canada as a delegate from Trois-Rivières, but when he insisted on taking his official oath on the Old Testament, chaos erupted in the chamber. Member after member stood to say that Jews had no right to sit in Parliament. They were still awaiting the arrival of the Messiah when everyone knew that He had already arrived. Because Jews were not citizens in European countries, it was obvious that they did not *want* to be citizens, and therefore shouldn't be so in Lower Canada. Finally, since Jews were not allowed to serve in the British Parliament, a British colony was under no obligation to change the rules. Then they expelled Ezekiel Hart from the Assembly.

Hart tried again in 1808 without success; but the wave of liberalism that swept the West following the French and the American revolutions was also changing the *Zeitgeist* in Quebec, and in 1831 an English member of the Assembly of Lower Canada introduced a bill granting Jews the same rights and privileges as others. In 1832 this Jewish "Magna Carta," as it was called, became law, making Lower Canada the first jurisdiction in the British Empire to legally emancipate Jews. "What a good colony," Baron Lionel de Rothschild is purported to have said when he learned about the bill, for he too had been prevented from taking a seat in the British House of Commons after successful election victories. "I love it without knowing it."

The story of the integration of minorities into any society is an up-and-down affair as historical events determine social change, but Ezekiel Hart's misfortunes clearly foreshadowed conflicts in Quebec over majority-minority relations which continue to this day. I hadn't set out to explore xenophobia, but discovering its presence in early Canada made me think I was on track to something important. It had already become apparent to me that discriminatory attitudes to women were like exclusion on grounds of religion, in that both women and non-Christians were seen as "other," and I was beginning to think that I might be looking at a single, deep-rooted human impulse expressing itself in a variety of situations.

If the Harts and their British-cultured progeny marked the beginnings of Jewish life in Canada as well as the first faltering steps towards the legal equality of minorities, what happened next definitively changed the nature of the community itself. Around 1850, several families from Russia and Poland arrived in Quebec, among them Abraham Jacobs, Moses Vineberg, and Lazarus Cohen. Like many later arrivals from places in Eastern Europe, they peddled wares among the farmers, and when they saved enough money, they opened general stores.

Lazarus Cohen, for example. When he looked around him, he saw trees stretching as far as the horizon. So, he went into the lumber business. Soon he was dredging the St. Lawrence River—thus facilitating passage along what remains the most important commercial waterway in Canada. As Quebec industrialized in the mid-to-late nineteenth century, several of these original families entered the emerging needle trades. Flush with success, they moved to the leafy streets of Westmount alongside the stone mansions of the Scottish fur barons. Assimilationists to the core, they purposely adopted the British ways of the small community of established Anglo Jews such as the Harts, some of whom had settled in Montreal. They educated their children in the best schools—and if these happened to be Catholic schools, so be it. They compensated with after-hours Hebrew school programmes.

The new arrivals also built the Canadian Jewish community's first institutions, such as the Young Men's Hebrew Benevolent Society, which in turn created the Baron de Hirsch Institute, the organization that would later be called upon to help the thousands of Eastern European Jewish immigrants who poured into Canada following the deadly Russian pogroms of the 1880s. Their children married one another, knitting families even closer together. More than a century later, we know the names of their descendants: the late singer-poet Leonard Cohen was a direct descendant of Lazarus, as is Andrew Cohen, one of Canada's finest journalists. Sam Jacobs, the son of Abraham Jacobs, became the first Jew to be elected to the Canadian House of Commons, although in significant ways he fared only marginally better than his political forerunner, Ezekiel Hart, a telling story about integration and acceptance I'll return to.

The poverty-stricken Jewish escapees from the Russian pogroms did *not* have English airs, and they certainly did not wear top hats or carry fashionable walking sticks. In overcrowded slums around St. Lawrence Boulevard ("the Main," an area subsequently made famous by Mordechai Richler), they were numerous and destitute. They needed help; and, to their credit, the Westmount Jews rose to the challenge. Between 1881 and 1921, after which date immigration to Canada incrementally closed, more than 126,000 Jews arrived in Canada from Eastern Europe—my grandparents among them.

In November 2005, the staff programmer of a Toronto retirement home (where my widowed mother then lived) invited me to speak to the residents about the origins of the Canadian Jewish community. Many of the men and women seated before me had been part of this early migration, or were the children of the migrants, and to talk to them about the early days was to allude to their own lives. I knew that when I talked about the teeming slums of Montreal, some of them would think of Toronto's Ward district, which was also the heart of the arrival community. I watched my mother as she sat proudly in the front row, wondering whether she might be thinking about my long-dead grandparents, whose momentous lives had carried them through the failed Russian revolution of 1905 and imprisonment in the Tsar's jail in St. Petersburg before they successfully escaped to London, where she was born.

Other thoughts also crossed my mind that day—thoughts about the striving for acceptance which the generation I was addressing had had to navigate; thoughts about my father, who rode to the hounds at the Eglinton Hunt Club, anxiously hoping his Jewish origins would pass unnoticed; and about my mother, who had joined the Toronto Symphony Orchestra's Women's Committee with the same ultimately futile hope for acceptance in mind. Such were the ways of Canada when the people facing me were at their prime.

In Montreal, the so-called downtown Jews—the new arrivals from Eastern Europe—and the so-called uptown Jews, their wealthy patrons, clashed over just about everything, holding in common little more than their ancient religious affiliation. The uptowners wanted to promote assimilation and the ways of the British Empire. Their newspaper, *The Jewish Times,* published by Lazarus Cohen's son Lyon, spoke for the noblesse-oblige philanthropists whose job it was to help the needy and to advise the newcomers about how to comport themselves properly in this place called Canada.

But the downtowners occupied a different mind-space. They seethed with the left-wing ideas they had brought with them from Russia as supporters of the revolutions that would, or already had, overthrown the Tsars; and from other countries where their search for safety as Jews had led to splintered internecine politics. Their Yiddish-language newspaper, the *Keneder Adler,* adamantly opposed the assimilationist tendencies of the uptown Jews. British-style restraint was not their style: the *Keneder Adler* writers were intellectually inclined and emotionally excitable. They fought over issues with full-blown rhetoric and high drama.

That the two communities communicated at all was something of a miracle. What did the downtowners know of Westmount and the dignified ways of the Cohens and their friends? Why should they care? they asked themselves, except out of gratitude for the assistance they had received.

Problems outside the community also hindered integration. In the early twentieth century, a new wave of religious and ethnic intolerance in Quebec swept away the liberal attitudes that had characterized official Quebec for almost a century and had granted legal rights to the Jewish minority. In 1910, Jacques-Édouard Plamondon, an influential Quebec City lawyer and journalist, gave a speech in which he revived the slumbering calumny that all Jews were enemies of Christians. It was a stark throwback to the era of Ezekiel Hart, who had been denied permission to sit in the Assembly of Lower Canada a century before.

Plamondon also revived the medieval blood libel: the charge that Jews murdered Christian children to get blood for the baking of Passover unleavened breads. Not surprisingly, there were repercussions: vandals broke synagogue windows in Quebec City; Jews were molested and stoned.

I read the Plamondon story at my desk in the Archives on Wellington Street and was disquieted, for I believed that this event was then largely unknown. I included it in *Jews: An Account of their Experience in Canada*, which was published in 1980, but Quebec did not begin to grapple publicly with this subject until the early 1990s, when Esther Delisle published her controversial doctoral thesis from Laval University, titled *The Traitor and the Jew: Antisemitism and the Delirium of Extremist Right-Wing Nationalism in French Canada from 1929 to 1939*. And Plamondon, I learned from my archival study, was just the beginning. Over the next years, particularly during the Great Depression and the simultaneous rise of Nazi ideology, francophone elites turned inward, and in the damp breeding grounds of their frustration extremism took root.

My research was carrying me to unforeseen places as I explored the pervasiveness of fascism in pre-Second World War Quebec. I wasn't yet ready to confront the antisemitic social movements that had taken place in France, starting with the Dreyfus Affair at the end of the nineteenth century, although what I was learning about Quebec would soon lead me there.

As I write these words, my book *Jews* lies open before me. I read my own text about the rise of copycat fascism in Quebec and the impulse to find a scapegoat for the woes of the age, and reflect that in subsequent years I have seen this same phenomenon emerge incrementally in many places. A sudden or simmering disruption of the usual course of events triggers the emergence of a strongman, or a charismatic intellectual, or a populist who purposely exacerbates anxieties then promises a self-serving remedy. In Quebec, starting in 1930, there were two such men: Adrien Arcand, a journalist and orator, and his collaborator, the printer Joseph Menard. Menard's role was essential, since every effort at influencing opinion must be propagandized to the public.

Arcand and Menard didn't invent the idea of religious nationalism; they didn't need to. Rather, they dipped into the underground stream of Quebec intellectual life that had re-emerged with Jacques-Edouard Plamondon. As nations industrialized during the nineteenth century, new economic insecurities created rivalries; Jews were being emancipated into the larger society and were considered competitors.

The Quebec intelligentsia had ready access to antisemitic materials from France and Germany. For example, as early as 1886, during a period of social and economic turmoil exacerbated by France's defeat during the Franco-Prussian War (for which "Jewish influence" in French life was blamed), the French nationalist Édouard Drumont had published *La France juive, Essai d'histoire contemporaine*, then a second work in 1891: *Le testament d'un antisémite*. Drumont's themes were racial (Jews and "Aryans" were incompatible races—a foreshadowing of Hitler); economic (the intimidating new world of finance and capitalism was controlled by Jews); and religious (the Jews had killed Christ). At this writing, *La France juive* has only rarely been out of print; in 2012 it was republished by Kontre Kulture, an imprint financed by the right-wing nationalist group *Equality and Reconciliation* with connections to the French National Front party.

Quebec had easy access to *La France juive,* but it was also producing its own racist literature. In 1922, *L'Appel de la race*, a novel by Lionel Groulx, a Catholic priest, portrayed a transcendent nationalism in which the spiritual well-being of the hero is tied to his rejection of everything foreign. Groulx's work echoed nineteenth-century German writings featuring the ethno-racialist idea of the *Volk,* a concept that invoked a mystical community based on shared blood ties that excluded the Jewish minority.

The most influential article written about the Jews in Quebec had appeared in *L'Action nationale*, a far-right nationalist journal inaugurated in 1917 under the name *L'Action française,* another copycat facsimile of an ultra-right French publication (and organization) with the same name. (The Canadian journal shrewdly changed its name in 1933, shortly after Charles Maurras, the editor of the French publication, was condemned by the Pope for using Catholicism as a tool for political change). The content of *L'Action nationale* was controlled by Groulx himself, but the pivotal article in question—"*Les Juifs au Canada*"—was penned by the prominent lawyer Anatole Vanier in September 1933, the year Hitler became Chancellor of Germany. Vanier wrote that, with the Nazi takeover of Germany, the Jews in Germany were getting what they deserved. He predicted that a similar fate awaited them in Quebec.

"What is happening in the new Germany is germinating everywhere where Jews are considered intruders," he wrote. "And where, one may well ask, are they considered otherwise?"

I caught my breath as I read these words in Canada's public archives on that long-ago day. For decades this material had been hiding in public view.

I try to be careful. In 1933, no one was predicting the Holocaust, and there is certainly no evidence that the prominent antisemites of Quebec had death camps and gas chambers in mind. But the racism of early Quebec nationalism has trailed visible tendrils into our own era. When former premier and Parti Québécois leader Jacques Parizeau notoriously blamed "money and ethnic votes" in October 1995 after the close failure of a referendum to separate Quebec from Canada, he was speaking recognizable code to his fellow Québécois. When Parti Québécois leaders Bernard Drainville and Pauline Marois introduced the Quebec Charter of Values in September 2013, in which they sought to ban Muslim headscarves, they, too, were dipping into a familiar stream of xenophobia under the pretended veneer of secularism—a political debate that continues today under the umbrella of "values." When a Laval student who was known to hate "foreigners" attacked a mosque in Quebec City in 2017, after U.S. president Donald Trump initiated exclusionary acts against Muslims, it could have been 1910, when Jacques-Edouard Plamondon excited the populace, and a Quebec City synagogue was attacked. The old underground stream of ethno-nationalism resurfaced again in 2021 as a raging torrent when Quebec premier François Legault availed himself of Canada's constitutional override, the "notwithstanding clause," to legislate Bills 21 and 96 regarding religious apparel and the imagined impoverished status of the French language.

In a January 2017 article in *Le Devoir* celebrating the one hundredth year of the journal *L'Action nationale,* publishers Robert Laplante et Denis Monière dismissed the ugly beginnings of the publication with anodyne clichés: "The history of a review is not always a calm river," they opined; the journal would have "its highs and its lows." But the past bleeds into the present most visibly in the person of Jean-Claude Dupuis, a Laval University-educated expert on the era who postulated that "from the start, *L'Action française* made it clear that its nationalism was above all an economic nationalism." This was a selective, exculpatory view. Dupuis made himself a lot clearer when he wrote that the identity-based nationalism of *L'Action francaise* and its successor publication intended to prune away "foreign vegetation" to reattach Quebec to its true, traditional sources. Dupuis, who was born in 1961, considers himself "an inheritor of Groulxian nationalism."

Since 1917, at least 17,000 authors have appeared in *L'Action francaise/L'Action nationale* (including Pierre Elliott Trudeau in his early nationalist phase), and its incremental embrace of secularism made it an intellectual pivot of the 1960s and 1970s separatist movement. Not surprisingly, the journal's influence has faded in lockstep with the failing fortunes of separatism in Quebec, although that deep-rooted nationalist desire is unlikely ever to disappear entirely. Nonetheless, the fact that *L'Action nationale* continues to exist at all in the third decade of the twenty-first century is witness to the tenacity of historical association, and to the intellectual sources that inform Quebec history.

I have focused on Adrien Arcand not simply because he was an important polemicist, but because what he sought went far beyond social discrimination. When Arcand argued that there were only two *lawful* minorities in Canada—the English in Quebec and the French in the rest of the country—he was arguing for the delegitimization of minority rights that had been in place since the Emancipation Act of 1832. For if Jews were not entitled to legal minority status, they had no legitimate claim to equal treatment under the law.

Arcand and Quebec fascism were discredited in 1939, when Canada went to war against Nazi Germany. Minority rights were not withdrawn. But in retrospect, Arcand's challenge foreshadowed Canada's long historical debate over the accommodation of minorities, a discussion that reached its apogee in 1971 with the creation of the Official Multiculturalism Act, which recognized—indeed celebrated—cultural diversity.

ANOTHER STORY I STUMBLED upon from the layered history of the Jewish minority in Quebec touched me deeply: that of Sam Jacobs, who in 1917 was the first Jew elected to the Canadian House of Commons. Although his family held membership in the uptown Westmount compact, his "downtown" Yiddish-speaking constituents adored him. He was a respected lawyer, and well assimilated into the fabric of Montreal professional society—the very man to represent their interests in Ottawa.

Jacobs was a Liberal—of course. Everyone at the time knew that in America the Democratic Party was friendlier to the Jews than the Republicans, who supported the established order. The same held true in Canada, the Jews believed. The Liberals were progressive; the Conservatives were hidebound to Empire. The established order, wherever it was found, was the enemy of the downtown immigrants from Russia who had fled pogroms and Tsar alike. Furthermore, it was Liberal leader Wilfrid Laurier who had been prime minister during the era of mass migrations. He had welcomed them into the country.

I wrote an entire chapter about Sam Jacobs in *Jews*—about the rejection he faced from the Ottawa public service as he tried to pry open Canada's closed doors to Jewish refugees from Hitler, and about his painful personal rejection by Prime Minister Mackenzie King, with whom he had believed he had a close relationship. As it happened, I came across his papers almost accidentally. They had been in Library and Archives Canada since his death in 1938, but had been barely touched in the interim, according to the documents in my hands. Jacobs seemed to reach out to me from the yellowing pages spread on the table before me—a fine man who had been rebuffed at his core.

Jacobs is important to Canadian history because his personal saga embodied yet another singular moment in the long process of minority integration into the country. He did not suffer literal ejection from Parliament, as did Ezekiel Hart in Quebec—by the teen years of the twentieth century, immigration into Canada was already well established. But what he did suffer was open and covert discrimination. He served his constituents and his country with demonstrable honour, but he did so during an era of rapidly increasing antisemitism and xenophobia—and he died a defeated man.

Jacobs had dual obsessions. The first was immigration. His concern was initially with the victims of pogroms who were seeking admittance to Canada, but his worries intensified in the 1920s and 1930s as growing numbers of people poured through his Montreal constituency office pleading for help in getting relatives out of Europe as the Canadian Department of Immigration incrementally closed its doors. As early as 1921 he wrote to a friend in Winnipeg that he believed that "everyone in the Department [of Immigration] is strongly and bitterly opposed to our people."

Still, he remained optimistic. The young William Lyon McKenzie King was contesting his first election as Liberal leader. Jacobs had admired Wilfred Laurier intensely, but after the latter's death, he had shifted his loyalty to King, who had campaigned on a platform of reopening immigration. McKenzie King's Liberals won a landslide victory, and so did Sam Jacobs. The *Montreal Gazette* called him "the rising star of Montreal." Everyone was certain Jacobs would be brought into King's cabinet, to highlight Quebec's distinction of being the cradle of Jewish political emancipation in the British Empire.

Jacobs was not appointed to cabinet; nor was Prime Minister McKenzie King any more open to immigration than his predecessor. In fact, a new order-in-council further restricted immigration from so-called non-preferred countries—essentially everywhere outside of the British Isles.

In the 1920s, Sam Jacobs was on his feet in the House of Commons arguing that nativism was impeding Canada's development, that closing the doors to immigration was harmful to the country. He claimed, demonstrating a certain courage given the times, that poor immigrants from southern and eastern Europe worked harder than the British remittance men "who thought they owned this country." Throughout, his elected colleagues listened in stony-faced silence. Their constituents didn't want Jews or other foreigners in the country, and they were elected by their constituents.

Jacobs began to send his colleagues small gifts he hoped would jog their consciences. Many contained biblical allusions, since most people had at least a passing acquaintance with major quotations from the Bible. He offered R. B. Bennett, leader of the Conservative opposition, a book on Jewish history, perhaps hoping he would make the oblique connection between the Jews who escaped slavery in Egypt and the increasingly growing plight of European Jews in the contemporary world. He sent a box of matzos, the unleavened bread of the ancient Israelites baked during the flight out of Egypt, to the Minister of Immigration. What he got back was a puzzled note thanking him for the Passover biscuits, "which were very good."

In 1933, the year Hitler came to power, it seemed that the entirety of Canadian Jewry was turning to Jacobs for help. Already in his early sixties, he was being called upon to do what he had failed to accomplish during his sixteen years as a member of the House of Commons. There were thousands of homeless Jews in Germany. Refugee aid organizations in Europe also wrote for help. After trying unsuccessfully to meet with R.B. Bennett, he did meet with W.A. Gordon, the Minister of Immigration, who told him that Jews were not farmers, and only farmers could be admitted to Canada. Meanwhile, the Quebec City Council passed a resolution that said it was "in the interest of the two Mother Christian races of this country to prevent the immigration of non-Christian persons." It was 1807 again in Quebec, the year Ezekiel Hart, an elected representative, had been expelled from the Legislative Assembly of Lower Canada because he was a Jew.

At the highest level of the land, Sam Jacobs struggled alone.

Because R.B. Bennett was the prime minister of Canada as the calls to help Jewish refugees grew more urgent, I requested his archived papers. In them I found a poignant set of letters, likely one of hundreds of desperate pleas sent to politicians in those years. They were written in Yiddish-English by a member of the Davidman family in Calgary, who was trying to rescue a sixteen-year-old niece and granddaughter, Figa Birenbaum, from Poland. They are worth repeating here, as they were written:

> *To Mr. Bennett*
> *Ottawa*
> *...Please Mr. Bennett, I'm sure you can get the papers if you try and please do try as you know whots going on in Poland now...Please Mr. Bennett don't be mad at me. You don't know what this means to us, especially my old parents...*
> *Yours very truly,*
> *Mrs. A Davidman*

> Dear Mrs. Davidman,
> With respect to Miss Figa Birenbaum, it did not appear clear to the Department [of Immigration] that Miss Birenbaum would not eventually seek employment in this country if she were admitted...I'm afraid there is nothing Mr. Bennett can do.
> Yours faithfully,
> Secretary

> *To Mr. Bennett,*
> *Ottawa*
> *Dear Sir,*
> *I'm sorry to bother you again but you musnt get tired of me...you are the only man who can help us.... Please let this mater be one of so many things you have to atend to, as you know how Poland is now, we must get this girl out of there and if you don't help us there is no chence.*
> *Yours very truly,*
> *Mrs. A. Davidman*

> Dear Mrs. Davidman,
> ...I greatly regret that it was not possible to secure the required consent for the entry of your niece into this country.
> Yours faithfully,
> Secretary

Figa Birenbaum lived in the city of Radom. Before the war's end, 90 percent of the 30,000 Jews who lived there were exterminated.

I opened *Jews* with a quotation from R.B. Bennett written in 1935, the same year that Mrs. Davidman wrote to him to save her niece. Hitler had been chancellor of Germany for two years; darkness was closing in.

Bennett wrote:

> But what can one man, however able and advanced, do against the current of his age? History shows us constantly that the

> great reformers have been those who felt and followed the general feeling of their times, who became mouthpieces for the great mass of thought and effort behind them, not those who struggled against the tide.

I feel as sad now as I did then about these words from Canada's prime minister, for if they were misguided and cowardly when I first transcribed them, they appear even more so today. In desperate times Canada was not well served by its political leaders.

WHEN I WAS GROWING up in the forties and early fifties, the Communist Party of Canada was flying high. The Depression had propelled thousands of people into its ranks. Low wages and abysmal working conditions—in the so-called needle trades, girls as young as eight did piece work from home for as many hours as they could train their eyes on a sewing needle—led to the embryonic beginnings of trade unions and, eventually, to legislated work hours and a minimum wage. The Party attracted those among the immigrant minorities who saw the written constitution of the Soviet Union as a utopian hope for equality. Whatever was rumoured to be happening "over there," including tales of atrocities, remained unconfirmed until February 25, 1956, when Nikita Khrushchev shocked the delegates to the 20th Congress of the Communist Party of the Soviet Union by informing them about the brutal realities of Joseph Stalin's rule.

Given the catastrophic history of their people, it is not surprising that Jewish communists were seized by the promise of equality. Sam Lipshitz, who sat on the Canadian party's central committee from 1943 to 1946, memorably expressed his passion the day we met in 1979. "The world was as now—people were burning books and murdering," he told me in a quiet voice. "But then, on the dark horizon, there was a light. The Soviet Union and the communist movement were that light."

Many Jewish Canadians, it is clear, sympathized with the internationalist values of the movement without formally joining the Party. However,

I doubt whether these sympathizers included my parents, except for their tangential commitment to universal values. My immigrant grandfather Isaac Lipkin had joined the Workman's Circle socialists in Toronto, but socialists in those days were emphatically *not* communists—in fact, factional fighting between them absorbed much of their energies. His daughter, my mother, kept a safe distance from the nitty-gritty of politics, especially Jewish identity politics. My father was a vague supporter of the CCF, the forerunner of the NDP, but his interests were not sectarian.

Still, I understood the impulse to "believe"—a word I use advisedly because to join the Communist Party was indeed to adopt an alternative theology, the difference being that in the case of communism the promised paradise was purportedly achievable here on earth. Marxism and the foundational ideals of Soviet communism were familiar to most Jews, in that they mirrored the messianic beliefs at the core of their own ancient religion—the primal longing for an end-of-days messiah turned out to be fairly easily transferable to the "paradise now" promised by communism.

I was fascinated by the thinking of the time and the psychology underlying it. One of the things I have loved about journalism, and then book-length non-fiction writing, is the gift of a passport to enter the lives of strangers once I have won their trust. With this passport I have indeed "swallowed the world"—a wish I voiced in my twenties to the uncomprehending ears of my boyfriend, Jean Riffaud—in ways that have opened me to new ideas and different realms of experience.

The men and women who lived the entirety of their adult lives at the heart of the Canadian communist movement were especially interesting to me, and of the dozens who told me of their hopes and disappointments, three whose public careers intersected with the story of Canada stand out all these years later. They are Joe (J.B.) Salsberg, Fred Rose, and Sam Carr. Each of these men desired to better Canada and the world—and each chose means that were ultimately self-defeating.

Joe Salsberg was in his late seventies in 1979 when I interviewed him at his Toronto apartment. His seminal work as a union organizer, then as an Ontario MPP representing the Labour Progressive Party (as the then-outlawed Communist Party of Canada had renamed itself), underpinned early labour and human rights legislation that nudged Canada leftward in a liberal direction. On the day we met, more than 20 years had elapsed since May 1957, when he had dramatically left the Communist Party a year after Nikita Khrushchev had made his famous speech. Leaving the Party had left a chasm in Salsberg's life. Since 1957, he had sold insurance, written a column for a Jewish publication, and metamorphosed into a fervent Zionist. He confided to me that on lonely nights he singed orange peels on his kitchen stove, closed his eyes, and dreamed he was in Israel.

He seemed very old to me then, slightly stooped, his famous shock of red hair now grey and sparse on his head, but his eyes sparkled with whimsy—like my father's. He made us tea. He showed me his balcony garden of potted plants. We talked about his rupture from the Party, after which he had been shunned by his former comrades for having abandoned them, and by many in the mainstream Jewish community for having joined in the first place. But he offered little when I asked him why he had not exposed Stalin's lies about the experience of Soviet Jews under communism, and why, knowing what he did, he had not left the Party sooner. Because Joe Salsberg knew the truth when others did not.

He had visited Moscow in August 1939, immediately following Stalin's purges of the Communist Party leadership, government bureaucrats, military leaders, peasants, and the intelligentsia, including many Jews. After summary trials based on invented evidence, hundreds of people were executed or sent to the gulag. These murders and expulsions had been explained away as a housekeeping tool for eliminating "enemies of the people"—a justification that was repeated by sycophantic communist parties in the West.

Antisemitism had never disappeared after the 1917 Revolution, except on paper. Salsberg had worried about what was happening to the hope for Jewish integration and equality; and especially to the promise of Birobidzhan, a remote area on the eastern border of the Soviet Union that had been designated as an autonomous region where Jews could escape the Pale of Settlement ghettos that had characterized the Tsarist regime. During this 1939 trip to Moscow, Salsberg had concluded that the Birobidzhan plan was going nowhere, but he had said nothing public about this on his return to Canada. In response to my own question on the matter, he told me what he had consistently told others: "I couldn't come out and cry publicly without destroying my own credibility." This was an honest, if self-incriminating, admission containing layers of self-protectiveness. He had been unwilling to raise questions for fear of jeopardizing his career in the Canadian Communist Party. But his silence was not innocent, and he knew it. Birobidzhan signalled the beginning of the repression of Soviet Jews and Jewish institutions. Thousands in Canada and elsewhere needed to know what he knew.

Over the next years, Soviet-Jewish writers and other intellectuals disappeared, never to be seen again. What was happening? Some in Canada left the Party. Joe Salsberg did not. Although he was preoccupied by worry, his public rationalization was a familiar one: he would have more influence inside the Party than outside. Despite my private cajoling—during which I told him I could find a more complete answer to my question elsewhere but preferred to hear it from him (a dubious interviewing "incentive" I had learned from Peter C. Newman)—he adamantly refused to say more. I suppose he was too kind to laugh out loud, but in retrospect I can't imagine why I thought he might reveal his secrets to me, an audacious young writer he had never heard of.

It seems self-evident that the *Zeitgeist* of the era in which we grow to maturity is as likely to shape our adult selves as the values of our respective families. This was certainly true for me and my generation: the Canadian postwar era of prosperity and optimism powered hope, but also, among many of us, outrage at injustice. It was equally true for Salsberg, whose lifelong social commitments were formed by the lives of hapless misery he witnessed in the sweatshops of Spadina Avenue, the heart of Canada's clothing industry, where he worked from the age of fourteen, and especially by the beginnings of resistance to these conditions.

Salsberg was just fifteen when the October Revolution of 1917 exploded like a supernova in the heart of a Canadian immigrant community already seething with left-wing ideas for improving the world. He was just seventeen when the seminal Winnipeg general strike of 1919 took place. The strike, which was triggered by returning First World War soldiers who found themselves unable to recover their jobs, attracted tens of thousands of protesters. It was the largest strike action in Canadian history—and when the police fired live ammunition, killing two, something had to give. Although the federal government was fiercely unsympathetic to the strikers, the idea of federal assistance to municipalities responsible for relief payments to the hungry was broached for the first time.

When Salsberg joined the fledgling Communist Party of Canada in 1926 (it had been created in 1921), industrial unionism looked like a path to better labour conditions. He was still in his formative twenties when the 1929 Depression cracked open the economy, propelling millions more into poverty. The Communist Party of Canada benefitted from this crisis. Its pro-worker social policies gained legitimacy (although emphatically not in Ottawa, where Prime Minister R.B. Bennett outlawed the CPC in 1931, arrested several of its leaders, and deported others to their countries of origin). The Party's reputation soared even further in 1941, when the Soviet Union commanded its militants to fight Hitler's fascism—a policy turnaround that allowed Jewish-Canadian communists like Salsberg to metamorphose into hyper-patriots in the fight against the Nazis. In 1943, the newly popular Communist Party of Canada (now renamed the Labour Progressive Party) elected two individuals to parliament: Joe Salsberg was elected to the Ontario Legislature; Fred Rose of Montreal, who was later convicted of recruiting spies for Russia, was elected to Canada's House of Commons.

There was no one quite like Joe Salsberg. Having arrived in Canada from Poland in 1912 as a ten-year-old child, he had lived with his devoutly Orthodox family in the Ward, the same poverty-stricken district of Toronto my grandparents had first inhabited. When his father failed to eke out an adequate living as a peddler, young Joe went to work in a leather-goods factory where he had a front-row view of the desperation that characterized life in the needle trades. His family's religious Orthodoxy, he thought, did not address the reality of this new Canadian world.

One day Joe's grieving father told him that his ceaseless talk about workers' rights and the secular books he was leaving around the house were affecting the other children in the family. He said somebody had *seen* young Joe seated with boys and girls his age reading aloud from one of these offending works. The chief rabbi of Polish Jewry in Toronto was called in to adjudicate. "All right," Rabbi Graubart told the wilful fifteen-year-old. "You want socialism? Fine. But do it the way the *prophets* wanted to do it. Think of *Amos*. Who is this Marx, anyhow?"

When the pleading failed, the father asked the son to leave home. Joe's mother fainted. In the ensuing chaos, an aunt came running over. "What are you doing to your *mother?*" she shrieked.

In the end, it was decided that Joe would remain at home, and that he could pursue his burgeoning career as a union organizer as long as he respected the ethos of the Orthodox household. It was an extraordinary concession on the part of parents whose child had rejected their core beliefs.

I retell Joe's story because the generational struggle of the Salsberg family was mirrored in hundreds of immigrant homes, Jewish and non-Jewish, and because it continues to be the case as new arrivals to Canada negotiate family crises when their Canadian-born children deviate from traditional values. It is an ongoing truth that the general tolerance of difference that characterizes Canadian society has frequently found its source in private pain.

During our conversation, Joe Salsberg told me how much his father's principled dedication to ethics had influenced his life. "You believe in what you are doing, I know you do," the father told his son. That mattered most.

Joe Salsberg served in the Ontario legislature from 1943 until 1955, when he was effectively defeated by prosperity: his downtown electors had moved north and into the middle class. He was also defeated by the fall-out from the 1947 Igor Gouzenko spy trials and its revelation of a Soviet spy ring in Canada, quite likely the most sensational political scandal ever to beset the country, something I'll come back to. If organizing labour unions had marked his earlier career, Joe's life as a Member of Provincial Parliament opened up undreamed of possibilities, including what became his most important contribution: his fight to pass the 1944 Ontario legislative bill known as the Racial Discrimination Act.

The Act's objective was to do away with current prohibitions against selling land to Jews, Orientals, and Blacks, and with notices around Toronto banning Jews from swimming pools and from living in certain neighbourhoods. (As an adult, I learned that my parents had been forced to vacate their home on Toronto's Centre Island.) With the passage of the Racial Discrimination Act on March 14, 1944, Ontario became the first Canadian province to formally address racial and religious intolerance, prohibiting the public display or publication of any notice, sign, or symbol expressing ethnic, racial, or religious discrimination. Importantly, it was a precursor of Ontario's official Human Rights Code, which was proclaimed on June 15, 1962, a full two decades later.

The changing social attitudes that have buttressed the evolution of Canada's civil and human rights legislation become boldly visible when one reaches back to a time when prejudice was mainstream and minority rights were unheard of. By paying attention to the abject working conditions of immigrants and by championing human and labour rights, Salsberg changed the Canadian map of human dignity. This longing for respect and equality had led him to communism, though he would eventually pay heavily for his choice. Seven decades later, Kathleen Wynne, the former premier of Ontario, was partnered in marriage with another woman, and few seem to care. On the contrary, most, if asked, would describe her as personifying the trajectory of social change that Joe Salsberg helped spur into being.

Then there was the Igor Gouzenko affair I mentioned earlier. It seems barely out of date today, when one considers the Russian internet infiltration scandals that currently threaten the integrity of Western democratic elections. The Affair was also a milestone that carried major repercussions for Canada and for Jewish communist dreams.

When Igor Gouzenko, a cipher clerk for the Soviet Embassy in Ottawa, defected to the West on September 5, 1945, he was carrying with him 109 documents on Soviet espionage activities in Canada. The Second World War had ended just three days earlier, and Joseph Stalin was a purported ally. So shocked was then-Prime Minister Mackenzie King that he called a Royal Commission to investigate espionage in Canada. The investigation led to the trials of twenty Canadian communists. Of the eight who were convicted for passing nuclear secrets to the Soviet Union and for recruiting Soviet spies in Canada, two were high-ranking Party members who were Jewish, Fred Rose and Sam Carr, the latter widely considered to be the brains of the Party.

The (renamed) Labour Progressive Party survived by fiercely denouncing all eight convicted spies—although, given the elevated status of Rose and Carr, the idea that the Party's upper echelon was unaware of their activities continues to strain credulity. Rose and Carr were both convicted of treason.

What motivated these men to betray their country? Like Joe Salsberg, Fred Rose and Sam Carr were true believers who thought the Soviet experiment would usher in a world of greater equality. Rose, like Salsberg, came to Canada from Poland as a child; he, too, had worked in the sweat shops (this time, of Montreal), where he was subjected to the appalling labour conditions of the day. Rose's radicalization would have been compounded by Quebec's home-grown fascism, personified by Adrien Arcand and others. He also had a habit of speaking publicly about a presumed relationship between Quebec premier Maurice Duplessis and Hitler, a stance that earned him the support of anti-fascists in the province, including Jews, but the scorn of others. For his part, Sam Carr always denied that being Jewish informed his politics, yet he had spent his early childhood in the Ukraine, where one single event had set him on his life's course. When I interviewed him in 1979, he confided that he had witnessed the murder of his father during a pogrom, an event which, he said, "set me in a certain relationship to my fellow man. That has remained all my life and is still true. I believe what I believed when I was thirteen years old, that man should not exploit man..."

I understood him when he said that a single event could shape a life. My own personal history suggested the same.

There are doubtless many reasons for committing treason. They may be monetary, or they may hinge on an expectation of personal advancement. It's an understatement to say that betraying one's country is an unwise career move. Nevertheless, it is possible to understand how one's personal past, coupled with the mood of an era, can inform individual choices, including poor choices.

Today, a foreign state that seeks covert influence and classified intelligence is no longer dependent on men in trench coats carrying state secrets in leather satchels. In the hydra-headed digital world we now inhabit, a nation can be destroyed from within by an enemy that hacks computers and orchestrates false news stories that erode trust in the institutions of governance. In the United States, a special counsel was appointed to examine not whether, but how, the contemporary Russian government interfered with the November 2016 election that carried Donald Trump to the presidency.

Joe Salsberg, Fred Rose, and Sam Carr were complicated individuals who were committed to changing not just Canada but the entire world. But only one of them, Joe Salsberg, moved the country in the direction of the defense of human rights. Through my study of homegrown fascism and communism, I was learning about the occasional successes, like that of Salsberg, but also the overall perils of these immutable ideologies.

WHEN COMMUNISM FAILED ITS Jewish devotees, an identity void plunged the community of believers into an abyss. Who were they now? What was left in the suitcase of ideas and cherished history that they had brought with them to the new country? What were their options?

They had a choice: they could stay in the Party, or they could leave. But to acknowledge that one's entire life had been spent in the service of a mirage was unutterably painful. Those who could not do so stayed put, to their personal detriment, because the known lies they continued to propagate about the glories of the Soviet Union corroded their integrity. Joseph Gershman, the editor of the longstanding Yiddish-language communist newspaper *Der Vochenblatt*, who stayed on despite his personal fears for his family in the Soviet Union, was one such individual. Like Salsberg, he rationalized that he could be of more use on the inside than the outside; he tried a balancing act by writing articles attacking antisemitism counterbalanced with pro-Soviet pieces that churned out the latest Party line.

According to Salsberg, Gershman, who had close relatives in the Soviet Union, frequently arrived at his house crying, "They're killing them! They're killing my family!" But at a meeting of the Canadian Party's central committee in the early 1950s, Gershman rose to his feet to speak against accusations Salsberg had just raised regarding antisemitism in the Soviet Union. He said: "I too have doubts, but now I see clearly." "Gershman," Salsberg rebuked him angrily, "you either cry or you make speeches. You can't do both." The two men never spoke to each other again.

Gershman had more than Salsberg's ire to worry about. The Party's central committee was watching him. They warned him about his side criticisms. Then, in 1977, they forced him out of the Party. Joe Gershman was seventy-four years old, and had devoted fifty-four years to the movement that capriciously discarded him.

The communist true believers were a twentieth-century manifestation of utopian longing for an ideal world that has characterized humans from their beginnings. Such dreams fail because their universal flaw is a passion for perfection. The danger they pose to their societies lies in their willingness to justify their desired ends by any means possible, including violence. Such fatal choices in the service of unrealizable ideals have inspired conflict across history. It is closer to the truth to acknowledge that a better life is possible; a perfect one is not.

The late Leonard Cohen said it with great simplicity in his song "Anthem":

Ring the bells that still can ring
Forget your perfect offering
There's a crack in everything,
That's how the light gets in.

Just as the *Sex and Civilization* series had allowed me to explore the subject of discrimination with a tangential glance back at my still-unassimilated student year in France, writing *Jews* was a harbinger of my emerging interest in pluralism and ethnic diversity. Before long I would intuit that assimilation was a lot more complex than my parents' yearning to be embraced by mainstream Anglo-Saxon Canada—and that it, too, presaged danger when advanced as a precondition for belonging.

On June 11, 1967, I happened to be shopping at the Lawrence Plaza in what was then Toronto's north end. A large television screen had been mounted on the side of one of the buildings. It was broadcasting pictures of triumphant shouting and dancing in the streets of Jerusalem, and soldiers praying fervently at the newly liberated Western Wall in the Old City, Judaism's holiest site. They posed for pictures in front of the nearby Dome of the Rock, Islam's holy shrine that had been built over the ruins of the destroyed Second Temple. The Six-Day War had just ended. Israel had won. The symbols of contested ownership—of what would come to define Israel-Palestine relations in the decades to come—were already on view: sanctified militarism, hyper-nationalism, the crushing of enemies, and the birth of a military occupation that is still in place half a century later. Zionism was being reborn as a powerful secular religion.

Prior to the Six-Day War, I hadn't paid a lot of attention to the new state of Israel. After teaching at David and Mary Thompson Collegiate, I had returned to the University of Toronto to begin a master's programme in French literature. I was parenting my four-year-old daughter. And I had my own new birth to contend with: I was pregnant with my second child, Roland, who was due at the end of that month.

But I was mesmerized by the triumphant passion I had just witnessed, and by the immediate transformation that had taken place in many Jews of my acquaintance. In what seemed like an instant, the left-wing liberal Zionist ideology that had characterized the first twenty years of the new state of Israel was seamlessly adopted. The ideal Israeli—the *sabra*: thorny, tough, but sweet on the inside—had long been touted by Zionists, in contrast with those who had died in the Nazi Holocaust: people who, they said, did not work with their hands to build a land, and who, according to some, had not fought hard enough to defend themselves. The charge was grossly unfair, and unrealistic, too, given the nature of Nazi genocide. Nonetheless, it served to define the "new Jew"—men and women who would defend their homeland to the death. Following the victory of 1967, it was only a short step to another, more militaristic vision of Zionism.

Two decades would pass before I set out to explore the complexities of Israeli society for a book that I would title *The Garden and the Gun*. Two decades during which I would negotiate an inevitable divorce, tend to my children whose lives were disrupted, cement a new, enduring relationship with Tom Robinson, and, by the publication of *Jews*, establish myself as a "real" writer at last.

While I was still bothered by old unresolved questions about history, identity, and plural societies, having finally written a book thrilled me, and had likely nudged me forward. While I was drawn to the shifting complexities of Israel, what I didn't know then was that a new opportunity to look deeply into France's troubled history would soon open itself to me. And that I would jump at the chance to penetrate the remaining layers of haze that obscured my earlier view of that history.

CHAPTER SEVEN

INTO THE FRENCH MAELSTROM

IT WAS FEBRUARY 1983—A time when winter in its glowering prime dares the most weather-hardened Canadians to step outdoors. Including Tom and myself. On the sixth day of the month, we are seated on our living room sofa preparing to hear the evening news.

The CBC announcer's words drift hazily towards us from another room; there's nothing of particular interest...until a startling item catches our attention: a man named Klaus Barbie, a German Gestapo chief who'd been based in Lyon, France during the Nazi occupation, was at that very moment being flown to France in a French government aircraft. He had been living for decades in La Paz, Bolivia under the assumed name of Klaus Altmann. A mere day or so ago, the Bolivian government had agreed to arrest and extradite him to Lyon. According to the news report, the French public was awaiting his arrival with unparalleled excitement, for Barbie had twice been convicted *in absentia* for committing atrocities against members of the wartime Resistance. Now it seemed he would face charges for concerted attacks on France's civilian Jews, including the deportations of men, women, and children to Auschwitz.

I experience a moment of startled recognition. More than two decades have passed since I unexpectedly looked upon a human dissection table at the Natzweiler-Struthof death camp, and at the furnace in the next room. More than two decades have passed since I began my intermittent, formless attempts to fully understand what I had seen. During those years I had married, borne two children, divorced, then married again. I'd started, then abandoned, a teaching career in the elusive hope of realizing my youthful fantasy of becoming a writer. I'd been occupied, in other words. But now, listening intently to the radio on this winter evening, I intuit the possibility of something new, as I ask myself whether I might now find answers to questions that haunted me still, despite the revelations of Marcel Ophuls' *The Sorrow and the Pity*.

I turn to Tom: "That's my next book."

"I know," he replies unhesitatingly.

I run to the kitchen phone and call my agent. "I have my next book!" I tell her excitedly. "This story will have international importance. If this person Klaus Barbie comes to trial, what happens in court will set a precedent for the prosecution of other fugitive Nazis. His arrival is already challenging wartime memories."

"I could *never* sell that in New York," she drawls when I stop for breath.

I make a quick decision. She will no longer represent me.

"Thanks," I said, and hang up the phone.

❦

"YOU WON'T BE ABLE to do that!" says Malcolm Lester, looking perplexed. Malcolm is a childhood friend who has built a fine publishing house: Lester & Orpen Dennys. He has expressed interest in publishing me, but given the nature of my previous work, he seems to think me incapable of this project. He doesn't mention sales directly, but that must be a factor. How many books on the politics of French historical memory would he be likely to sell in Canada?

I understand. Yes, it was true that I had never written anything remotely related to the book I was proposing. But I didn't care. Except for Tom, few would have understood my compulsion to research this story. It wasn't easy to explain, even to close friends, many of whom seemed as puzzled as Malcolm.

In the *Sex and Civilization* radio series a few years before, I had explored the origins of sexism and the perceived otherness of women in a first, albeit oblique, exploration of marginalization and its effects—a work that was, in retrospect, a trial run for the story that now offered itself to me. Would uncovering the record of Klaus Barbie in France pry open some hitherto closed doors? Would it lead me to understand the path which majority-minority relations in that country had travelled?

Once the initial excitement subsided, I had to admit that I had no idea how to proceed. Just go there, I told myself. You've got a history in France, and at least language won't be a problem. With luck, your insider-outsider view on events will give you a unique perspective. So, I booked a ticket to Paris and checked into a cheap hotel on the *rue Monsieur-le-Prince* in the Latin Quarter, close to the Luxembourg Gardens and the *boulevard Saint-Michel*, where I had once marched against the Algerian War. I also followed the seminal teachings of my mother and started reading what the daily newspapers were saying about Barbie's return.

It was the right move: column after column evoked shock at the realization that Klaus Barbie, whose name continued to burn on an unfinished page of history, had been returned to French soil. In typically sonorous language, journalists and historians spoke of long-repressed memories of the war era, when Barbie and his colleagues had terrorized the area surrounding Nazi-occupied Lyon. Barbie had murdered Jean Moulin, a hero of the French Resistance. It was this act that most people remembered.

Some called for vengeance: resistance against the occupying Nazis was the ideological grounding of postwar France, and now that Barbie was at hand, they wanted him to pay for his crimes. I noted that, although widely known by now, the deportation of tens of thousands of Jews remained officially unacknowledged. Yes, large numbers of people had seen *The Sorrow and the Pity* by now, but it remained blacklisted for television by government order.

Palpable fear accompanied the formerly taboo subject of the Collaboration, which was also being openly discussed in the press. What would happen now to the many people who had worked directly for the Nazis, either out of ideological conviction (usually anti-communism) or from opportunism (in the expectation that Germany would win the war)? Or the innumerable citizens who had supported the Vichy-led collaborationist government of Marshal Philippe Pétain, the hero of Verdun? Would they be exposed? Klaus Barbie, I read, was already chuckling over this possibility, claiming to remember the names of every one of his French "helpers."

Among the few who boldly confronted the new reality was Guy Baret, writing in *France Soir*. "Are We Ready?" he asked.

> Forty years after the death of Jean Moulin, Klaus Barbie will appear before his judges. Are we ready? No, we are not ready to hear the atrocious accounting.... We are not ready to hear, in sorrow and pity, the witnesses whose eyes are still filled with horror. The history of genocide will become current news again.
>
> Are we ready to look at the true face of France, at the dark years reflected in the mirror of this trial?
>
> Are we ready to see old wounds reopened and the unextinguished fire of yesterday's passion relit?...
>
> Are we ready to renounce the image of Épinal, whereby the entire population of France rose against the occupier and only a handful collaborated?...
>
> All this will be a part of the trial of Klaus Barbie. It will be an ordeal for our country...but it will be to our honour to attempt to confront our past.

I avidly read this column, which I later quoted in *Unhealed Wounds: France and the Klaus Barbie Affair.* Beyond the possibility that my title derived from his phrase "old wounds," which lodged in my memory, what he had written encapsulated some of the central themes I would pursue.

Not everyone agreed with him, and that too would be central to my story, for resurrecting the past meant reviving the pre-war social fissures that had facilitated collaboration with the Nazis. How did this happen? I asked myself. What social processes had contributed to altering the consensus such that home-grown atrocities could occur?

Among the political Right—still virulently anti-communist in 1983, and (more covertly) antisemitic—only 15 percent thought Jews were people like any other, and many now claimed that crimes had been committed on both sides, and that you had to have been on the losing side to be prosecuted (an argument that was echoed by Klaus Barbie in interviews and is still heard today). For others on the Right, the issue was a pseudo-moral one: "When will France stop trying to win the last war?" sighed one journalist. "I feel nauseous when I contemplate the barbarous national sacrifice we're preparing [for this old man]. I'd prefer a little more charity..."

One riveting strain in this deluge of words—as the transformation of Klaus Barbie and his prospective trial became a metaphor for the past, present, and future of France—was this: the trial would, many claimed, "condemn Nazism itself," as all of Hitler's crimes crowded into the prisoner's box along with those of the accused. It would be the trial of *all* crimes against humanity, including the Soviet gulag and the atrocities of Cambodia's Pol Pot. It would "demonstrate what happens when power is unchecked, and democracies give up before a totalitarian system.... All this is more important than the fate of a retired monster like Barbie," opined one writer, after listing a series of other appalling world events.

It was evident that the charges against Barbie were going to be divisive. In the immediate postwar years, the French government had passed a general amnesty law that had allowed thousands of small and big-time collaborators to hide their deeds and re-establish themselves in society.

These people might now be outed. The other minefield would certainly be the Jews. The French penal code contained a statute of limitations that automatically "prescribed" (exempted from prosecution) any crime that had gone unpunished for ten years (a law which had brought to light the startling possibility that former SS officers might enter France as tourists to show off the sites of their former "operations" to friends and family). The legislature had, however, also ratified the law of "crimes against humanity" that had been written into international law at the Nuremberg Trials specifically to deal with Nazis. And crimes against humanity—among them genocide, murder on a massive scale, and the forcible transfer of populations—were *not* circumscribed by time limitations, meaning that such charges could be brought against Klaus Barbie.

But there was a rub: according to the Nuremberg definition, crimes against the Resistance were "war crimes"—and they did fall within the statute of limitations. Only crimes against the Jews met the "crimes against humanity" criterion. Given the anguish being expressed by surviving members of the Resistance who had been tortured by Barbie, there could be trouble ahead.

I felt electrified with energy and excitement. It seemed increasingly possible that the Furies unleashed by this impending trial might open a window on collective memory and enhance my own understanding of it.

I still remember that Paris was perfumed, as usual, by the heady aromas of freshly baked croissants, espresso coffee, garlic on the post-prandial breath of salespeople in the shops, and still the fumes of Gitanes, all of which lovingly evoked my early life here. Art deco lanterns and the diffused yellow light emanating from the interior of favourite *quartier* restaurants illuminated the February nights. Friends from my student days appeared to understand my project, but they seemed less than pleased that I, a foreigner, was planning to stick my nose into this story. The most common word that had come up in my reading to describe the unwelcome past was "mud"—and it had been generally agreed, until now, that this was not to be "stirred." There was hardly a family in France that had not been touched by the Resistance or the Collaboration, including my ex-husband's, and my friends were as wary as anyone about the outcome of Klaus Barbie's return.

I had to start meeting people, but whom? Probably those whose names were appearing most often in the press, such as Serge and Beate Klarsfeld. It was they who were responsible for the extradition of Klaus Barbie from Bolivia to France, and Serge didn't mince words. He had been quoted as saying that "the heroes of the Resistance" had done little to help him and Beate during the twelve years it took them to find Barbie in his Bolivian haven. He also didn't hesitate to suggest that the reason the French were interested in Barbie "had less to do with the murder of Jews than with Mr. Barbie's mistake of killing the hero of the Resistance, Jean Moulin. What interests us now are crimes against humanity, which until now have been hushed up or ignored. One of the darkest moments in French history was the role of the French in the deportation of the Jews," he charged.

Hushed up or ignored. The "mud" of the deliberately opaque past was meant to remain "unstirred." Was this why I had been unable to find answers to my questions (albeit poorly articulated) after my traumatic visit to Natzweiler-Struthof?

I placed a telephone call.

The capture of Klaus Barbie had made the Klarsfelds world famous—a notoriety that would grow over the next years as they strategized how to bring other Nazis and major French collaborators to trial. They agreed to meet me, but when I arrived at their modest Paris apartment, tape recorder in hand, Serge looked disappointed. Was it because I was young, female, small of stature, and working independently?

He was tired of talking to journalists, he said dismissively. Barbie had been apprehended—now it was time to move on to other "operations," like the case of Jean Leguay, a chief of the Vichy police in the Nazi-occupied zone who had since enjoyed a successful business career on three continents. There was also the important case of Maurice Papon. We met him earlier: he was Paris's prefect of police who ordered the violent crackdown against anti-Algerian War protesters in 1961. But during the Second World War, as general secretary of the Vichy prefecture in Bordeaux,

Papon had personally signed deportation orders for 1,500 Jews—including those in Bayonne.

I had to secure Serge's attention and respect. Luckily his wife Beate entered the room.

"What gives you the courage to do this risky work?" I quickly asked them.

He bristled. "The very fact of the Holocaust. After what happened, I don't have the right to be afraid. Besides, it would give too much pleasure to my enemies. Sometimes I think of King Louis Philippe. When there was an attack and everyone flattened themselves on the floor, he remained standing saying, 'These are the risks of the trade.' I simply refuse to be afraid."

Their work was perilous indeed. Beate had located the history of Klaus Barbie in dusty archives in France and Germany. She had followed his trail through meetings with German prosecutors who showed reluctant interest, then through meetings with French politicians. A Socialist government led by François Mitterrand had recently come to power, and it was purportedly sympathetic to capturing "the Butcher of Lyon," as Barbie was called. The road to Bolivia had been even more fraught: Beate had travelled there with a Jewish survivor who had lost her children to torture and deportation at Barbie's hands. The two women chained themselves behind hand-made signs that outed the identity of the locally known Klaus Altmann as SS-*Hauptsturmführer* Klaus Barbie. For years they pursued him in acts beset with danger as their prey successfully eluded them. Finally, a brief liberal moment in Bolivian politics, in tandem with the presence of a Socialist government in France, had made Barbie's arrest and deportation possible.

I am impressed, but the Klarsfelds were the parents of two young children. Why would they risk their lives? I ask them.

It was personal, they said—for each of them. When Serge was a child of eight, his father, Arno, was torn from their home in Lyon by Klaus Barbie's men while the rest of the family listened and trembled behind a false wall. Just prior to the banging on their door they had heard their neighbours scream, "Help! We are French citizens!" Arno Klarsfeld had offered himself to the Gestapo as a foil to protect his hidden family. He never returned.

But the impetus to track down Barbie came from Beate. She was a German national, and in the conventional family that raised her no one had ever spoken about the war. She had no knowledge of what had taken place in her country.

In 1960, at age twenty-one, she had come to Paris to learn a second language. She and Serge met on the platform of the *Saint-Cloud* metro station. It was his Jewish friends who confronted her with the recent past of Nazi Germany.

Beate had responded with shame. She and Serge wanted to marry, but any children born of their union would have a dual heritage. Because she wanted them to be proud of their origins, she committed herself to an extraordinary course of action—"to restoring my country's honour," as she put it to me. When she was criticized for "stirring the mud," her response was to avow that the dead cannot rest, nor can the historical page be turned, until people who have committed monstrous crimes against humanity are brought to account. Anything less, she argued, was tacit approval of their acts.

"Everything I do is as a German who is not a Jew," she said, staring at me with steely blue eyes.

One thing they said that day surprised me and continues to do so. At bottom, they wanted Klaus Barbie and the other Nazis and French collaborators *to apologize* for what they had done. I quoted Serge's exact words in *Unhealed Wounds*:

> If Barbie had come back to France of his own accord and said he regretted what he did...hat would have been enough for us. There would have been a trial, but it would have been conducted in a spirit of cooperation...
>
> But I'm a realist. They never change. They look younger than their age, and they live much longer than their victims who survived, and they never have trouble sleeping at night.

> Something inside me is revolted by the knowledge that human beings can do such things to each other. I am sickened. We always give them the chance to express regret—and they never do.

These many years later, his words that day continue to surprise me: that all that mattered to him was a statement of regret—one that never came. I ask myself if regret is the same as accountability. And I think not. Saying one is sorry for being a major criminal is, shall we say, a nice thing to do, but accountability for crimes against humanity necessitates a public iteration of deeds done, and should carry consequences as determined by law. A trial, in other words.

As it happened, Klaus Barbie was eventually brought to trial in a courtroom spectacle that was broadcast internationally. And he appropriately spent the rest of his days in prison. All the same, I have also come to appreciate the power of apology and remorse in world affairs—the formal recognition that what happened did actually happen; and the potency of speaking truth in the face of lies and denial.

By bringing Barbie "home," so to speak, the Klarsfelds were effectively challenging the entirety of French society. For to acknowledge the hidden story of the Nazis, the Collaboration, and the Jews was a bold undertaking in a country that revered the wartime Resistance—that multiplicity of armed groups with differing political proclivities that had refused to accept the fall of France to the Germans on June 22, 1940. The most successful among them were communists, and the least likely to be caught, since individuals usually knew only their immediate superior, and then only by code name—hence they were less likely to provide information under torture. Charles de Gaulle, the leader of the Free French based in London, won the day. When he arrived back in France on June 14, 1944, the myth that just about everyone had resisted the Nazis, including collaborators who now claimed to have been covert *résistants* playing a "double game," took root.

The name Lucie Aubrac appeared most often in news stories about the Resistance. She was famous for having performed the most daring rescue of the occupation—that of her husband Raymond from the Montluc prison in Lyon, where Klaus Barbie corralled his hostages. Between 7,500 and 10,000 people were incarcerated at Montluc. Only Lucie Aubrac's escape plan was successful.

Under an aristocratic-sounding pseudonym (Guislaine de Barbantane), Lucie presented herself to Barbie as Raymond's disgraced, pregnant girlfriend. She told him she only wanted her unborn child to have its father's name, even if the "traitor" (Raymond) had to die. It was a long shot, but in the 1940s a vestige of pre-war chivalry remained. Remarkably, the ploy worked. Although he reportedly tortured women sexually with dogs and a whip, Barbie expressed sympathy for the plight of a high-born "fallen woman."

"Ah, Mademoiselle," he said to her. "Men, men, you should never trust them." Astonishingly, he agreed to allow her to speak with Raymond in his presence.

"You are a bastard!" Lucie shouted at her husband for Barbie's benefit. "I am expecting your child, and it must have a name. I don't care if they deport or shoot you, but you must marry me first."

Raymond Aubrac realized an escape plan was being acted out.

That night, as a truck transported prisoners back to Montluc from their daily torture sessions in Barbie's SS headquarters, a van with Lucie inside edged its way in front of the vehicle. Another van and car took up position in the rear. Inside the truck, the prisoners were chained together in pairs. After a few minutes the van behind moved up to pass the truck, and as it drew level, three machine guns with silencers sprayed bullets at the driver. The guards at the back of the truck leaped out. All but one was killed on the spot. A lone guard escaped, as did all fourteen prisoners, including Raymond Aubrac.

She was tall and elegant, a woman whose intensity had never wavered over forty years. She seemed wary of me, as was Raymond, who was also present the day we met. Why was a young Canadian interested in this story? They had reason to be cautious; they had long claimed publicly that they knew which turncoat in the Resistance had betrayed Jean Moulin to Klaus Barbie.

Ancient schisms within the Resistance were reborn as now-elderly people stepped forward to have their say—including René Hardy, a controversial figure within the Resistance, who had been arrested by Klaus Barbie in 1943 and released under mysterious circumstances. During the war, Lucie had sent Hardy a sweet laced with cyanide, but, having divined its source, he had refused to touch it. Now an old man, Hardy had recently published a book, *Last Words,* in which he made the explosive claim that Lucie and Raymond had been in cahoots with Barbie himself. In the fragile environment that now characterized French society, the Hardy book had become an instant *cause célèbre*. The Aubracs charged Hardy with slander. Hardy responded with a counter charge.

"We're devastated," Lucie told me once she was assured of my bona fides. "I'm still in perfect health. I could be travelling or dabbling in archaeology, which has always been my passion. Instead, *I* have become the defendant in this case."

It was as a young history teacher that Lucie first felt compelled to resist the Germans and the Vichy regime. The impetus came from a Nazi exhibition called "The Jew" that was travelling through France. As an historian, she was appalled by the distortion and the racism. Other shocks followed. "When you run through roll call in your class and the little girl whose name is Levy is afraid to reply, then the next day in roll call someone says, 'Oh, she's gone. She's with her parents and they're all gone.' Or when your Jewish colleague is fired..."

One single event hardened her resolve. A train of prisoners was leaving Lyon. Friendly railway workers hid Lucie and several friends in a boxcar from which they could spy on another track in the station that was hidden from view. A convoy of Jews was being loaded. She recounted the experience:

> I saw one of my former students. Her name was Jeannine Cremieux. She had married, and she was holding a baby on one arm. With her other hand she was carrying a package of her belongings.
>
> When she put her package down to grab a railing and pull

> herself up the steps onto the train, a German who was standing behind her kicked her. She and the baby both fell. The baby rolled on the track and its clothes reddened with blood. That day I wanted to kill. Do you understand? I saw that with my own eyes, that horror, and even now, when I speak of it, I feel distraught.
>
> Jeanine picked up the baby and her package and got onto the train. She was gassed when she arrived at Auschwitz. After the war I went back to the school, and her name was on the wall in the list of students who never returned.
>
> When you see a thing like that you cannot *not* join the Resistance. After you feel that kind of hatred, anything is possible.

I quote this interview at length because I never forgot it. I still see the passion that contorted her face as she recounted this story, see her forehead wrinkle, hear her voice break. She exposed me to something that would increasingly absorb me in the years to come—a curiosity about the kind of people who act in spite of facing personal risk. Like other rescuers of the endangered and the oppressed, Lucie Aubrac was enraged by injustice. She was independent and autonomous, altruistic, capable of empathy, and courageous—and a woman who despised authoritarianism. Most importantly, she felt a strong sense of duty.

One day in 1985, not long after the Canadian publication of *Unhealed Wounds*, an extraordinary event occurred, the sort of rare happening that instantly makes the years spent writing a difficult book worthwhile. I had just given a talk in Ottawa, during which I told the story of Lucie Aubrac. As I was autographing copies, a middle-aged woman who'd been waiting in line reached me. "Lucie Aubrac was my teacher," she told me in a barely audible whisper. "I too was deported from that station, but I survived."

Now knowing Lucie was still alive, she wanted to see her again. I put them in touch with one another. And the woman who had remade her life in Ottawa flew to Paris.

I WAS ENCOUNTERING PIECES of hidden history I could never have guessed at during my student days in France: that of the Gestapo, of the occulted fate of the Jews, of the internecine wars of the Resistance. I remembered that long ago a Jewish man in a shop had asked me, "How is it for 'us' in Canada?" What comparison had he been hinting at? I didn't know then. There had been frightening antisemitic scrawls on the walls of the Metro. There was my neighbour and would-be friend who had punched her fist into the air and cried, "*Je suis fasciste*!" The indecipherable background to these events had alarmed and puzzled me. Now the murkiness was clearing, as it was clearing for the French themselves.

The daily diet of war trauma was starting to affect me emotionally. I became preoccupied by the horrors of torture, something I had never consciously thought about. I'd always been interested in the psychology of outlier behaviour, perhaps because of my father's sharp observations. I recalled that as a university student I'd once picked up a remaindered book titled *The Mind of the Murderer.* It was both the psychology of the perpetrator and the lasting effects on the victim that absorbed me then and now: the intimate physical relationship they shared through the exercise of raw power by one of them.

I would continue this pursuit of the origins of extreme human behaviour, and what always struck me, especially when there were photographs, was the pleasure on the face of the torturer. For years I was perplexed by this. Eventually I began to believe the enjoyment might embody liberated blood lust, or perhaps the simple thrill of unmitigated power over a captive human being. To understand the psychology of torture would become part of a larger attempt to separate out the different threads of social change that could lead to this behaviour.

Lucie and Raymond Aubrac encouraged me to learn more about Klaus Barbie's treatment of captured Resistance fighters and the wartime environment of Lyon. I agreed, and that was how I met Jean Gay.

A tall, gaunt man lowers himself into the chair beside me on the terrace of a small café in Montparnasse. Like other survivors from that era, he is a man in his sixties, or older. He wants to dispense with initial pleasantries, and he begins talking immediately.

He was arrested by Klaus Barbie's Gestapo on March 7, 1944, after someone had denounced him as a Resistance fighter. Denunciations of *résistants* and hidden Jews had rained upon Barbie's office—a universal phenomenon when the chance to curry favour with the powerful presents itself. For several hours during two consecutive days, Gay was submerged in freezing, then extremely hot, water; but his worst memory was of psychic pain. During one session, Barbie told him his two sons were downstairs, and they would be tortured in front of him the next day—unless he provided information about his resistance network. That night Gay tried unsuccessfully to kill himself. The next day, to his surprise, he was deported to a prison camp.

Under a gray winter sky, he tells me about his experience in Montluc. "When you saw your friends return a mass of bleeding and torn flesh, eyes torn from sockets, fingers and toes hacked off, this was part of the ongoing torture. Especially when you were offered, in return for information, regular access to food for yourself and your family, protection, and money. You never knew who had been 'turned,' or who was listening to your account of what had happened to you that day."

As I have not forgotten my encounter with Lucie Aubrac, so have I remembered my meeting with Jean Gay on the terrace of that small nondescript Parisian café. Perhaps it was then that I first intuited two seemingly contradictory things. The first is that our psyches are vulnerable; few among us can withstand the destruction of self that is the outcome of the experience of torture. I have never been tortured, nor am I a survivor of the Holocaust; but the shock I experienced when I was young and unsuspecting of the world has haunted me. I cannot imagine experiencing torture and staying sane. But resilience is the other side of suffering. Jean Gay would subsequently tell his story at the trial of Klaus Barbie. He couldn't wait, he told me. The act of bearing witness against his torturer would help restore his humanity.

As I delved deeper into these stories and their kaleidoscopic complexities, phantasmagorical images assailed me at night. In one dream, I found myself addressing a crowd of thousands, in a language I did not know, about a subject I knew nothing about. Fortunately, I woke up laughing. I didn't need Sigmund Freud to interpret my unconscious fears about the book I was trying to construct. All the same, I clearly needed to pause, to consolidate.

I settled into a few weeks of quiet reading, and what I learned was illuminating. In 1845, Benjamin Disraeli had described Britain as a country of "two nations," in a description of the British class system. Half a century later, in his massive study *Histoire de France,* the French scholar Ernest Lavisse spoke similarly of "*les deux France*"—of two distinct value systems separating those who prized order above justice and the state above its members from those whose priorities were the reverse. These competing worldviews had sporadically erupted into conflict since the 1789 French Revolution. They had resurfaced during the wartime Occupation, with the Vichy regime that prized "work, family, and fatherland" on one side of the divide and the Resistance prizing universal rights and republicanism on the other.

Lavisse's seminal work appeared during the first decade of the twentieth century—as the Dreyfus Affair tore through France. Alfred Dreyfus, an unremarkable Jewish army officer from an old Alsatian family, was unjustly accused and convicted of treason because of a series of byzantine happenings involving forged documents, wastepaper baskets, and a cleaning lady who happened to discover the planted "evidence." The discovery of the forgery triggered a virulent outbreak of the malaise of *les deux France,* in which Dreyfus the Jew became almost irrelevant, except that it was he who was suffering.

Newspapers published attacks and counterattacks of fabulous dimensions. On one side were right-wing elements composed of monarchists, unhappy aristocrats, the army, the church, antisemites, and ultra-nationalists who perceived themselves as France incarnate. For these people, the guilt or innocence of one man was simply not paramount; of far greater importance was the fate of the nation. Dreyfus, they said, was guilty because the evidence pointed to his guilt. He was guilty because, once designated as such, the honour of the army demanded that he remain condemned.

On the other side were those who held more recognizably modern ideas of guilt and innocence: people committed to justice for the individual. The best known among these was Émile Zola, whose book *J'Accuse* led to his being publicly reviled, and tried for libel.

The Affair, as many were aware, was a transformative event; it had led both to the creation of the French League of Human Rights *and* to the Vichy collaboration, as over decades *les deux France* fought each other. It had also established antisemitism as a deeply embedded national malaise—long periods of liberal openness notwithstanding.

Jean-Denis Bredin's superb book, simply titled *L'Affaire,* helped me understand the pandemonium surrounding the return of Klaus Barbie by opening a window onto the larger issues of the war era, such as the effects of propaganda and hate speech on a receptive population, and their connection to the Dreyfus Affair. There had been an economic recession just prior to the 1894 accusation against Dreyfus—a common trigger for a scape-goat attack on a minority. Additionally, something then known as "modernity," in which capital wealth had begun to replace historical land ownership and raise unemployment, badly frightened the old guard. *Fin de siècle* political anarchism and socialism further upset the established order. The Jews were said to be at fault.

The story of poor Alfred Dreyfus is a well-known cautionary tale with remarkably interesting implications. When he was, of necessity, found guilty, riots broke out all over France. A joyful mob of supporters of the verdict heaved through the courtroom doors screaming their approval. But in the end the *Dreyfusards*, as Alfred's supporters were called, prevailed: they managed to get the verdict overturned, and organized the League for the Rights of Man, a body that came to symbolize republican France's commitment to universal human rights. Their successes inspired the Jews to believe that they belonged to the polity. But the "other" France was not to be crushed. It re-appear with a vengeance at the time of the Vichy government during the Second World War.

During my 1983 research trip "Dreyfus" was still a loaded word. Later that year, as xenophobic France re-emerged in the person of National Front leader Jean-Marie Le Pen (whose legacy continues today in the person of his daughter Marine), a chauvinistic National Front supporter produced a diatribe titled "Dreyfus the Scum."

KLAUS BARBIE'S LEGAL DEFENSE added to the public cacophony in that winter of 1983. France was a democracy where everyone had the right to a fair trial, but there was nothing conventional about what was happening now. A notorious lawyer named Jacques Vergès had taken on the case.

Vergès had personal knowledge of racism: he was born in Thailand in 1925 of a French doctor attached to the French embassy and a Vietnamese mother. The marriage had ended his father's career. In those days, Frenchmen did not marry Asian women. The family moved to Reunion Island, where Jacques experienced the worst of colonial bigotry. As a young man he had joined the French Resistance against the Nazis. That was before he knew about the violence of the Algerian War, before he knew about the torture of other colonized people carried out by the French, some of them former members of the wartime Resistance and themselves victims of Klaus Barbie.

The Algerian War, which had been my own introduction to political violence twenty years earlier, was also emerging as a piece of the proverbial "mud." Algeria had gained independence in 1962, and by now diplomatic relations between the two countries were longstanding. But, like the buried truths of the Collaboration, knowledge of the atrocities committed during that conflict had been interred along with the unresolved schisms of the era.

Jacques Vergès was publicly licking his chops at the prospect of defending Klaus Barbie. His strategy, he announced, would be to turn the tables on the prosecution. In what way, he wanted to know, was SS-*Hauptsturmführer* Klaus Barbie worse than the murderous, lying hypocrites of the Algerian War? Vergès already had a public connection with the Algerian conflict: he had been a hero of the Left as far back as September 1960, when luminaries such as Jean-Paul Sartre and Simone de Beauvoir signed the famous "Manifesto of the 121," demanding that the French government recognize the Algerian uprising as an authentic fight for self-determination. That year, Vergès had defended pro-Algerian militants in court.

There was palpable shock at the news he had become Klaus Barbie's lawyer. How had this happened? More importantly, who was paying him? A conventional French lawyer had already been assigned to the case before Vergès swooped in—Alain de la Servette, the head of the Lyon bar association. De la Servette denied that he was receiving remuneration beyond payment provided by legal aid, but it was openly rumoured that he had met François Genoud, a mysterious Swiss-Nazi banker who was, people whispered, planning to bankroll the Klaus Barbie defense.

I telephoned Alain de la Servette. He hesitated, then agreed to meet me. I had never been to Lyon, a city internationally renowned for its gastronomy and now for more infamous reasons. Since I arrived early, I took the chance to visit the notorious fortress prison of Montluc, where Jean Gay had been held, and the Hotel Terminus, which had been Klaus Barbie's SS headquarters. Merely to see these places, the nerve centres of the Gestapo, made me catch my breath.

Alain de la Servette looked about sixty—and worried. Deep furrows carved horizontal grooves between his eyes, which were large, and exaggerated by round horn-rimmed glasses. He seemed immediately eager to set the record straight. He did not deny the rumour that he had been contacted during the days following Barbie's return to France. Yes, he had received letters from "lawyers in Germany" offering "help," but they had subsequently withdrawn their offer, he insisted. Yes, he admitted, he had been in touch with François Genoud, who had come to Lyon to meet him; and yes, he had travelled to Lausanne on at least one occasion. During meetings with interested parties from outside France, he had been advised that there would be plenty of money available for Barbie's defense, but, he added, looking visibly uncomfortable, the fee had been offered, not asked for.

I was surprised that he was willing to talk so freely. He was clearly in distress. What happened next remains unclear, but within days of our meeting, the press reported that Alain de la Servette was out and Jacques Vergès was in. No one was a match for the mercurial Vergès. And his defense of Klaus Barbie would be financed by François Genoud.

Genoud is worth a detour. A mysterious figure who stalked the world of international intrigue for fifty years, he had been a convinced Nazi since the 1930s, when he fell under the personal spell of Adolf Hitler after his "law and order" family had sent him to Berlin, hoping he'd pick up the emerging *Zeitgeist*. As a youth he had also travelled to Palestine where he met the ex-Grand Mufti of Jerusalem, who became his link to the Arab world and to the simmering hub of anti-Western, anti-Zionist, anti-colonial radicalism presided over by President Gamal Abdel Nasser in postwar Cairo.

Genoud and the ex-Grand Mufti personified a hybrid of ultra-left and neo-Nazi extremism that underpinned the terror movements in Europe that started in the late 1960s. One might even say they invented it. Genoud personally managed the stolen treasury of the Nazis after the fall of the Third Reich through numbered Swiss bank accounts deposited through a clandestine club of former SS officers called *Die Spinne* (The Spider). He also financed the cause of Arab nationalism, including the North African liberation armies of Morocco, Tunisia, and Algeria. His contributions to ex- and neo-Nazis were legendary among the few people in the know. He became a publisher of important Nazi materials, acquiring the rights to the writings of Hitler, Martin Bormann, and the Nazi propaganda minister Joseph Goebbels. He financed the defense of PLO and other Palestinian terrorists of the day, including the notorious Carlos the Jackal. And for several decades his partner in law and cross-over ideology had been none other than Jacques Vergès.

I wrote two chapters on Jacques Vergès in *Unhealed Wounds*, one titled "The Making of a Radical," the other, "Through the Looking Glass." As for the latter title, there was no other way to describe a man who disarmed his enemies by dancing circles around them while holding up mirrors that distorted conventional opinion. He had used the Lewis Carrol phrase to "explain" his strange disappearance from Paris between 1970 and 1978, which merely served to stoke rumours that he had joined his old student friend, the murderous Pol Pot, in Cambodia.

Deliberately enigmatic and utterly calculating, he performed verbal pirouettes around his opponents, his magic mirrors reflecting the "hypocrisy" of Klaus Barbie's accusers by confounding the linear truths they cleaved to. And they fell for it—all of them, from the gutter tabloids to the distinguished magazine *L'Express*. How *dare* he undermine the narrative of the heroic Resistance? they fulminated. How *dare* he raise the spectre of Algeria in the context of the trial of a German Nazi? Fine questions, but what *was* reality if you could reflect it, stretch it, expand it, distort it, then "explain" it in words that continued to sound confusingly familiar to the ears of ordinary people? Who among them would rise and say that the emperor wore no clothes?

Klaus Barbie would indeed be tried on specific charges, but Vergès's "strategy of disruption," as he so aptly called it, successfully targeted the national soft spot. His contrived charges against "France" contained enough unnerving truths to make everyone uncomfortable. He and his client were the lone principled defenders of democracy against a transgressor state, he proclaimed. Were Nazi torturers worse than the French torturers and murderers in Algeria? Vergès wasn't sure.

IN THE SPRING OF 1984, I flew back to Toronto for a few months to assimilate my work to date, then returned to Paris in the fall to resume my research and write the book. This time I would be accompanied for part of my stay by Tom, and by my son Roland. Tom was beginning a five-year term as dean of the School of Graduate Studies at the University of Toronto, but he had made his acceptance of the position dependent on an initial half-sabbatical so we could be together. Roland, who was about to enter his last year of high school, had opted to earn his final credits in the summer of 1984 so he could join us for the school year in France. He, too, would register in the *Cours de civilisation française* at the *Sorbonne*—the same programme I had taken almost a quarter century earlier at the start of my own adult life.

Just before leaving for Paris, I strained my back foolishly trying to win a swimming race against one of my nieces, and I spent the next weeks lying flat on my back. I was far from better when my departure date arrived, but I was scheduled to leave, and leave I would. We had rented an apartment called Villa Adrienne near the *place Denfert-Rochereau*, once again in the 14th *arrondissement*. I already had interview appointments. I had to get there.

I arrived alone (Tom and Roland would join me later) and was immediately taken in charge by my student-days friend Dominique, who sent her son to stock my kitchen. For several weeks I lay prone on the living room floor reading my research. It was lonely; one memorable day I shuffled into the kitchen and comforted myself with spoonsful of sweet jam—something I would never ordinarily have done. I signed up for physiotherapy at a nearby hospital, where I was treated daily by bored practitioners who wanted nothing more than to be rid of me. Roland arrived and I roasted a welcome chicken, my customary way of pacifying new territory wherever I temporarily establish myself.

Soon I was well enough to venture out—and my first port-of-call was the Montparnasse office of Jacques Vergès.

It was a large, high-ceilinged space decorated with a magnificent Flemish wall tapestry and a beautifully preserved sixteenth-century edition of the Code of Justinian. Exquisite pieces of African art embellished nooks and crannies. The radical-left lawyer wore an expensive-looking grey suit with an argyle cashmere sweater. This was no Che Guevara. He was perfectly tailored and perfectly self-contained, with the faultless manners of Frenchmen of his generation.

He leaned back in his chair behind a polished wood desk, drew deeply on a thin cigar, and looked at me appraisingly.

Something about his demeanour amused me. "Some people call you a destabilizer. Is that a compliment?" I asked.

"Oh, yes," he laughed. "A tremendous compliment."

He wants to talk about his tactics and underlying beliefs (I'm tempted to put ironic quotes around the latter word), but what interests me most is his avowedly calculated use of passion. The passion for the underdogs of the Third World and against the "hypocrites of the Resistance"; the passion for the unorthodox, violent solution; his passion against "Zionism." He had proclaimed to the media that the French government was in the service of Israel, and that Barbie had been returned to woo the "Jewish vote." He denies being an antisemite. "Some of my Jewish friends are antisemites," he offers casually. Even anger is a calculated response, he tells me.

As for his beliefs, he is convinced that crime makes the world beautiful. "The subject of crimes attracts me as it attracts all the novelists. A society without crime would be a dead society," he explains, adding that he identifies with Julien Sorel, the young murderer portrayed with psychological acuity by Stendhal in *Le Rouge et le Noir.* "My law is to oppose the law," he declares. His true pleasure seems to be the joy of anarchy. Of being bad. Breaking the rules. Confounding the public. The thrill of danger.

His friend Jacques Derogy, then a senior reporter at *L'Express*, confirmed this to me with a telling story. Several years earlier, Derogy's phone rang in the middle of the night. It was Vergès. "Come over," he said. "Something's happening."

Derogy made his way across the darkened city. Vergès opened his door wearing a yellow and black silk bathrobe and brandishing a revolver.

"What's this about?" panted Derogy.

"There was some sort of threat," Vergès replied vaguely and happily. Then he happened to catch sight of himself in the hall mirror. The reflected image of the lawyer-anarchist-revolutionary in silk, revolver in hand, was irresistible. The two men laughed till they ached.

Unhealed Wounds: France and the Klaus Barbie Affair was published in Canada, the United States, and France in the fall of 1985. The French edition had a provocative title: *L'affaire Barbie: analyse d'un mal français* (The Barbie Affair: Analysis of a French Malaise). I flew to Paris for the launch, an experience as baroque as the research itself.

Just prior to publication, the telephone had rung in my Toronto home at 3 a.m. I leaped out of bed, fearing the worst: my parents were now elderly. It was my editor from *Éditions Ramsay* in Paris, which was publishing of the French version of my book. Ominously, the company's lawyer was also on the line. Without apologizing for the hour, he demanded the removal of two sentences in which I described the lawyer Alain de la Servette's evident discomfort regarding the fee he had been offered by François Genoud for the defense of Klaus Barbie. If I refused, the lawyer said, my book would not be published.

It was a middle-of-the-night ambush. Caught off-guard, still half-asleep, I made my way to my desk, found the manuscript, and opened it to the relevant pages. The excision made little difference—de la Servette's complicity was evident regardless. Okay, I said, and returned to my bed, where I lay sleepless until morning.

When I arrived in Paris in October, I learned that word of the publication of *L'affaire Barbie* had reached the Élysée Palace, and that a limousine had arrived at the publisher's office to collect the first copies. Following this startling news, I received a frantic telephone call from Jacques Derogy. "Where are you?" he asked. A live panel discussion about my book was taking place at that moment, he told me; he was on the set, and the chair reserved for me was empty. The publisher had neglected to inform me.

Later that same day I met with Fred Bild, then second-in-command at the Canadian Embassy. Fred had been supportive during the research process, and he was very welcoming. That evening he and his wife, Eva, hosted an embassy dinner in my honour, which delighted me. He also accompanied me to the local police station, where it was suggested that, for reasons of safety, I not sleep in the same bed twice. Why? I had been called as a witness by the newspaper *Le Monde* regarding an upcoming trial in Lausanne, Switzerland. François Genoud had sued the newspaper, and since my book included the Genoud connection to the Barbie case as well as his connections with international terrorism, I too was implicated.

No one knew who Genoud's friends were or how they might respond—including Jacques Vergès, although I was quite certain he would be chuckling heartily at the publicity. He would have been especially pleased to note that *L'Express* had excerpted my chapter on him, and that it had made it that week's cover story. The police gave me a special phone number to use if I felt the need. Luckily, I did not, and in retrospect I think my fears were likely unsupported, but it was an anxious moment.

The promotion for *L'affaire Barbie* was ordinary enough—although one event did have long-ranging consequences. A television show that everyone watched, hosted by the legendary Bernard Pivot, passingly displayed the cover of my book. Watching that day was Chantal Sanglier, my former roommate at the *Maison Néerlandaise*, with whom I had lost touch years before. We found one another and resumed our youthful friendship, which persists to this day.

Two other things happened—one amusing, the other less so. The former took place during a reception for the book hosted by Adrienne Clarkson, then Ontario's agent general in Paris. The room was filled with French and foreign journalists, including Flora Lewis from *The New York Times*. She wanted to know whether the book contained breaking news—something to hook a story on—such as new information about the U.S. involvement in the infamous Rat Line that had spirited Nazis, newly viewed as anti-communist allies in the emerging Cold War, out of Europe. I hadn't included that story, but what *was* truly new in my work was the unexpected linkage between Palestinian and neo-Nazi extremists in the European terror attacks of the era, including the pivotal role of François Genoud, a man who was unknown to English-language readers. (Flora Lewis wasn't interested, but that aspect of the book was picked up in the United States by *Mother Jones* magazine in 1987, then by *The Philadelphia Inquirer* in 1997.)

The funny happening was the presence of a CBC Television W5 crew that had flown to Paris to film the event. They embarrassedly admitted that their photography equipment had been held up in customs, so they couldn't do the job they'd been sent to do—but they enjoyed the meal!

The less amusing development was my reaction to the trial in Lausanne. Tom (who had joined me) and I flew there from Paris with the journalists from *Le Monde*; and when the plane landed (in the middle of the tarmac) everyone casually sauntered off. Except me. I was terrified of being exposed as I stood on that airfield, and of laying eyes on the Nazi, François Genoud. Suddenly panic-stricken, I couldn't move my legs. Slowly and gently, my husband coaxed me off the aircraft.

Now at the courtroom, we witnesses were in an anteroom waiting to be called in. Each time the door opened, my heart pounded. But the call was always for someone else. Hours passed; a well-known writer sitting beside me filed and polished her nails. Then came the announcement: an agreement had been reached between the parties. The trial was over.

Then François Genoud walked through the open door into the witness anteroom. He was thin. A smile hovered around his lips. Only I seemed to have found this experience an ordeal. Afterwards, Tom and I joined the *Le Monde* crowd in a local bar across the road. Everyone laughed uproariously and told their war stories.

AMIDST GENERAL TREPIDATION, KLAUS Barbie was charged with forty-one separate counts of crimes against humanity (crimes against Jews) and war crimes (crimes against Resistance fighters). It was impossible to guess what might happen. A conviction based on witness testimony would crack open the contrived amnesia that had obscured the truth about the Holocaust in France, including the truth about the Collaboration. But an acquittal of Barbie was also not impossible. Either way, the country would be forced to pay attention to hidden truths. And to truths about that other war as well—the one in Algeria.

On May 11, 1987, the day the Klaus Barbie trial opened, I was in Washington, D.C., being interviewed on CBS network television. What happened felt surreal: on a studio monitor I watched a reporter delivering a stand-up report in front of the Lyon courthouse. I intimately recognized his script: he was mouthing my words, an entire paragraph lifted directly from my book.

On July 4 that year SS-*Hauptsturmführer* Klaus Barbie was sentenced to life in prison. He died there four years later at the age of seventy-seven.

In the immediate aftermath of Klaus Barbie's return to France, the journalist Guy Baret had asked the most pertinent question of all: "Are we ready to look at the true face of France, at the dark years reflected in the mirror of this trial?" From my perspective, the Barbie *affaire* and the subsequent trial had imposed that introspection. It was true that many people still refused to look. After the publication of the French edition of *Unhealed Wounds*, someone mailed me an anonymous postcard containing just three words: "You don't understand." It was postmarked Bayonne.

I thought I did understand. And I sympathized with the fact that people who had spent four decades justifying the actions of those they loved would be greatly pained by the unexpected unsealing of lips. And I understood that the new situation might require a re-evaluation of family narratives, and that not everyone was willing, or able, to manage such reversals.

For me, the Sisyphean stone I had carried on my back for two decades seemed a little less heavy, but it would take another twenty years, and several more exploratory books, before I felt free. Only in retrospect did I come to understand that *Unhealed Wounds: France and the Klaus Barbie Affair* was the beginning of my recovery from my unexpected visit to Natzweiler-Struthof two decades earlier.

I met people whose experiences taught me lessons I would later draw on—lessons I would never have learnt otherwise. Torture, and the questions it raises about our capacity to inflict harm; the unbearable anger one may feel when children are victimized by the unscrupulous; and the importance of the struggle for criminal accountability. Also, the power of acknowledgement and apology; the formidable strength of character one must possess in order to move from thought to action, as Lucie Aubrac and the Klarsfelds had demonstrated; and, from Jacques Vergès, the proof of what I had learned in my long-ago undergraduate class about interpreting and distorting history.

Vergès astonished me, as he did millions of others. What I absorbed from him was the power of propaganda in the hands of an expert strategist. I thought he was a slick showman with a personal mission—a smarter, outsized, more practiced version of Robert Lemieux in Quebec. Klaus Barbie hardly mattered to Jacques Vergès; what counted was his own assault on France itself. Ironically, it was he, in conjunction with the Klarsfelds, who would prick the balloon of lies the French had taught their children for forty years.

France was not the same after the trial of Klaus Barbie. The shameful story of French collusion in the deportations of the Jews was now public, as was at least partial truth about the Collaboration and the atrocities of the Algerian War. In the years to come there would be more criminal charges and more trials, moving from Barbie, the German Nazi, to Paul Touvier, a pre-eminent French collaborator, to Maurice Papon, the Vichy bureaucrat responsible for sending Jewish families to their deaths.

But the learning that influenced me most while researching and writing this book may have been my first glimpse of the threads that weave their way, often invisibly, across history—including those directly linking the fervid social divisions of the Dreyfus Affair to the veritable civil war of the Occupation. On this larger tableau I began to absorb the complexities of societal consensus, how they are created, and where they may lead.

As Bronwyn Drainie noted in her review of *Unhealed Wounds* in *The Globe and Mail*, I had not chosen this book. It had chosen me.

CHAPTER EIGHT

ENCOUNTERING ISRAEL

BRONWYN DRAINIE HAD INTUITED my passion. Yes, the story of French historical memory had chosen me, commanded me to pay attention to the murmurings that routinely broke through the mundanity of daily life. The writing of that book had felt like a small breakthrough. It had carried me further than I had thought possible, and it had whetted my appetite for an unmediated encounter with history.

During the three years I lived with the story of Klaus Barbie, I'd been too preoccupied to acknowledge the depth of my emotional reactions to the work I was engaged in. Looking back, I think it may have newly traumatized me, in that it presented me with a much clearer historical context for my visit to the Natzweiler-Struthof camp. It had taken more than a decade, after that initial encounter in 1960, for me to feel that I'd acquired even a minimal perception of the social, then legal, transformations that had incrementally threatened the safety of the French Jewish minority—transformations such as increasing public rejection, then eventual loss of citizenship, with the loss of fundamental rights that this entailed.

While I was still married to Claude and living in France as a housewife and new mother, it was the so-called Jewish Question that had unsettled me. Given my hyper-sensitivity to the subject, those two words had appeared to be omnipresent in the books and newspapers I was reading—although they likely were not. In any case, I had had no idea what they signified, and probably thought that translating Jean-Paul Sartre's famous book of that title might magically inform me.

I seemed to flounder once the excitement of publishing *Unhealed Wounds* evaporated. I felt the need to continue my work, but I didn't know where to direct my thoughts and energies. Was I still a writer if I wasn't writing? I even consulted a hypnotist, which had no discernible effect beyond rendering me dizzy, and flattening my slim bank account.

During this fallow period in the mid-1980s, I was offered the chance to write the authorized biography of the late Sam Bronfman, the patriarch of the famed family who had made his fortune in the distilled beverage business during Prohibition and founded the Seagram Company. Michael Levine, a prominent Toronto entertainment lawyer who had been a school friend of my younger siblings, was a relative of the Bronfmans, and he was certain I was the right person for this commission.

So, Michael and I travelled to Montreal, to the Peel Street headquarters of Seagram, with its stained-glass windows and elegant interior. In a majestic wood-panelled boardroom I was introduced to Charles Bronfman, his widowed mother Saidye, and Robert Rabinovitch, then Executive Vice-President and Chief Operating Officer of Claridge, Inc.—a Bronfman family holding company—who would later head the CBC. I thought the meeting went well. I liked Saidye, and she seemed to like me.

Within days, I was offered the job. That is, until Charles's sister, Phyllis Lambert, dismissed me outright in the notoriously choice language she was known for. She wouldn't hear of anyone other than an academic historian writing her father's biography.

The commission eventually went to Michael Marrus of the University of Toronto, but my consolation prize was far better than the job itself.

So bothered was Charles Bronfman by his sister's rebuff that he agreed to pay me a fee of tens of thousands of dollars, presumably to assuage my hurt feelings—a windfall that became the underpinning of Tom's and my retirement savings.

"Erna, you should *not-write* more books more often!" quipped my friend David Stein. The unlikely story even merited a small mention in *The Globe and Mail*.

Gradually, my focus returned. Given what I had learned about France and what I knew about Canadian social history, the historic Jewish experience of living as a minority in Christian cultures—a subject I'd begun to explore in *Jews: An Account of their Experience in Canada*—continued to intrigue me. I'd become particularly attentive to the Zionist-nationalistic shift in Jewish-Canadian identity during the 1970s, after the Israeli victory in the Six-Day War of 1967 and the creation of the Occupied Territories.

There was a background to this ideological shift: massive immigration from Eastern Europe had long ceased, as had the ideological passions of that generation. The pithy Yiddish language had been discarded by the second generation as an archaic reminder of the Old Country. The dream of universal equality promised by Karl Marx had also failed. In 1948, at the creation of the State of Israel, most Canadian Jews had rejoiced as partakers in an historic feast—but it wasn't until the new army of Israel emerged victorious over the Arabs during the Six-Day War of 1967 that the national creed of Zionism became a litmus test of belonging. Diaspora Jews had been waiting for a new identity to supplant those that had failed or been rejected.

I'd watched these changes happen with some fascination, but from a writerly distance. In 1982, I wrote an article about the infamous Lebanon war for *Quest* magazine, then edited by Michael Enright, titled "Canada's Jews and the Summer of Lebanon," which won a gold medal at the National Magazine Awards (including a cheque for $1000 that thrilled me) as well as a mixed reception from the Jewish community. Soon I began to think that if I wanted to understand the core of contemporary Jewish identity, I would need to visit Israel itself.

Coming from an assimilationist family, I didn't feel the emotional pull towards Zionism that others seemed to experience, although I did agree that having a country of one's own might be a good idea should future tyrants show interest in unleashing another Holocaust. As with *Unhealed Wounds,* I knew I'd have to write if I wanted to understand, and, as with *Unhealed Wounds*, I wasn't sure how to proceed. When I closed my eyes and focused, I knew I wanted to experience Israel directly and independently, beyond the propaganda and counterpropaganda that depicted the country either as a Paradise whose leaders could do no wrong or as the abode of war-lusty evildoers who could do no right.

Throughout the summer of 1986, I wrestled with various scenarios, none of which seemed promising—until the day Malcolm Lester invited me to lunch. I must have been boring him with my concerns because he interrupted me. "People always respect honesty," he said. I was startled by this simply spoken truth; I had forgotten about the power of authenticity. So, I decided to proceed. As did Malcolm; he said he'd publish me.

I had just a few contacts at the start, but they were central. Patrick Martin, *The Globe and Mail*'s excellent Middle East correspondent, generously opened his rolodex and gave me the names of dozens of sources. Shira Herzog, the former chair of the Canada-Israel committee, a friend of nuanced mind and resolute passion, briefed me on social conditions in Israel and contacted people on my behalf. Until her untimely death in 2014, she was one of Canada's most respected analysts on Israel affairs, and an unfailing activist for peace in the Middle East.

For six months I read both histories and polemics (many of the latter hopelessly biased one way or another, it turned out, and useless for my purposes). I studied the founding Zionists as well as their self-described successors, the religious militants who had populated settlements in the Occupied Territories after the 1967 war and were already beginning to change the face of Israeli politics. I also immersed myself in the Return-to-Religion movement that was targeting North American Jewish youth, and I looked with interest at the world of the ultra-Orthodox who lived in segregated neighbourhoods in Jerusalem. The more I read, the more positive I felt about the planned book. I wanted to visit these likely idealized places. I wanted to have direct experience of the territories, both Jewish and Palestinian; I wanted, at the very least, to try to understand the peace process, which was as elusive then as it is today, although possibly less an object of cynicism. Finally, given my personal obsessions, I wanted to comprehend the role of Holocaust memory in Israeli society.

I tried not to feel overwhelmed. I knew then, as now, that if I permitted myself to dwell on the immensity of the book's scope I might back off, so I practiced a sort of wilful blindness as protection. I decided to be ruthless; on a few occasions, this meant avoiding friends who had been honest enough to express perhaps understandable skepticism about the breadth of my subject. What kept me going was a core of stubborn determination known to many writers. And perhaps the conviction that I was engaged on a path I continually needed to define.

During my initial reading, I began to perceive Israel as a "country of the mind." In this interior space, Israel is not just a tiny land mass situated in the conflicted Middle East. It is not merely a democracy with a fine judiciary, or the place where creative science, such as the desalination of seawater and other important innovations, take place. This country of the mind is more—much more—for within its imagined cosmos "Israel" is a mythic entity. For almost two thousand years—since the destruction of the Temple in Jerusalem in 70 CE and the dispersal of the Jews throughout the world—the religious orthodox had yearned for the end of exile and the coming of the Messiah who would lead them back to *Eretz Yisrael*, the Land of Israel.

When nineteenth-century pogroms shattered the ancient Jewish communities of Eastern Europe, this redemptive dream metamorphosed into a nationalism that would appeal to the growing numbers who had abandoned orthodoxy. Asher Zvi Hirsch Ginsberg (1856-1927), a Ukrainian Jew known as Ahad Ha'am, taught that, in order to survive, Jews needed to strengthen their "national spirit," as seen in the teachings of the biblical prophets. This spirit, he argued, depended on reason and ethics, not religion. Ahad Ha'am had followers: early migrants began to leave for what was then called the Holy Land; but it wasn't until the end of the nineteenth century that yet another antisemitic attack—this time against the innocent Frenchman, Alfred Dreyfus—triggered into another notable figure into action: Theodor Herzl, a true political revolutionary, armed himself with a practical plan.

I was struck by the Dreyfus connection to Zionism, for as I have noted, I'd been intensely moved by his suffering during my research for *Unhealed Wounds,* and by the centrality of the Affair to the entirety of twentieth-century French history. It was no surprise to me that Herzl, an Austrian who lived in France during the Dreyfus debacle, would understand the Affair as a *raison d'être* for a Jewish state. His vision was of a return to Palestine that would transform idealism into action; Israel would be a secular homeland in which Jews would be free at last from King, Cossack, and Tsar.

Soon a more militaristic conception of a Jewish state emerged. In the 1920s, Vladimir Jabotinsky, another Ukrainian Jew, claimed that a future Jewish state in Palestine must include land on both sides of the Jordan River, including a permanent garrison of troops for defence. And this militant reorientation within Zionism became mainstream after the 1967 war.

These multiple beliefs had rivalled one another from the start: the religious paradigm of a return to Zion and "The Land"; the dream of the coming of the Messiah; the prophetic vision of the Jews as a spiritual "light unto the nations"; and, on the practical side, Israel as a refuge, as a Jewish national state. From Canada it was difficult to know how exactly they related to one another.

I made choices. In addition to meeting representative individuals with distinct points of view, along with scholars who might possibly offer a broader perspective, I would visit Kibbutz Yiftah, one of Israel's older kibbutzim. I would also spend time in an ultra-Orthodox community in Jerusalem; stay in a yeshiva (school) for North American returnees to the faith; visit at least one militant Orthodox-Zionist Jewish settlement in the Occupied Territories; find a way, if possible, to see the Israeli-Palestinian conflict through Palestinian as well as Jewish eyes; and, finally, explore the memory of the Holocaust.

On a warm spring-like day in March 1987, I boarded an airplane destined for Ben Gurion airport. Re-reading what I later wrote about my departure, I now laugh aloud. I was, I wrote, a "stubbornly curious, old-fashioned traveller." (I remember half-imagining myself as a nineteenth-century British explorer, minus the helmet.) "Walking shoes broken in, knapsack packed, modern accoutrements of tape recorder and other assorted paraphernalia at the ready," I continued with a flourish, "I was ready to explore the vagaries of settlement and ideology forty years after the creation of the state."

Following my romantic departure, I was relieved to find on arrival that most of my trip had already been organized by my contacts. What they could not control, however, was my first encounter with Israeli society. The shared taxicab that was supposed to carry me from Ben-Gurion airport into Jerusalem seemed to be stalled. A furious argument was taking place in Hebrew. Not understanding the language, I settled down to wait it out—until one of the passengers informed me that the shouting concerned me: an Orthodox male passenger was refusing to take the trip with a woman in the cab. The kerfuffle was eventually resolved when the irked individual chose to wait for the next car. It was, however, a portent of some of the strangeness inherent in Israeli society.

My contacts had rented a tiny home-base apartment on my behalf in the Yemin Moshe neighbourhood of Jerusalem, from which I could look down a hillside at the golden-hued stones of the Old City. That pleasure, though, was short-lived, for I was slapped by reality just moments after I entered my front door, for it was then that I encountered the distress endemic to Israeli families. Naturally, I knew that every Israeli under the age of fifty was in the active or reserve army, meaning they were either on a war front, or engaged in duties in the Occupied Territories, or on call; but it was my landlady Miriam, there to welcome me, who introduced me in an instant to a major dynamic of Israeli life. As she arranged a bouquet of flowers she'd bought for me, she spoke of her son.

He was fourteen, she said, and not long ago, during an adolescent argument, he had reminded her that not all young Israelis *live* long enough to stop "being stupid" and learn to "act like a grown-up," as she had reprimanded him to do. Her daughter, she told me, was just eighteen, and about to leave for her first army stint. She would be overseeing women prisoners at a West Bank holding facility. The daughter was afraid and tearful. She did not *want* to be an overseer of other women. Miriam had looked away when she said to me that she hoped that the lessons of empathy and compassion she had tried to teach her children would not be eroded in the rough, militaristic environment of the Occupation.

It was a shocking introduction to the country. I can still see us in my mind's eye two women in their forties, both of us mothers, standing beside a bouquet of flowers. I remember all these years later how thoughts of my own children filled my mind that afternoon, including the knowledge that they brimmed with hope for a life they were certain they *would* live to see. Whatever empathy and compassion they felt for others would not be tested by having to become an unwilling jailer in a brutal place.

Miriam interrupted my reverie. "The old woman upstairs is crazy," she warned me. Her son, it seemed, had been killed during the Six-Day War.

Miriam left, and I had barely stepped outside my door when the woman in question entered my ken. She glared at me, her hands on her hips. Had I locked the front door? she demanded to know. Had I let in an Arab?

I was a stranger intruding upon her grief. For the rest of my stay, she deliberately swept the dirt from her upstairs steps onto mine.

The places I'd wanted to visit seemed to comprise separate realms, like cocoons within which radically different worlds existed. As it turned out, many of these worlds were rejected by other Israelis. The "country of the mind" was effectively composed of many minds, some of which couldn't abide other ones.

It felt right to start with a visit to a kibbutz, the incarnation of the nation's ideological beginnings. Kibbutz Yiftah was a foundational settlement located near Metula, on the northern boundary with Lebanon. Some of its older members had fought with the Palmach during the 1948

War of Independence, and, as I drove my rented car north towards the dangerous border, the patriotic songs of hope and sacrifice I'd been taught as a child at Holy Blossom Temple took residence in my mind. I warbled aloud, sailing past the tree-clad rounded mountains and steep valleys of the Upper Galilee:

From Metula clear across the Negev,
Desert lands unto the sea,
All our friends are called to arms now,
Every man goes willingly....

The communal nature of the lyrics evoked Israel's origins, as they were meant to; and the language conjured up images of the "new Jew" who would inform Israeli identity. The idealized "new Jew" was intended to be everything his European parent was not: he was a strong-bodied warrior who sought peace, but would fight to defend his community if called upon; he was anti-religious; and he was a physical worker, not an intellectual—unlike those pathetic Talmudic scholars who went "like sheep" to their deaths under Hitler. He was also a pioneer in and a builder of the empty land that had been waiting for his return. "Ideology played the greatest role in the development of the modern Israeli psyche," wrote Amos Elon in *The Israelis: Founders and Builders,* in 1971. During my trip I would learn that the verb "to build" was the central feature of the new syntax, and that the idea of a civilian army—the Palmach of my adolescent playlist—would morph into that of the IDF, the Israel Defense Forces, a military body with spiritual roots in the dual national ethos of "building," and of willing sacrifice in the name of self-defence.

I see Kibbutz Yiftah now as I did then, in vivid detail. With its landscaped flower beds, sandy "streets," identical cottage homes, and its large barn-like communal hall, the kibbutz looked like the summer camps of my youth. On the paths, everyone was dressed in no-nonsense work attire, their faces sunburned and natural. Five hundred people resided here, of whom almost half were children who lived together, separately from their parents, until they entered the army at age eighteen. Yoram, my guide, had arranged a schedule that would, he said, introduce me to every aspect of kibbutz life—but what he really wanted to know before we began was my life plan. "Are you planning to move to Israel? Might you move to a kibbutz?" he asked, before our acquaintance was a quarter-hour old. The first of these questions—Would I move to Israel—was repeated by almost everyone I met during my months in Israel. After first establishing that I was a Jew, that is.

Decades later, writing these words from notes that were unused in the final text of *The Garden and the Gun*, as well as from the published book, it seems self-evident to me that the idealized world of the kibbutz (today unrecognizably changed) was destined to end. Its underlying belief-system and practices were too inflexible to survive. In retrospect, Yoram, my guide, was an example of what went wrong. Hungarian by birth and a true believer in the Zionist cause, he had moved to Israel in 1956 after the Soviets returned to his country. Yoram didn't just believe that Jews everywhere ought to move to Israel because sooner or later the diaspora would throw up a new Hitler. He went further still in his conviction that within Israel only the kibbutzim could offer safety, that only the civilian soldiers of the kibbutz fighting alongside the IDF could and would protect the Jews of the world. And just in case I might heed his warnings and decide to move to Israel, he had another admonition: I should just forget about Tel Aviv, he warned ominously. The "new Jew" was not meant to sip lattes in decadent cafés on Dizengoff Street.

Yoram was not unfamiliar to me. He might have been an ideological communist, or socialist, or fascist for that matter, for what sets such people apart, it seems to me, is the inflexibility of their views. Such individuals have always interested me; in fact, they seem closer to one another in the style, if not the content, of their thinking than they are to thinkers who find comfort closer to the more relativist-looking centre of the political spectrum.

Yoram had a store of anecdotes to shore up his message; for example, he recounted a telling, perhaps apocryphal, story about an American woman of his acquaintance who had once admitted to him that she hid her Star of David necklace when she left her home, a tale meant to illuminate the dangers of diaspora life. What he did not know was that, unbeknownst to him, all the people he would introduce me to on Kibbutz Yiftah would acknowledge during the course of our conversations that life on the kibbutz was not what it used to be. Members of the founding generation worried aloud about their children, many of whom no longer subscribed to the socialist ideology of their parents. This didn't surprise me. In researching the Jewish communist movement in Canada—a similarly utopian movement—I'd learned the identical thing: the adults were the believers; their children just wanted to be ordinary, capitalist Canadians.

Memories of my Yiftah encounters remain as sharp today as they were then. For example, Yeshayahu (who had fought with the Palmach) and Tamar spoke to me about change while insisting that the underlying values of kibbutz life remained constant. "You live not only for yourself and not only for today," they insisted in a heartfelt refrain that sounded just a little too practiced. Their own children had lived twenty-four hours a day, seven days a week in the children's house; but today, they said, children slept at home with their parents. The younger adults had insisted on this; they wanted more family closeness. But the shift in sleeping arrangements had triggered a new problem. Because money could not be exchanged for services rendered, and few were willing to volunteer their time, there were no available babysitters. Parents were now unable to have an evening alone together.

Issues surrounding "women's work" were also beginning to rankle. On the kibbutz, men fought the battles, worked the fields, and tended whatever industry the kibbutz was engaged in. Women looked after children, laundry, and food preparation. But feminism was sweeping the world, and the kibbutz was hearing unprecedented complaints about enforced gender roles. Furthermore, the young were now daring to think as individuals. For example, a group of seventeen-year-olds I was introduced to—children who had grown up together largely without their parents—giggled and looked sideways at one another while avowing that most of them would not return to Yiftah after their military service. Not until they were in their forties were Tamar and Yeshayahu allowed to pursue their own interests off the kibbutz. "There has always been an inner struggle between the self and the group," Yeshayahu explained, looking downcast. "For years I asked myself why I didn't leave to study in the United States or Canada. But then I asked myself, 'Who will build this place?'"

There it was again, that word "build." No matter how many decades the country had been in existence, no matter how often endemic conflict diminished hope, the sustaining pioneer ethos of building could be called upon to banish doubt.

Another memorable scene. Yiftah was surrounded by barbed wire. I understood that it sat in a dangerous neighbourhood, but to me a barbed wire enclosure signalled defeat, or at least the continuation of conflict—an absence of peace. But this was not the intent. Yoram handed me a promotional pamphlet about Yiftah. Inside, I read that the wire represented "the kibbutz's sense of purpose."

There was an explanation for this: "The Holocaust in Europe strengthened the resolve of [the] Jewish settlers.... Many left the barbed wire of the concentrations camps that closed them in and found the barbed wire of a people able and willing to defend themselves and their communities." Barbed wire had apparently mutated into something positive—the heart of the pioneer vision, a symbol of captivity transformed into a glorified symbol of self-defence. I wasn't convinced.

Early the next morning Yoram introduced me to Yossi, the senior army officer in charge of security for the twenty-nine kibbutzim and small farm communities that hugged a Lebanese border that was indisputably dangerous. The 1982 Lebanon war had formally ended a few years earlier, but Hezbollah had recently intensified its incursions into the region. There had been an attack on a neighbouring kibbutz.

I still recall the disarming beauty of the Lebanese countryside. Rounded mountains undulated under a blanket of spring green; pools of water reflected the morning sunlight from the bottom of deep gorges.

This was, of course, deceptive. It was the job of Yossi and his colleagues to advise the border populations of imminent danger. "Children living here cry with anxiety at night," he told me. Some wailed as they were led into bomb shelters, he said. Others retreated into a mute, traumatized silence.

"What do you tell the children about where they live?"

"The truth. We live near the border. Sometimes that can be...sometimes conditions can be dangerous. We tell them they must know what to do."

We passed by Moshavim. Years earlier a school bus filled with children from this village was attacked just yards away before their parents' eyes. The landmarks remain in place: the tree, the large rock, the hill behind which the killers hid. I think it was at that moment that I began to acquire a visceral sense of what it must mean to live here. Nothing was as it seemed. Unless they were actively revealed to the visitor, the peaceful-looking borderland held on to its secrets.

Most interesting was the memorial just over a nearby hill that commemorated the members of the 1948 Yiftah Brigade of the Palmach. Children from across the country were brought here on pilgrimage to pay homage to the heroes of the nation. Families held Bar Mitzvah ceremonies here.

I watched Yoram and Yossi fight back tears as they stood side by side. Their emotion was contagious, but I was also unnerved by the conflation of religion and nationalism. My studies of France and the Holocaust had already made me wary of this perilous synthesis, and, as I write these words, I know I have not changed.

I was certainly not immune to the chronic anxiety of life here. Yoram had billeted me in a little house that had once belonged to a young couple with three small children. The husband had been killed just over this border during the Lebanon war. After a few years the kibbutz had sent the woman and her children to Tel Aviv, ostensibly so she could study, but really, it was whispered to me, so she could remake her life with another man. The house was exactly as she had left it. Her winter jacket hung on a hook; books collected dust on a shelf; the kitchen cupboard was stocked with coffee and tea; faded children's drawings were tacked to the wall.

Each night, I lay in the bed where they had slept together for the last time, the bed where they had conceived their children, and each night I felt intimately close to peril. Their family, my family.... Devastation hovered in the stillness as I held my breath and listened to the sounds of the night.

My own night terrors helped me understand why the rhetoric of heroism and a new land waiting to be built was unendingly rehearsed by adults and pounded into the ears of children. Simply said, it was not rational to live here in the kibbutz. Yeshayahu had hinted at this when he admitted asking himself why he didn't leave. His answer was the resonant verb "to build." To leave the kibbutz that he had helped to found would have been to betray the convictions of a lifetime, something he could not do.

Listening to him, I remembered the poignant, mostly elderly Jewish communists who had allowed me to enter their lives. Their experience had been very much the same. When the dream of an egalitarian society began to crumble, few among them were able to abandon the beliefs that had given meaning to their lives.

As I write these words, the transformation of the kibbutz movement is almost complete. Most have been privatized and are paying salaries to their members. People own their homes; they have investment portfolios and private bank accounts. At Yiftah, only the longstanding industry of drip irrigation systems remains a communal enterprise, and among the kibbutz facilities, only the dining hall is still under collective ownership.

A century after their founding, the iconic settlements have abandoned socialism, although, as utopian experiments go, they did last longer than most.

SOMETHING NEW WAS ADDED to the rhetorical mix in the early twenty-first century as long-occulted Palestinian history slowly infiltrated the conventional Zionist narrative. Abandoned memory-holes stirred with new life as both Israeli and foreign scholars published revisionist works.

If early Zionist ideology had held that Palestine was "a land without a people for a people without a land," what now entered the public realm was the knowledge that the belief-system of the kibbutzim—stressing "self-defence" and "building"—had concealed a submerged reality. The famed egalitarian society had been constructed after the forced removal of a large Arab population that had inhabited the territory for centuries. This event, known by Palestinians as the Nakba, was the centrepiece of modern Palestinian identity, just as Zionism informed contemporary Jewish identity. In contemporary scholarship, the two were now beginning to converge, not as comparable happenings, but as foundational historical events that had become the narrative underpinnings of both national identities.

The emerging twenty-first-century literature also included a belated recognition that these competing narratives had equal value. Authors such as Ari Shavit (*My Promised Land: The Triumph and Tragedy of Israel*), John B. Judis (*Genesis: Truman, American Jews, and the Origins of the Arab/Israeli Conflict*), and Amos Goldberg and Bashir Bashir (the joint Jewish and Palestinian editors of *The Holocaust and the Nakba: Memory, National Identity and Jewish-Arab Partnership*), among others, had researched forgotten archives and revised the story. Although the peace process had effectively ground to a stop during the leadership years of Israeli Prime Minister Benyamin Netanyahu and U.S. President Barack Obama, there had been change, nonetheless. None of the above-cited works would have been published in mainstream venues when I was writing *The Garden and the Gun* in the 1980s.

The Arab expulsions were not unknown, of course—in Israel, in the Jewish diaspora, and in the world at large. Taboo remembrance is always present, which is why those who seek to re-shape the collective memory of a nation must work so diligently to create a thick narrative of myth, however improbable. I think back to postwar France, and the efforts expended by General Charles de Gaulle and others to imbed in the collective consciousness the fable that every Frenchman had resisted the Nazis, when the truth was quite the contrary. I think about the great efforts put into teaching mythologized war history to the postwar generations, and about the fierce struggle to suppress the truth on the part of those who had a stake in the outcome. One of the illustrations I had included in the French-language edition of *Unhealed Wounds* was a newspaper cartoon from the chaotic days following Klaus Barbie's return to France. It depicted an outsized book of history, opened to the year 1942. On one side of the image on the page, a crowd of pint-sized people, representing half the population, pushed to close the enormous volume; on the other side of the image, a crowd representing the other half of the population strained to hold it open.

A similar confrontation is poised to emerge regarding the 1948 War of Independence. It takes time, perhaps generations, for evidence-based historical revision to surface. And even longer to be accepted.

To place the founding events of Israel in their proper context, the concept of *terra nullius* (land owned by no-one), and the imperial notion that the world was comprised of civilized Europeans and uncivilized "others," was commonplace in the late-nineteenth century—and these colonial assumptions imparted strength to the Jewish claim to Palestine. The Jews needed a home. After two thousand years of dispersal marked by expulsions, pogroms, and finally genocide, the appeal for such a home was not unjustified.

Unfortunately, the era of imperialism and colonialism was effectively ending just as Israel came into being. The Indochinese war against the French had already started in 1946. India became independent in 1947. The Algerian War began in 1954. By 1960, seventeen sub-Saharan African nations had gained independence from their former European overlords. The old world-order was changing. Major international institutions were coming into being, the most important of which was the United Nations. There was a new emphasis on universal human rights.

In other words, Israel was established according to a consensus that was already disappearing: state-building by means of expulsion and repression was becoming an anachronism. To acknowledge this is not to call into question Israel's ongoing right to exist; one can examine the circumstances of its creation in terms of then-prevalent political assumptions without calling the subsequent establishment of a vibrant state into question. It is, rather, to recognize that in terms of their shared geography, both Jews and Palestinians have rights. And that a bilateral acknowledgement of this truth is the only rational route to a lasting peace.

The anti-religious, leftist, kibbutz movement may have been in decline in the mid-1980s, but at the time of my visit the ideology of building and defending of borders was already morphing into something far less innocent. Following Israel's occupation of Arab territory after the 1967 Six-Day War, the settlers who moved to the West Bank announced that *they* were the true pioneers of Israel; *they* were the inheritors of the land after the morally bankrupt, socialist kibbutzim, whose glory days were gone. Forget about the horrors of socialism. *They* were the new defenders of The Land, inspired by God himself.

How had these people so successfully appropriated the language of the kibbutz? What made them willing to raise their children in this dangerous environment? The founding kibbutzim, such as Yiftah, had also raised children in dangerous places out of conviction, but the West Bank settlers were literally *surrounded* by Palestinians under military occupation who hated them.

I was curious about these zealots and their choices. I would meet them if I could arrange it.

THE RELIGIOUS-SETTLER MOVEMENT HAD begun under the British Mandate decades earlier. Their leader was Rabbi Abraham Isaac Kook, who argued that Jewish settlement in Palestine was the first stage in the prophesied redemption of the Jews.

Unlike the atheist kibbutzniks, and the apolitical ultra-Orthodox who were content to wait until the Messiah decided to make an appearance, Rabbi Kook saw the historical trajectory of Zionism as part of an irreversible messianic trend. His son, Rabbi Zvi Yehuda Kook, carried his father's mystical thinking further still by assigning to God an active role in Middle East politics. When Israel won the Six-Day War, then occupied the biblical lands of Judea and Samaria on the west bank of the Jordan River, Rabbi Kook the Younger and his followers rejoiced. The biblical cities of Hebron, Nablus, and Jericho would at last be accessible to the historic Jewish people—a miracle Kook and the others interpreted as concrete evidence of God's active presence in history.

So, in 1968, a small group of fundamentalists known as Gush Emunim (The Bloc of the Faithful) moved into the ancient heart of Hebron, a city holy to both Jews and Arabs located in the Judean mountains thirty kilometres south of Jerusalem. Hebron was the site of the Tomb of the Patriarchs, purportedly purchased by Abraham to bury his wife, Sarah. Isaac and Jacob were also buried there along with their wives Rebecca and Leah. David had founded his kingdom in Hebron before conquering Jerusalem.

But there was a catch to this liturgy: Muslims also venerated the Tomb of the Patriarchs, asserting that Abraham, a Quranic as well as a Biblical prophet, was also the father of Ishmael, who is believed to be an ancestor of Mohammed. The locale had always been contentious; way back in the twelfth century, the warrior-sultan, Saladin, had converted the site of the tomb into a mosque, and as relatively recently as 1929 the beautiful Abraham Avinu synagogue there had been burnt down. Hebron, in other words, was ground zero for past and present Jewish-Muslim antipathies; and the Gush Emunim settlers who moved there were raring for a God-inspired battle.

At the time of my visit to Israel, the 65,000 settlers who lived on the West Bank were estimated to possess no fewer than 10,000 firearms of all types. (By 2021, about 470,000 people had created settlements across the map of the territory, effectively making a Palestinian state impossible.) In the summer of 1983, Jewish settlers had murdered three Arab students. That same summer, a settler was stabbed to death in the Hebron market. The territory seethed with hatred: some of the settlers hatched plots to blow up the Dome of the Rock Mosque in Jerusalem, to attack Palestinian buses, and to assassinate Palestinian mayors. The director of Israel's Shin Bet intelligence service was reported to have called the Gush settlements "psychological hothouses for the growth of Jewish terror."

On the other hand, some of the settlers were not religious nationalists, but secular Jews taking advantage of state-sponsored financial incentives to move to the territory. This too was a political endgame, for their presence there effectively consolidated the Occupation as a *de facto* annexation.

Life on the west side of the Jordan was undeniably more dangerous than living in Tel Aviv, for example, but the hilly terrain was beautiful, and the Jewish settlers were protected by the Israeli military. Furthermore, they never had to see a Palestinian if they preferred not to: the government had built a highway that linked the Jewish settlements while simultaneously bypassing the Arab communities along the route, making the latter invisible.

In 1979, eleven years after the first settlers had arrived, seven hard-line families had moved into the heart of the Hebron casbah, where they were granted special military protection. Among them were Gush Emunim leaders Rabbi Moshe Levinger, his wife, Miriam, and their eleven children. The Levingers were militant believers who purposefully engaged in violence. Since his arrival, Rabbi Levinger had been arrested at least ten times regarding incidents in Hebron. In 1985 he had attacked a six-year-old Palestinian child he accused of throwing stones; in 1988, he fired at local shop windows, killing a Palestinian store owner; on another occasion he was convicted of assaulting a Palestinian woman and her two children. Each time he was duly fined and sentenced, then released after days or months. This was fine with him; secular laws, he said, were secondary. What mattered was the Word of God—and dominance.

On the other hand, I'd been advised by a Jerusalem acquaintance that the real spokesman for the movement was Levinger's American-born wife, Miriam. One morning I telephoned her. She sounded tired—tired of being approached by people like me.

"Do you know the Bible?" she asked. "It's all there." Why not go directly to the source and get the story in half the time?

My visit to her guarded enclave at the heart of the Hebron souk remains one of my most memorable experiences. I was frankly scared. I'm presently reading what I wrote all those years ago and remembering just how unsettling was the bus ride out of Jerusalem. Few civilian non-residents ventured into the Occupied Territories, making my fellow passengers an unlikely lot: a young female soldier with a rifle slung casually over her shoulder like a tote bag simultaneously chewed a wad of gum and smoked a cigarillo; a wild-looking obese man with long unkempt hair sang rousing songs from the early Palmach in a booming baritone; and the driver looked at the road only occasionally, when he wasn't engaged in conversation with a friend seated at the back of the bus.

I got off at the Hebron bus stop along with two Arab women. They approached me. "Aren't you afraid?" they asked me in English.

"Should I be?" I replied nervously. They laughed, and patted me like a child before disappearing into the crowd.

A crush of people milled about the central marketplace of the city where the bus had stopped, the men in keffiyehs and the women in long embroidered dresses. Carts overflowed with oranges, avocados, and eggplants. A delicious aroma of grilling shish kabobs wafted from portable grills. I was surrounded by large tables displaying trays of flaky baklava dripping with honey.

I didn't know where to go. Mrs. Levinger had given me only vague directions. Where was the Israeli military post that guarded the Jewish enclave? I knew I was being watched. I felt it at the back of my neck.

Out of the corner of my eye I saw two Israeli soldiers disappearing at the end of a narrow road lined with more food stalls. I ran after them. "Excuse me! Excuse me!" I shouted. They didn't hear me, and I was attracting a lot of unwanted attention. I wove around the shoppers, wary of inadvertently touching anyone lest a misunderstanding occur.

Out of breath, I caught up with them.

"Mrs. Levinger, please!" I panted.

They pointed in the direction I'd just come from—the heart of the market. *Toda*. Thank you. I sucked in my breath and turned back into the crowd.

And there it was. The military kiosk. The guards asked for my identification, then indicated a small gate that opened into a narrow pathway. Like Alice leaving one world for another, I entered a small tranquil courtyard where several wooden doors stood ajar. I located the name Levinger and "knocked" on a sheet of plastic.

She was seated at a long table in her kitchen, peeling potatoes. I guessed she was fifty or more. Her face looked open and friendly; wisps of greying hair escaped from the scarf that covered her head, and she wore an apron over her dress. How relieved I was to have found her. There was even an unexpected commonality to our meeting, for despite the unique physical and social geography of her home, the circumstance felt oddly familiar. When I sat down with her at the table (she had switched to peeling carrots and garlic) we were, for a moment, two women in a kitchen sharing the ancient ritual of meal preparation: a unanimity across millennia.

She acknowledged, but was undisturbed by, the conflict her family's move to the Hebron souk had created. The facts were simple, she said. The Arabs had come here seven hundred years after the destruction of the Second Temple in 70 C.E, but more than four thousand years of Jewish history had preceded their arrival. Therefore, they had no valid claim to the land. They could stay, she graciously allowed, but only if they didn't cause trouble. In any case, they would eventually leave. The Bible promised that the enemies of the Jews would do that, although not necessarily immediately.

I was not surprised that her radical vision defied all compromise of a contemporary political sort, but what did pique my interest was her appropriation of liberal political language. For example, she wanted to talk about pluralism and democracy, prized liberal concepts.

"People always ask me, 'How can you live here?' Well, that's just provocative. If they are pluralists, why *shouldn't* I have the right to live in Hebron? It's *democratic* for me to live here."

I almost admired her for this proud effort to outwit her critics, but her argument had a gaping hole at its centre. Pluralism is not just the presence of different peoples in a shared space; it is an inclusive agreement according to which all members of the polity hold equal rights. Her understanding entailed only physical juxtaposition; in fact, when she spoke of the biblical entitlements that presumably favoured the Jews, the other inhabitants of her geographical space seem oddly non-specific. The generic Arabs who surrounded her compound were merely the most recent enemies of the Jews—the latest in a long line starting with the ancient Amalekites.

I found her calculated inversion of democracy similarly deceptive. The state of Israel was, she maintained, a good thing for the Jews, and so was its military, but there was a caveat: the Jewish soldier was inherently defined by the Bible, not by the secular state. Soldiers were Jews, she said, before they were servants of the nation. In other words, democracy was a useful tool, but only if elected leaders acted in accordance with God's directives. "We are the vanguard," she summed up with practiced emphasis, looking meaningfully at her watch. "We came here because God told us to come, and we stay because that is what He ordained."

I felt grateful when she accompanied me to the bus, as the IDF watched us from their nearby station. As if reading my thoughts she said, "We are safer here than in London, Paris, or Manhattan."

Really? What a fantasy, I thought as we waved goodbye. The safety of her family and that of the others squatting at the heart of Arab Hebron depended entirely upon the soldiers who defended their enclave—and a willing government that enabled their presence.

By 2020, approximately 800 Jews lived in Hebron, surrounded by more than 782,000 Palestinian Arabs. The settlement had expanded into three separate areas of the city. The old souk I once threaded my way through had been closed by the Israeli military, and some houses there were occupied by settlers and soldiers. Palestinians whose houses fronted the ridge of one of the settlements were unable to enter their front doors; they were forced to climb across buildings and flat roofs to access the rear entrance of their homes.

In a 2010 documentary titled "*This Is My Land...Hebron*", directed by Giulia Amati and Stephen Natanson, the Israeli journalist Gideon Levy described the town as "cruel and crazy," and the place under military occupation that he despised most. Looking at it, I was shocked to see what had become of Hebron since I visited Miriam Levinger there. The two communities still lived side by side, one in army-secured freedom, the other under exceptional duress, surrounded by walls and watchtowers, and within wire enclosures. They were close enough to scream at one another, to throw stones (young Palestinians) and to fire guns (adult Israelis). I was happy to observe that the documentary makers seemed to have been motivated by a desire to understand how such hatreds grow, as well as just report them.

What etched itself into my memory was one scene. A young Orthodox Jewish mother wearing a head covering and rimless glasses holds a baby on one arm while gesticulating wildly with the other. She is shrieking at several Palestinians who are separated from her by only a few feet. "This is our land!" she screams. Three adult men standing by her are smirking with pleasure. The baby in her arms is crying with fear.

I shall never forget that baby. Not yet old enough to hate, but old enough to be terrified by the sounds and gestures of hatred.

Today, the peace process is more remote than ever. In the immediate aftermath of his 2016 election, the American president, Donald Trump, appointed as ambassador to Israel a man whose personal views lay far to the right of those held by most right-wing Israelis, and the then-government of Prime Minister Benjamin Netanyahu announced plans to annex the settlements. For decades, these settlements had been understood as illegal outposts under international law. Israel had feared fanning international condemnation by challenging this status quo, although it continued to build in the Territories. Some said that the political move to annex might lead to an indictment of Israel's leadership by the International Criminal Court. What did seem likely was a further erosion of empathy and human rights within Israel itself, a process of moral shrivelling that was already long underway.

The country had long prided itself on its unbiased judiciary, a key to its vaunted democracy, but courts had to be obeyed if the rule of law was to be more than a fig leaf for autocracy or special interests, and the signs were not good. That the Hebron settlers had ignored a Supreme Court ruling ordering them to cease and desist from their harassment of the Palestinians, who were their neighbours but lived effectively under military rule, suggested a breakdown in the functioning order of the secular state itself. As Miriam Levinger had made clear to me decades earlier, the settlers did not accept the authority of the state when it conflicted with their understanding of God's will.

From the earliest planning stages for this book, I had hoped to visit the Occupied Territories from both sides of the divide, but after I had seen Hebron what had been a wish was transformed into a need. I had many questions—basic questions—including whether I even wanted to identify as a Jew if that included admiring this society. It was true that the country was an economic powerhouse, and, I thought once again, a reasonably normal place if one lived in Tel Aviv, for example, and if one deliberately shut out the rest as a matter of self-protection. But as someone whose life seemed to have willed itself in a certain direction after experiencing a hallucination of personal destruction at the hands of group haters, I didn't feel free to ignore reality in the way others seemed able to.

Hebron behind me, I set out to find a refugee camp.

I'D ACQUIRED A PALESTINIAN guide and interpreter on my very first night in Jerusalem. I suppose my method was somewhat unorthodox. I didn't have a "fixer" or even a source, so I had opened an exploratory conversation with the young waiter in my hotel dining room. Once we'd both ascertained that I wasn't on an "Explore Israel" tour, and that I didn't want to have a drink after work so apparently wasn't there for sex, a silence had fallen between us. He was trying to figure out who I might be, and I was sizing him up too. Eventually I told him I was a writer, and I asked if I could hire him to guide me in the West Bank. He was wary, stepping away to whisper something to a colleague, then he agreed.

"I'm a son of the city," he boasted. "I know everyone." But be careful, he warned me in a whisper. Don't tell them you're a writer. Just say you're a teacher. They will respect that.

I wrote about Naim at length in *The Garden and the Gun*, about our path through the byways of East Jerusalem, where I drank mint tea in tiny hole-in-the-wall shops while he smoothed the way for an informal interview. But the most important office he provided was to introduce me to his friend Mohammed, who lived in the Balata refugee camp near the city of Nablus. Mohammed was a student at An-Najah University, where we met. He was shy and slight in stature—and he told me he was studying the Old English poem *Beowulf.* I was beyond surprise. He wanted to be a teacher of English literature.

Mohammed looked nervous as we entered the gates and stepped onto the muddy clay path that was the central street of the camp. He must have been wondering how I would be received, for I was accompanied only by himself, and were I to be rejected by the people living there, his own status might have been questioned.

I am aware that I am clearly under his protection in this place of fifteen thousand people, who live in the squat concrete row houses lining the narrow paths that radiate from the main street. Children emerge from doorways like a moving flock; they giggle, whisper, and point. Men and women step out of storefront shops to stare. I am immediately surrounded by five or six tough-looking youths—possibly the radical heart of the camp. They watch me closely.

Mohammed has intimated to me that the programming of the young starts early here. His younger brother is named Tha'ir—meaning "revolution," he explains—and he adds, "Anyone who has amassed the means is free to live elsewhere, but it is forbidden to leave the camp until the revolution."

"Forbidden by whom?" I asked.

"It is a holy thing to remain here."

Our growing entourage has now arrived at the shop of Hatem, the camp barber, where about fifteen young men mill about smoking cigarettes. They invite me inside and offer me one of the two chairs in the room. I say I am prepared to listen, and they tell me about the conditions of their lives—that tear gas is lobbed into the camp daily, that stone-throwing children are beaten by soldiers, that people fear to leave their homes after dark.

I plunge in: "How many of you have taken part in military actions?" I ask, using their own glamorized expression. They glance at each other, smirk, and raise their hands as though they are in a classroom and I am their teacher. Two of them speak up. Hatem, the barber, was arrested for "security reasons" and sentenced to nine years in prison. He looks thirty-five and brutal. Faisal served six months for attempting to take revenge on a Palestinian "collaborator." In what sounds like a well-rehearsed chorus, they recite, "We will fight to our own death. We will hope forever. Death to Israel!" A boy of fourteen with a smooth child's face enthusiastically assures me he is willing to die. "I am permitted to do anything to attack my enemy," another boy I hadn't noticed hisses in my ear. I turn abruptly to look at him. His hands shake as he raises his cigarette to his lips. "We must find the cruel Zionists who do these things and kill them."

The question I must now ask catches in my mouth: "Is it Israelis you hate, or Jews wherever they are?" What I have asked prompts a long, animated discussion in Arabic. Finally, Hatem speaks: "It's the Zionists we hate, not Jews in general. The Zionists led the Jews to Palestine. They said it was an empty land, but we were here."

I understand that this considered reply may be a strategic, partial truth.

"Do you all think that?" I ask.

"We all think the same," Hatem states firmly.

Suddenly, there is a crack of gunfire. The men rush to the window and look down the road. The Israeli military has arrived. I, too, jump up to look. Just a few metres away, soldiers are pointing guns. They are wearing riot helmets with plastic face shields. A little girl of four or five scurries down a narrow path just opposite; a teenager appears, hurls a stone, then runs to hide. Someone grabs my arm, pushes me to my chair at the back of the room. No one breathes.

A soldier takes up position directly in front of the window, his back to us, one foot before the other in a position of readiness. He points his gun down the lane where the child and the stone-thrower fled. I note that he is the same age as the young men who are protecting me in a confusing, topsy-turvy reversal of ethnic allegiance.

My heart is pounding. Then the soldiers leave—as abruptly as they had arrived.

For several moments I cannot speak. "This is our daily life," says Mohammed, the lover of *Beowulf*.

Outside my apartment that night, there is the strangled sound of someone going berserk in the street. His voice is garbled, but I think the language is Arabic.

Why is he here? What is happening to him? Is my door properly locked?

Earlier in the day I cowered with Palestinians before an armed Israeli patrol. Tonight, I am vulnerable, as a Jew, to a Palestinian at the end of his tether

Writing these words, I am transported back to that day. To shared fright. To group identity. To the barrier of "otherness." And to the seldom-revealed complexities that can change the way we perceive the world.

WHEN I REFLECT ON my explorations in Israel, it is the diversity of national passions that come to mind. I've described just a few of these: kibbutzniks struggling to maintain their ideological zeal in a changing world; religious nationalists intent on capturing ever more state support for their biblically inspired enterprise; young Palestinians united in despair. In 1988, uncompromising narratives and single-minded certainties already pointed to internecine conflict. Tellingly, early signs of the first Intifada had already emerged in nearby Ramallah several months before my visit to the Balata camp.

But beyond the search to comprehend the conflicting narratives that competed for primacy in Israel, I had set myself another task: an encounter with a different aspect of Jewish historical memory—the Holocaust.

The Holocaust informed Israeli society, as it did the world of the Diaspora, shaping a collective consciousness that effectively underscored the *raison d'être* for the state of Israel. The memorial museum Yad Vashem was the locus of this remembrance. Michelle, who was then volunteering on a kibbutz in northern Israel, agreed to join me there.

I retain three outstanding memories from my visit to Yad Vashem. The first is the tree-lined entrance lane where each tree had been planted in the name of a Righteous Gentile. I found it comforting to learn that some individuals did care. Who were they? I wondered. What kind of people were willing to risk their lives, and even the lives of their families, to help the persecuted? The question intrigued me then, as it has ever since.

Luckily, I would encounter many such individuals during my career, either in person or in books; and although they may have lived in different times and places, it has seemed to me that they are, in essence, very similar. They are strongly principled individuals who are impervious to propaganda, people who are willing to take risks to preserve their ethical core. Some have operated from religious conviction, others were humanists. But if the Jews who survived the Holocaust are a remnant, so are these defiant objectors a remnant of civilized humanity whenever crises strike.

My second memory is the pictures on the museum wall. Because the history of the Holocaust was already familiar to me when I travelled to Israel, it was the faces of the oppressors and their victims that drew my close attention. And here, too, I encountered a paradox I would subsequently ponder over: the obvious pleasure on the faces of the perpetrators, such as the smile on the face of a Nazi soldier as he cuts off the beard of a religious Jew whose eyes are half-closed in suffering.

Two photos stood out from the rest, both scenes from Babi Yar, the infamous ravine on the outskirts of Kiev where more than 33,000 Jews were shot in September 1941.

I subsequently wrote this in *The Garden and the Gun*:

> Three young women with terror-filled eyes stand together before a pit. Pathetically, they try to hide their nakedness. Behind them are soldiers, their guns already raised, positioned, aimed. In another picture an entire family of naked women—old mother, adult daughters, a tiny granddaughter, and a small baby—huddle together, gripping one another by the arms.

I stared at these photographs, allowing myself to move closer to the vortex of something I still cannot name. In an act of imaginative projection, I entered the photographs, penetrated their grainy detail, gazed into the stricken faces. My maternal grandfather's family almost certainly died at Babi Yar. Is this family of women holding each other during their last panicked moments my own? But for an accident of fate, that child cringing at the brink of the abyss might have been me.

There remained one last room to visit—my third memory—a place where the lights were low, where all the known names of the victims were recorded. The walls were lined with books containing millions of names; they were the concrete instantiation of my private hallucination repeated into infinity.

A clerk perches on a stool behind a desk. He looks impatient. Suddenly I am afraid to ask the question that brought me to him.

I should have foreseen this failure. My parents and grandparents had never told me the first names of those who remained in Europe. I have only surnames and the names of the cities where their families lived.

I asked the man about the family of my maternal grandfather, Isaac Lipkin.

"Do you know how many Lipkins the Germans killed in Kiev?" he asked dismissively, peering at me with disdain.

I turn away. To lose names was to lose the slender thread that linked me and my children to our familial past.

I left Yad Vashem, sought out a quiet place where I might feel calm, and wrote this:

> They are twice lost, my unknown relatives. Murdered some four decades ago, they have slipped into oblivion, not to be mourned by their great-granddaughter and great-great granddaughter who stand here in Jerusalem wanting to weep for them.
>
> I shall weep regardless. I shall adopt the wide-eyed, terror-stricken family of women on the wall in the next room. I shall rock them in my arms and sing softly to them from across the decades. I shall remember them.

Since I wrote *The Garden and the Gun,* the only observable change in Israel has been a worsening of the problems I observed in the 1980s. These include the assassination of Prime Minister Yitzhak Rabin in 1995 by an extremist settler. A quick Google search turns up three of Rabin's quotes that would have been anathema to the West Bank fundamentalists:

> *"We must think differently, look at things in a different way. Peace requires a world of new concepts, new definitions."*
>
> *"We do not celebrate the death of our enemies."*
>
> *"You don't make peace with friends. You make it with very unsavoury enemies."*

Unsurprisingly, the most toxic deterioration has been in the growing power of settler theocrats to shift the priorities of the secular state. For young men raised in the settlements who are entering Israel's compulsory military service the exclusionary, often hate-filled values of their communities' conflict with their presumed duty to the secular obligations of the modern state, and further undermine relations with Palestinians.

Because the settler communities have grown exponentially and acquired concomitant political power in the Knesset, their beliefs have infiltrated and altered the majority political *Zeitgeist* of the country at large. As I write these words in a world where the exclusion of minority populations is once again becoming mainstream, what were once marginal voices in Israel appear to have overtaken the rest.

Sorrow. Not long ago I listened to the Israeli novelist David Grossman speak of the country of his birth with unabashed pain. He spoke of empathy as the *sine qua non* of any future peace. He spoke of racism: Jewish-Israeli hatred for Arabs and Arab hatred for Israeli Jews. He said aloud that Israel should not be considered a democracy when it is available for only one part of the population, a part which considers the other inferior. He said that it was only possible to live a "good life" by shutting one's eyes to the suffering in what he openly called an "apartheid state." Grossman, like Amos Oz, A.B. Yehoshua, Gideon Levy, and many others, was one of a disappearing breed of modern-day prophets speaking truth to power. They were too well-known to be silenced, but increasingly, like their ancient antecedents, they were voices in the wilderness.

David Grossman's son Uri was killed in 2006 during the Israel-Hezbollah conflict when he was twenty—just as his father was finishing *To the End of the Land*, a novel about a mother who simply refuses to be available when the expected news of her son's death is brought to her door.

This parental fear—the looming potential of a young soldier's death on the morrow, a fear also expressed to me by my landlady Miriam on my first day in Israel—was the mirror-image of parental fear in the Occupied Territories, where the young, like those I had met in the Balata camp, dreamed of, and often carried out, resistance and revenge.

Does peace advocacy persist? Yes, it does, though now it is muted and often suppressed.

So, I return to the questions that first led me to visit Israel. I was exploring identity, in hopes of understanding the growing role Israel played in the Canadian diaspora imagination. Because I was deeply aware of the Holocaust, I understood the need for the new state. On the other hand, my family, my education, and my experiences as a young person living in France during the Algerian War had shaped my belief in human rights and equality as necessary conditions for peace—anywhere.

To accept the policies of the State of Israel as they had evolved challenged my most deeply held convictions of ethics and justice, both concepts I had—ironically—learnt early in my life from Judaism. Those policies continue to challenge them.

CHAPTER NINE

THE END OF DAYS

ALL THE PLACES I had researched by 1988, when *The Garden and the Gun* was published, had experienced fluctuations in the public consensus towards the minorities that lived in their midst. In Canada, attitudes had become slowly more progressive over the latter part of the twentieth century, although not without slippage. Twentieth-century France had undergone a major swing from widespread acceptance to xenophobia. In Israel, the original socialist-Zionist ideology of collectivism, including communal living, had hardened into right-wing rejection, as generations were born and educated during a period of sustained conflict with a competitor who claimed the same land.

With this history lodged at the back of my mind I was likely more than ready for my chance encounter with the Canadian author Matt Cohen's new novel, *The Spanish Doctor*, which I happened upon in the late 1980s. The setting of Cohen's tale was late medieval and early Renaissance Spain, an era that was characterized by *convivencia,* or what we would today call multiculturalism. By means of Cohen's fictional narrative I learned the history of the era in which Christians, Jews, and Muslims had successfully lived together in that European country for seven hundred years, starting with the Moorish conquest of Hispania in the eighth century C.E. I also learned that, during this remarkable period of almost unparalleled prosperity, scientific inventions and ideas that permanently changed the world were born: the compass, the mining of precious metals, nautical maps, the study of astronomy, and the foundations of everyday arithmetic, to name just a few.

This inter-cultural meeting of minds had seemingly been facilitated by open-minded rulers across the centuries, among them Alfonso the Tenth, a thirteenth-century King of Castile who was known in his lifetime as "Alfonso the Wise." This monarch had proudly named himself "King of the Three Religions." He had created a cosmopolitan court of Jews, Muslims, and Christians that encouraged learning, including the so-called "Toledan" School of Translators, where seminal works of philosophy and science were translated from the Arabic (itself often a translation from an original source in Classical Greek) into Hebrew, then Latin, Castilian, and finally other vernacular languages of Europe. The broad diffusion of these writings became the underpinning of the Renaissance in the West—and by extension of our world today.

How did this happen? I asked myself. And what became of this anomalous society that differed so profoundly from its rustic medieval neighbours? Cohen had the answer to the "what happened" question. He vividly described how *convivencia* was fatally damaged in the fourteenth century by a pogrom that destroyed the well-integrated Jewish community of the city of Valencia on the Mediterranean coast before spreading similar destruction across the land. Reading this, I immediately recalled my study of twentieth-century French cultural history, in which a once-welcoming country had also turned on a longstanding, well-integrated minority community.

I was intrigued. After centuries of peaceful cohabitation, what had happened to cause friendly neighbours to turn against one another? Was this a sudden event, or the endpoint of some process of social disintegration? Whatever the answer turned out to be, the question held major importance, for the world was becoming more ethnically and religiously mixed than ever before—as wars and accelerating climate change, along with the transborder migrations they often triggered, were starting to threaten our physical and economic survival.

Who were these long-ago people? What were the underlying structures of their society? Most importantly, were there visible commonalities with the troubled societies I had already explored that might help explain the unravelling of a longstanding plural social order? Although the Jewish connection to this story was still central to my interests, I intuited that I might be observing something universal.

I renewed my University of Toronto Robarts Library card and figuratively moved into the stacks, where I inhaled the familiar scent of thousands of books flirtatiously displaying their multi-coloured covers like wallflowers at a ball. The references I needed were in Spanish as well as other languages.

French would not present a problem, but Spanish was a worry. I had studied the language for a year as an undergraduate and had struggled to master it during frequent trips to Mexico, where my parents wintered in their later years, but I wasn't sure I had the linguistic competence to embark upon this work. Luckily, after some initial review, I found I could. Ironically, years of high school Latin had prepared me for Spanish, which had remained the closest of all Romance languages to its Latin roots—possibly because the Inquisition had effectively closed Spain's borders for four centuries, keeping out all modernizing influences. Furthermore, I had a resident classics scholar at home, and Tom declared himself willing to help. So, with some trepidation I jumped into the preliminary research—and before long the library on St. George Street in Toronto was yielding up its magic in the shape of books more than a century old.

Most of my previous works had included travel to the sites of my study, and this book would be no different. By autumn 1991, I felt ready to leave for a research trip, but not before having faced several hurdles. My publisher, Malcolm Lester, was encouraging, but when I submitted an outline and sample chapter before leaving Canada, one of his colleagues was unimpressed. She thought there weren't enough women in my story plan. She also seemed to misunderstand my underlying focus, which was the how and why of societal transformation. I adamantly declined to write the postmodern work she apparently had in mind, and to his credit Malcolm supported me. "It's Erna's book," he said simply as the three of us sat in tense silence.

I also had to disregard the disparaging remark of a friend whom I met for coffee just days before leaving the country. "No one will want to read that!" she exclaimed after I described my project. "Something on Andy Warhol would reach a bigger audience." I persevered, but I was learning that I would need to ignore the naysayers who didn't understand my larger purpose. Not that I entirely blamed them: the books I was writing confounded many people, including, sometimes, myself.

Tom (who had a sabbatical) and I rented a tiny studio near the centre of Madrid. It was so small that successive steps led from the kitchen (with its single burner) to the living room (a couch against the wall) to the study (a desk against the opposite wall) to the bed. There were also just two forks, two knives, two spoons, and two plates, but somehow it all worked. The city was alive with cafés featuring square-shaped women eating mountainous cream puffs; bars and tapas stalls where the drinking started in the morning before work; and the shouts of children playing ball at midnight. Butcher shops sold more varieties of ham than I had ever seen. (In the book I would eventually write, I would postulate a theory about why Spaniards still consume so much pork.) Happy after-work crowds coursing through the ancient Plaza Mayor.

I acquired a card for the *Biblioteca Nacional*, the National Library of Spain on the *Paseo de Recoletos*, where the country's history was preserved; and every morning I climbed the steps of the magnificent palace that had been founded by King Philip the Fifth in 1712, then converted into the present state library a century later. On my way I passed the statue of Alfonso the Wise and that of the sixteenth-century painter and sculptor Alonso Berruguete, whose pictorial depiction of an *auto-da-fé* I would later incorporate as an illustration for my book. His painterly imagination portrayed Spanish inquisitorial victims as tiny, insignificant, and almost invisible at the feet of somnolent inquisitors towering above them, nodding off even as the flames encompass their prey. It continues to speak volumes about the reign of terror incited by the Spanish Inquisition.

My visits to the library seemed to amuse the pasty-faced men behind the desk as I struggled to order the day's books from the stacks. I was taking conversation lessons a few times a week, but the capacity to express myself fluently was far behind my reading abilities. By force of having to deal with me so frequently, the pale-faced ones eventually decided to adopt me, bumbling speaker that I was. They directed me to ancient chronicles that had been edited and annotated by Spanish scholars centuries later, in the nineteenth and early-twentieth centuries. These, to my delight, contained dramatic narratives of people and striking events while simultaneously exposing the texture of lost eras. Most interesting to me, they also revealed the psychology of familiar human behaviour under stress.

But beyond these ancient documents, I knew that to write compellingly I would need to uncover medieval Spain in my own way, by attempting to project my imagination into the remote past. I'd need to talk to people—to historians; to archeologists who were digging up the physical structures and artefacts of the past; and to churchmen, the guardians of Inquisition history. I'd need to walk the still-vivible paths of this history. For months Tom and I travelled the streets and byways of Spain, directed by my reading. We "saw" with our mind's eye.

Following the trail of a story gleaned from an anonymously written sixteenth-century chronicle—*El libro verde de Aragon*—we visited the cathedral of Saragossa, where an inquisitor named Pedro de Arbues was assassinated in 1485 by some high-ranking, tragically misguided Jewish converts to Catholicism who were trying to stop the encroaching Inquisition. As we retraced the steps the perpetrators took on that fateful day, I suggested to Tom that we might be the only people in that busy city who were, at that moment, remembering this determining moment of Spanish history.

On a quiet street of shoemakers and merchants, we listened to the tap, tap, tap of a hammer repairing a heel, and recalled that 500 years earlier Saragossans on this same street had near-certainly engaged in these same activities. On another day a young historian who was guiding us opened a small door inside a nondescript apartment building and led us down a short, steep flight of stairs. Far below the modern street we entered a small hidden crypt: a twelfth-century synagogue still beautifully tiled in the ubiquitous Moorish architectural style of the day. And yet another memory surfaces: we are standing alone on the very road where, on July 31, 1492, thousands of Spanish Jews of all ages, who had refused to convert to Catholicism after the pogroms, walked in the staggering summer heat as the royal edict commanding their expulsion from Spain came into effect. It was a long straight Roman road leading now, as then, towards the Mediterranean. The scorching sun beat down on us as we stood in that now-empty place. Above us, black vultures flew. They would have been there then, waiting for the fatal stumble of a grandfather or a small child.

I would devote an entire chapter of *The End of Days: A Story of Tolerance, Tyranny and the Expulsion of the Jews from Spain* about the murder of Pedro de Arbues. It would discuss the inability of high-ranking Jewish converts to Catholicism, or *conversos*, to understand that the society into which they had been born, and within which they prospered, had irreversibly changed. Their self-protective certainty about their status had blinded them to unbearable truths, including about their own vulnerability, as they faced accusations of secretly practicing Judaism.

These tragically imprudent men reminded me of other examples of willing blindness in the face of the simply inexplicable. I thought of a letter I had come across (and wrote about in *Unhealed Wounds*) in which a long-assimilated French Jew expressed similar bewilderment that he and his family were no longer welcome in the country of their birth. On October 2, 1940, when he read that the Vichy government was preparing new laws regarding the Jews, Raymond Raoul Lambert wrote in his diary: "Is it possible that within a few days I shall be diminished as a citizen, and that my sons, French by birth, by culture, and by faith, will be cruelly cast outside the French community?...Is this possible? France is no longer France."

A similar blindness had characterized many Jews in early-Nazi Germany, who pointed to their service in the First World War as an example of their patriotism. The same mindset was apparent among high-ranking, non-converted Jews in fifteenth-century Spain. On March 31, 1492, the two leaders of the community knelt before King Ferdinand and Queen Isabella, begging them not to enact the Edict of Expulsion. They too cited the long, meritorious, thousand-year history of the Jews in the Iberian Peninsula, but to no avail. The times had changed under their noses.

Inside the cathedral were two memorials to the infamous assassination of Pedro de Arbues by *conversos*. The first was a marble mausoleum commissioned by Queen Isabella featuring a statue of the murdered inquisitor and scenes in bas-relief recounting the story of the killing. The second memorial displayed the original swords of the four perpetrators on a stone pillar (they had immediately been designated holy relics). On the stone floor of the church was the revered inquisitor's tombstone engraved with these words: "Here he fell, his throat cut by Jews."

That the "Jews" in question were in fact Catholics whose families had converted from Judaism generations earlier would become central to my pursuit as I explored the ways in which this once-plural society had reversed itself. Sadly, the murder of Pedro de Arbues had only quickened the momentum and cruelty of the Inquisition. It was a major accelerator in the continuing downward spiral that would eventually destroy Spanish *convivencia*.

THE BASIC QUESTIONS I had asked myself at the start was, how did *convivencia* emerge and then survive the way it did so long before Enlightenment ideas of equality and pluralism? How it started was clear enough. In the year 711 C.E. an army of Muslims ("Moors") from North Africa reached the Gibraltar coast of what was then known as Hispania. The country had previously been occupied by the Romans, who were indifferent to the minorities in their midst; what interested them was collecting taxes.

In the fifth century the Romans had been displaced by the Visigoths, a Germanic tribe that stormed in from the wilds of the north. As an aside, I enjoyed writing about the political machinations of these warrior Visigoths, whose material legacy seems to consist largely of shiny belt buckles that are today displayed in Spanish museums. Their cultural legacy, on the other hand, was more disturbing. The Visigoths converted to the new religion of Catholicism, then—importantly—made assimilation to this faith a prerequisite for belonging to the community. Their policy carried deadly implications, for when church and state merged into one entity, the historic Jewish challenge to Christianity—the claim that the Messiah had not yet arrived on earth—was redefined as a crime against the state, thus legalizing Visigoth persecution of the Jews.

After touching land at Gibraltar, Tariq, the Muslim leader, burned his ships. He was clearly planning to stay, and he and his army fought its way north, terrifying the Visigoths who had never witnessed such an enemy. Tariq handily defeated the army of their leader Rodrigo, leaving not a sign of the king or his white horse—and thus instigating a rumour that the Moor was the Devil incarnate. Many of the surviving Visigoths escaped to the northern reaches of the country, where they eventually reassembled as a crusade to retake the Iberian Peninsula known as the "Holy Christian Reconquest against the Infidel"—a campaign that culminated 700 years later in the defeat of King Boabdil, the last Moorish leader, by the armies of King Ferdinand and Queen Isabella in Granada.

Eighth-century rumours had also maintained that the Jews of Toledo secretly opened the gates of their city to Tariq the Moor—an allegation that may have been well-founded, since the invaders were offering unheard-of terms: They explicitly accepted both Jews and Christians as "people of the book," that is, as adherents to the other two monotheistic religions. They proclaimed that Christians and Jews would be free to practice their religions and to govern themselves according to their religious laws, provided they refrained from marching in processions (no potential mobs); did not insult the prophet Mohammed (no dangerous provocations); and paid a head tax. The result was a social peace that lasted almost three quarters of a millennium.

Living freely in an integrated society, Christians, Jews, and Muslims created the remarkable, diverse world I had first encountered in Matt Cohen's novel, including breakthrough creativity in every domain. Take reading, for example. By the tenth century, the university in Córdoba, the Andalusian capital, had become the most celebrated in the known world: an estimated 500,000 volumes populated the royal library of al-Hakam II, the contemporary caliph. (By comparison, the magnificent Abbey of Saint Gall in Switzerland contained just over 100 volumes.) Córdoba was reportedly a wonder to behold. The caliphs of the first Umayyad dynasty channelled water in pipes from mountain rivers. Fountains and baths graced the city. The magnificent eighth-century Mosque of Córdoba, which can still be visited today, was constructed of 856 multi-coloured columns of jasper, onyx, marble, and granite gathered from various parts of the ancient Roman Empire. And so magnificent was the sultan's palace that the head of a delegation from Constantinople is reported to have fainted at the sight of the caliph on his bejewelled throne.

But the crowning achievement of this civilization was the wide dissemination of the writings of the ancient Greeks, such as Aristotle, Euclid, and others—all of which were unknown in Europe—by means of multi-language translations.

These achievements were facilitated by wealth that derived from high literacy (a priority for both men and women), as well as trade with other Mediterranean countries. But tensions, even in a well-functioning plural society, were as inevitable then as they are today. To minimize these, legal frameworks safeguarded religious minorities, anticipating comparable protections in other societies more than a millennium later.

I was particularly struck by the wisdom of one early leader as I researched this material. Before his death in 788 C.E. the ruler, Abduh Rahman, called in the governors of the six provinces into which Andalusia had been divided to witness the royal succession. Then he addressed his son Hisham in language that remains striking:

> Remember, my son, that these are God's kingdoms...Be just to all men, equally to the poor and the rich, for injustice is the road to ruin; at the same time, be gentle and merciful with those who are dependent on you, for they are all creatures of God. Trust the government of the provinces to wise, experienced men and punish without pity those ministers who oppress the people. Treat soldiers with gentle firmness, so that they remain the defenders of the state and not its destroyers. Encourage and protect the cultivators, for it is they who provide us with our sustenance...Never cease to merit the affection of your people; in their good will is the security of the state, in their anger there is danger, and in their hatred certain ruin. And rule so that the people bless you, so that they live happily in the shadow of your protection; for in that is the glory and joy of a king.

I happened upon the above fragment in an ancient chronicle about the reign of Abduh Rahman that was translated into French by Louis Viardot in 1833. Viardot had relegated this remarkable expression of Enlightenment values to a footnote; after translating it into English, I included it in my text.

Though there were inevitable tensions, enlightened governance prevailed across most of the 400 years that the Umayyad caliphs ruled the Iberian Peninsula, but in the twelfth century they were displaced by a religiously orthodox Muslim army from North Africa, and this time Christians and Jews who refused to convert to Islam were exiled to the northern regions of Hispania, namely Castile and Aragon. What was striking in this history of caliphate succession was that the arrival of a militant orthodox regime mattered in terms of public policy, but seemed scarcely to matter at ground level, despite accompanying sword-rattling rhetoric. After four centuries, the habits of pluralism and the protection of minorities were already engrained in the national psyche. Although the Christian Holy Reconquest had been retaking territory in Castile and Aragon and installing Christian leaders, the ethos of inclusion had been normalized into a stable national identity which persisted regardless.

My second question—Why and when did social attitudes in Hispania eventually begin to mutate?—is more complex, for a reversal of this order had seemed unlikely up to and including the thirteenth century, which was, broadly speaking, one of the most fortunate in European history. The thirteenth century was the era of Dante, the Florentine writer and poet, and a time of expanding literacy; it was the age of Thomas Aquinas, the most influential medieval Western theologian and scholar; and in Spain it was the time of Alfonso the Wise.

What happened to destroy this? One clue, as I understand it, points to a recognizable pattern that has been repeated many times since. The transformation from tolerance to tyranny occurred not suddenly, but incrementally, often following a crisis of sorts, thus allowing people to accustom themselves slowly to a shift in norms. The downward spiral was a process, not an abrupt break with the past.

It may come as a surprise in our own age of accelerating climate change that the first trigger for social disruption in this long-ago era was environmental. During the first decade of the fourteenth century, what has been called "The Little Ice Age" froze most of Europe, shrinking or destroying agriculture. The result was localized starvation. In the second decade of that century, torrential rains again wiped out the crops. People prayed, and made entreaties to the king, and when these failed, the starving poor blamed the rich—especially those elites close to the king, such as the monarch's tax collectors, whose appearance at the door elicited fear. Most of the tax collectors happened to be Jews, simply because they were the best educated community in the country. There were poverty-stricken Jews as well, but many held responsible public service positions that appeared impossibly remote from the lives of ordinary people.

The mid-fourteenth century then saw the arrival of the bubonic plague—one of the most shattering pandemics in human history.

Although the entire world felt the force of the COVID-19 pandemic, making us somewhat more able to comprehend the fright experienced by Europeans so long ago, the science of medicine as we know it today eschews any comparison. We have vaccine remedies; the fourteenth century did not.

In Mediterranean Europe, including Spain, up to 75 percent of infected people died within days of infection. Helplessness, then callousness, became the norm as survivors watched the Grim Reaper take noble and pauper alike. Lawlessness and debauchery followed as the living ate, drank, and made merry on the expectation of death on the morrow. The rich escaped to the hills (to little avail), while the poor moved in, squatting in their abandoned mansions and emptying their wine cellars. People stepped over the dead in the streets. With no concept of the nature of infectious disease, they waved palm branches, sprinkled rose water, and beseeched God for deliverance.

Faced with unfathomable misery, humans did what they always do: they looked for scapegoats. Jews, as members of the educated elite, were suspect. But there was more. Unbaptized, and therefore considered not entitled to God's grace, the Jews were accused of causing the plague by poisoning the public wells.

In the 1990s, when I initially recounted this story, I believed that we might have left behind the propensity to invent conspiracy theories to explain and persuade. This has seemed especially true during the last seventy or so years since the end of the Second World War, a period that encompasses the lives of most people living today. The parallel intellectual universe that evolved in the United States during the years of the Trump presidency—a cocoon-world that embraced conspiracies and turned rationality on its head—was a sombre wake-up call. We still, it seems, have an intractable inclination to dream up enemies in times of economic and environmental crisis coupled with a relentless disease.

Seven hundred years ago, a newly emboldened clergy stepped into a world characterized by the disruptions of the bubonic plague and a resultant political void. Some of them knew exactly why God was punishing the people of Hispania with plague, cold, and floods. It was because there were still unconverted Jews in the land.

The first decades of the fourteenth century were akin to a long civil war: the bubonic plague had disrupted the functioning of the monarchy, and the Church had proved unable to stem massive death. But Christianity was the central pillar of medieval society, meaning that the Church's inability to staunch misfortune disoriented a population that was dependent upon it for guidance in distress. Some institution or strongman was going to seize control in such a fragile environment, and the Church, not the monarchy, was in the best position to do so. What was needed was to recreate a viable society, and for the Church that meant one with a common religious identity. The unifying tool would be conversions to Catholicism—a policy reminiscent of that of the Visigoths, who had similarly unified church and state by marginalizing non-Christians.

AS THE FOURTEENTH CENTURY progressed, so did the conversions of thousands of Jews. They were converted by intimidation; by choice, motivated by self-interested opportunism; and sometimes, although more rarely, by conviction. Charismatic preachers called for the eradication of Judaism itself. (Forceful anti-Arab rhetoric would emerge in later years, but at the start of the Church's campaign, it was the Jews who mattered. It was they who held high position and were envied for their success. Arabs were traditionally agriculturists, and not objects of economic resentment.)

The first populist attack on the Jews, which took place at the end of the calamitous century, telegraphed the eventual fate of the community, and was the first serious body blow delivered to the ancient ethos of *convivencia*.

The date was July 9, 1391, the place Valencia, on the Mediterranean coast. A preacher in Seville had recently instigated an attack on the Jews of his city, and the news of this shocking event has just reached Valencia. The messenger's words would fall on fertile soil: Friar Vicente Ferrer, a charismatic local preacher, had also been calling for conversions and the destruction of Judaism. In the way of such coded promptings, the priest had never overtly called for violence; his technique was to stir up others.

After the courier delivered his news, a few bored teenagers started to march towards the Jewish quarter, calling spiritedly for others to join them. They shouted at the Jews, taunting them with the threat of forced conversions. A young boy climbed up the wall of the quarter and accidentally slipped down inside; a rumour that he was dead spread like wildfire; an angry crowd breached the barriers, swords and daggers in hand.

I dramatized the scene this way:

> Inside the Jewish quarter men, women and children cower in hidden corners of their houses, or rush through back alleyways to take refuge in the synagogue. It is almost impossible to see for the dust in the air, impossible to know where one's family might be, impossible to hear over the cries of the dying and the shouts of the rioters... The Jews shoot crossbows from their houses, but they are vastly outnumbered, and now it seems that nothing will stop the madness...
>
> "Convert to the Holy Faith or die," cry the priests over the din. Conversion is the single key to survival. Some Jews will choose to die, but most want desperately to live. Thousands flee from the quarter to the cathedral and the baptismal font.
>
> Friar Vicente Ferrer joined the melee. He calmed the rioters, and invited the Jews to baptism. "He is saving them before God!" people cried. Before the day's end the massacre was being hailed as a divine event. By July 14, a report from the municipality of Valencia confirmed that, except for those still in hiding, all surviving Jews had been baptized. By August, the flames of the pogrom had spread across Castile and Aragon. Thousands were dead. Communities that had been integrated into the larger polity for centuries were destroyed, never to recover.

Slowly and incrementally, Spanish *convivencia* suffered further attacks and suppression, but another eighty years would pass before a new institution called The Holy Office of the Inquisition Against Heresy (better known now as "The Spanish Inquisition") would begin to arrest and try numbers of *conversos* on grounds of still secretly adhering to Judaism, and a century before Spain's unconverted Jews were finally expelled from their homeland in July 1492.

Why did this happen in the aftermath of mass conversions—or what we might today call an effort at forced assimilation? It is evident from reading the history that the Church's attempt to create national unity by means of religious homogeneity was a failure; there would have been no need for an Inquisition to root out "false" Christians if the policy had succeeded as hoped.

The problem was that baptism was believed to alter the soul: the *converso* was considered an instant (if unwilling) member of the Christian majority in an officially Christian land. In other words, the converted individual stopped being the person he or she was the day before baptism and became someone new.

That some "converted" Jews seemed to be still culturally Jewish was a puzzle. Why did they continue in the same high-prestige professions they had previously occupied? Why did they distinguish themselves from their countrymen by continuing to value learning? And why was it that they seemed rather less than pious in the way they practiced the new faith?

Since baptism included no instruction in the newly adopted faith, the latter was hardly a surprise, but it was true that many *conversos* did what they could to maintain the continuity of their emotional lives, often leading a painfully schizophrenic existence. Officially, they were Christians; in reality, they were often anything but. Many led secret double lives. They continued to practice Judaism, if only for reasons of comfort, family closeness, and companionship. They visited their unconverted relatives in the Jewish quarter, sharing meals with them in that unerring centrepiece of family life. And they were closely watched all the while.

The differences between so-called "Old Christians" and "New Christians" raised previously unimaginable questions. The *conversos* weren't "real" Christians, people whispered. Minor cultural differences that were once ignored became touchstone indicators of non-conformity—of otherness. And so it happened that, half a century after the 1391 Valencia pogrom, the long confusion over baptism and "changed souls" abruptly came to an end. It was a seminal historical moment, with implications that crossed borders and travelled forward in time.

I described it this way in *The End of Days*:

> On the 26th day of January, in the year 1449, something spontaneous and unexpected happens in the central square of the city of Toledo, Spain after two priests ring the bell of the church of Santa Maria La Blanca (formerly the Ibn Shushan Synagogue before being forcibly converted to a Christian edifice in 1411). A mob descends on the square. "The conversos are false Christians," cries Pero Sarmiento, the governor of the city's royal palace. "They are the enemies of Holy Mother Church!"
>
> The mob bellows its approval.
>
> At a public meeting on June 6, *Señor* Sarmiento reads aloud the new legislation, to be known as the Statute of Exclusion. The law, which comes into effect immediately, forbids any person descended from Jews from holding a public post. The statute affects thousands of Toledans who were converted to Christianity from Judaism over the preceding half-century, and many of whom had moved into important positions in municipal government and elsewhere. Some thirteen city councillors, judges, and notaries are immediately removed from their stations.

For the first time in European history, blood and race are at issue, not faith, as was previously the case. Soon "purity of blood" (*limpieza de sangre*) will explode into a national obsession.

When the Spanish Inquisition was created in the 1480s, *conversos* became, in the eyes of many, once again "Jews," and charges of "heresy" against "false Christians" started to be heard. All means possible, including torture, and death by burning for the pertinacious, were tried, in attempts to prune away the "false" Christians from the rest. Eventually all Jews, not just pseudo-*conversos*, were expelled from the realm, at which point the Inquisition turned its attention to Protestants, homosexuals, and so-called witches, among others. (The institution survived, remarkably, until the nineteenth century.)

I WAS HALFWAY THROUGH the five years during which I "lived in" medieval Spain before I realized that I had been writing not single works, as I had supposed, but a series of works on closely related themes. These were: the ambiguities of historical memory, cultural identity, and the fragility inherent in majority-minority relations; the uses of political propaganda; and the origins of racism, all of them seen through the lens of repeated human experience. I had been attempting to identify the "process" of social breakdown in multicultural societies.

Long after *The End of Days* was finished and published, I continued to think about my fully formed, humanly recognizable new acquaintances from the fifteenth century. I had brushed the dust off their ancient selves and encouraged them to speak to us through actual dialogue that I had uncovered in old chronicles. I missed them for a long time. I still do. And I feel changed by the experience of getting to know them.

They and their era taught me that policies of mandatory assimilation are a misguided means to achieving national unity. An ancient chronicle I encountered told of a Saragossa convert named Maria who dared to speak of what she had lost to a single trusted friend, Agueda. Maria admitted she had converted "not from devotion, but from fear," and that she continued to cook "the hot dish" on Fridays so it would last through the Sabbath on Saturday, but her "Old Christian" husband was so angry at this that he had destroyed her oven. When she was a Jewess, she had been in love with a Jewish man, she told her friend, but "they" had married her off to her present husband. Even now, she admitted, she and this man were lovers.

"Look at yourself, Agueda," Maria confided. "If you became a Jewess, how could you possibly give up following Christian ways? This is what you must understand. In these things one must do what comes naturally."

Culture cannot be shed by decree.

I was delighted, I must add, when the Spanish consul in Toronto attended the book launch of *The End of Days*, and I suspect my guests were as surprised as I was when he spoke regretfully about his country's sad history. In doing so, he was mirroring contemporary Spanish policy, as diplomats do. After the death of General Francisco Franco in 1975, Juan Carlos had become king of Spain and initiated a transition to democracy. Furthermore, on March 31, 1992, exactly five hundred years after King Ferdinand and Queen Isabella had signed the edict ordering the expulsion of the Jews from Spain, the king had stood before the ark of the Torah in Madrid's only synagogue, wearing a skull cap on his head. The building was crowded with foreign observers that day, and with as many of Spain's sixteen thousand Jews as were able to cram themselves inside. Chaim Herzog, the then-president of Israel, was also present.

King Juan Carlos expressed deep regret for the Expulsion, but he stopped short of apologizing, something many had hoped for. Although centuries had passed, Ferdinand and Isabella were still venerated as the parents of national unity, the vanquishers of Islamic Granada, and the sponsors of Christopher Columbus. He could not go further.

Nonetheless, I felt a surge of emotion as I typed the final words to *The End of Days,* in which I acknowledged the historic significance of that moment.

"It wasn't perfect," I wrote, "but with this symbolic reconciliation between the Jews of Spain and the kingdom that rejected them so long ago, a balm soothed old wounds. And when the synagogue filled with the sounds of Kaddish, the Jewish prayer for the dead, the ghosts of generations past wept to be remembered."

CHAPTER TEN

LONG SHADOWS

I NOW KNEW THAT I was moving forward in my search, even if I couldn't precisely delineate its parameters—and in 1996, just months after the publication of *The End of Days*, I began yet another piece of investigation. This time, with thoughts of France still in mind, I would direct my attention towards the way nations shape their collective memory of difficult historical periods, especially after times of crisis.

At the start, I wasn't quite as clear as the above may sound. The idea for the new book, as in the case of much of my earlier work, seemed to appear unbidden. Tom had been invited by the Japan Academy of Sciences to give a series of university lectures in that country, and the invitation included me. I leaped at the chance. My earliest memory of Japan, perhaps my only memory, was of having read John Hersey's remarkable book when I was a teenager, and still living on Rosemary Lane. All these years later I could still see my girl-self curled up in the "reading chair" in the book-lined den of our house, with its wide window looking out at the stone cherubs in the garden beyond, those lovely carved creatures that today reside on our tiny patch of inner-city green. This quiet room, with its floor-to-ceiling bookshelves, its chair, its window, and its magical Dictionary was where I mined the world of literature, unimpeded by parental constraints.

In 1996, when the invitation arrived, I could still recall John Hersey's dramatic images with vivid precision, especially his scenes of drowning people clogging the Ota River, gasping, and clutching at fallen debris as nuclear fires devoured their streets. And the special horror of the verb he chose to describe what happened to those who survived the initial seconds: their skin, he wrote, "sloughed" off their bodies.

I knew at once that I would travel to Hiroshima and Nagasaki, and that I would travel alone. I didn't ask myself why I wanted to see these places; it simply felt like an imperative. Only later would I consciously identify the link between this visit and some of the themes that preoccupied me. How did human beings survive catastrophes of this nature? I wondered. I had begun to explore France's historical response to its ambiguous wartime history, but how, I asked myself, did the Japanese remember this unique experience?

After our initial arrival in Osaka (and the culture shock of wearing a "bathrobe" to breakfast in the company of similarly attired strangers), Tom and I were introduced to his Japanese colleagues, all professors of ancient Greek philosophy. I tagged along to the lectures and events, including a seminar on Greek thought that Tom gave to the Buddhist monks on the sacred mountain Koya-san, near Osaka, where I was the only woman present and evidently displeased some of the eminent participants by asking a question of my husband. Twenty male heads had swivelled around to stare incredulously at the brazen wife at the back of the room.

Otherwise, I was ignored—until the morning I announced my personal plans to travel south, to Hiroshima and Nagasaki. The Japanese were disconcerted that I planned to travel alone—and to such places. Alongside the apparent impropriety of my behaviour, I didn't know a word of Japanese beyond thank you, hello, or goodbye.

Since I couldn't read the signage, the train station was admittedly a challenge, but as the Shinkansen bullet train travelled south, I delighted in entering another world. Perhaps such things have changed now, but in 1996 the rice paddies surrounding the traditional homes that abutted belching industrial chimneys struck me as a metaphor for an uneasy post-war transition. I wasn't overly worried about my arrival in Hiroshima; with the generous help of the Canadian embassy in Tokyo I had hired a guide and interpreter to locate the people I wanted to interview, and to deliver me to the sites I wanted to visit. But as the mythic Ota River came into view, I felt my breath catch unexpectedly in my throat. John Hersey's grotesque images crowded my mind, but oddly the waters looked peaceful, even beautiful. And beyond the river lay the city, a humming modern metropolis. The train entered an enormous station. Keiko, my guide and interpreter, was there waiting.

Among the many nuclear-bomb survivors I met whose stories I chronicled in, three stand out in my memory, possibly because their experiences became seminal to my understanding both of the nuclear catastrophe itself and of how it had been mentally archived by the Japanese. It could also be because each of them revealed something essential about the cultural and moral ethos of Japan before the war, during the war, and during the decades that followed.

The first was Chiyoko Watanabe, a retired nurse. We met on her 74th birthday; and after we had talked about that day, so long ago, when an atomic bomb had exploded into her young life, she invited me to join her for a birthday dinner. That evening her unpinned white hair floated about her face. She wore a print dress and a string of pearls around her neck, joyfully ordering the best sushi and sashimi on the menu for the two of us and for the hotel manager, who was our interpreter. Before we parted, she presented me with a gift, a blue ceramic flute-shaped cup made by her brother.

There seemed to be no barriers between Chiyoko Watanabe and me on that memorable day. This is some of what she told me, as I recounted it in. Her story spoke to me of bravery—and of attitudes I had not encountered in the West.

On August 6, 1945, the day the Enola Gay B-29 aircraft dropped an atomic bomb preciously named "Little Boy" over Hiroshima, Chiyoko was twenty-two years old and working at the Red Cross hospital just 1,650 yards from Ground Zero. Most of the doctors were instantly killed or wounded; her friend at the next desk simply vaporized into thin air. Glass shards speared Chiyoko's face, but she survived. Of 1,780 nurses on duty that day, 1,654 were killed. The others ran away or were too injured to walk.

Chiyoko Watanabe did not run, even as the city burst into flames, and thousands of wounded streamed into the hospital.

I remember how she waved her hands in the air as she animatedly recounted her story of massive death and slim rescue; and that I felt overwhelmed by her tears and the intense way she held my gaze. I remember that I held her gnarled hands. Her courage...She had been the same age I was when I entered the Natzweiler-Struthof death camp in Alsace, and although my experience was insignificant compared to hers, my life too had changed in a moment. She was an ordinary girl, she told me. Until then.

She also told me that she believed I understood her—a remark I have never forgotten. But something else has stayed with me all these years. Chiyoko said that she was able to rise to the occasion, to carry out what were, in effect, heroic deeds, because she believed in the divinity of Emperor Hirohito, who sat at the pinnacle of Japan's hierarchical world; and that the second most terrible day in her life had arrived on August 15, 1945, just nine days after the nuclear explosion. That was the day the emperor told his people, many of whom had never heard his voice, that Japan was surrendering. She whispered that, fifty years later, she still "adored" the emperor.

She wasn't alone. Adoration of the emperor was the foundation of pre-war Japanese society and the impetus for many wartime deeds, including atrocity crimes committed in China and the kamikaze suicide-attacks on American ships in 1945. To adore Emperor Hirohito was, by itself, a motivation for survival: people willingly endured hunger and deprivation for the ruler's sake. What struck me was not Chiyoko Watanabe's unfailing commitment during the war; it was that her unquestioning acceptance had continued during the subsequent half-century. In this she was perhaps lucky, if one can thus characterize unthinkingness. She had suffered unspeakably, lost her young husband on the Chinese front just days after their marriage, and fought the ongoing effects of radiation disease. Through it all she had never asked questions.

I would hear the rationale of emperor-worship repeated many times during my travels in Japan. I would learn that Chiyoko spoke for many when she said, "He was not the only one at fault, and he was never forced to admit to anything. So why should the Japanese people blame him?" In this, she acknowledged the possibility of his guilt and simultaneously forgave him.

My encounter with another survivor, Sunao Tsuboi, also opened my eyes to the synthesis of culture and war memory. He was a twenty-two-year-old student the day the Enola Gay passed like a shadow over his city—on his way to school when he saw the flash and felt his body fly through the air. He got up, bleeding profusely, numbly observing that his clothes had been blown away. He ran towards the River Ota, where he saw the human detritus that John Hersey's description had burned into my own childhood memory. On the way to the river he witnessed terrible things, he told me. Now, all these years later, he recalled having also terrible things: "Have courage, for the sake of the emperor!" he had shouted heroically to a screaming mother trying to rescue her burning child.

Tsuboi had been in and out of hospital most of his life; and at age 72, he still dreamed about the bombing. "Tsuboi!" his dreamland tormentors cried, "Why did you not help? Why were you chosen to live?"

He told me these things as we sat together in the back room of an inconspicuous storefront called "The Hiroshima Sufferers' Welfare Organization" that offered practical advice about medical referrals and how to access financial help; and, as he spoke, I was reminded of Holocaust survivors who also felt debilitating guilt at having survived when others did not. Tsuboi's response was diametrically different from that of Chiyoko Watanabe, which is one of the reasons I remember him so well. He did not continue to love the emperor; on the contrary, he began to read history and to reject the old thinking. He said he believed in "democracy and equality." He thought the Japanese government should apologize to its citizens for the years of war they were subjected to for reasons of false nationalism. Strangely, he did not blame the Americans for having dropped the bomb, and, on reflection, I think this anomaly may be tied to his belief that Japan, as a nation, was similarly guilty.

My travels in Japan would expose me to differing degrees of cultural fatalism; for example, one individual suggested that the nuclear bomb had no real physical origin, but merely incarnated the destructive forces of nature. There was a common expression in the language that surprised me: "*Shikata ga nai*," meaning "It can't be helped."

Although Tsuboi had educated himself to believe in responsibility and accountability, he was unable to say anything in public, for to voice strong opinions, even privately, was culturally taboo. Instead, he joined the officially sanctified Hiroshima Sufferers' Welfare Organization as an anti-nuclear peace activist. He was an internationally recognized leader of the movement—but his inability to deal with a lifetime of unresolved thoughts and emotions, including mental trauma, survivor guilt, continuing physical pain, and generalized anger at his country had left him profoundly unhappy.

Finally, there was Dr. Koso Matsuo, whom I visited at his cottage-like home surrounded by a garden of cascading flowers. Gardening, he told me, was his way of keeping his demons at bay.

What Dr. Matsuo wanted to talk to me about was his stapled-together manuscript titled "Too Much Worry Recently," which he had translated into (approximate) English himself. Dr. Matsuo worried about many things: Why did the United States not warn Japan about the possible nuclear bombing? Why wasn't the firebombing of Tokyo reprisal enough for Japanese war deeds? Did the bomb represent some sort of "balance" of victims, and was it necessary to achieve this balance? Or could the entire tragedy simply "couldn't be helped"? Cultural fatalism again...

Dr. Matsuo wanted me to know that he felt personally constrained by the conformity of Japanese society. He tried to show his writings to friends, but they only smiled appreciatively and exclaimed, "What a good writer you are!" He called this attitude *wa*. Keiko, my guide and translator, didn't have a ready translation and looked up the word for me. *Wa*, she explained, meant harmony. It meant "we will endure discussion, but always aim for the harmonious whole."

I thought I was perhaps beginning to grasp the reluctance to talk about wartime memory. This averseness was not unique to Japan; the struggles of the French and the Germans had taught me as much. But Japanese culture seemed to place additional roadblocks in the way of external and internal reconciliation. In avoiding critical reflections on the past, Chiyoko Watanabe had chosen the easiest route; Tsuboi Sunao and Dr. Matsuo, on the other side of the equation, had led lives of psychological as well as physical distress in a society where they risked social exclusion for expressing views that challenged the culture of *wa*.

The surprise inherent in my visit to the shrine-like Hiroshima Peace Museum, located at ground zero of the nuclear blast, further piqued my interest in Japanese historical memory. The relics of that awful day were preserved behind glass: twisted bottle caps, burned roof tiles, torn, burnt clothing, broken pottery. But these faded in comparison with a horrific, life-size wax display of a wounded family staggering towards the River Ota, their burnt arms raised to alleviate the pain. And yes, their skin had "sloughed off," as John Hersey had informed me all those years ago when I was innocent of the world.

The unmissable message of the Peace Museum was contained in its name. Peace—universal peace. All wartime suffering had been swept up and funneled into this place. Yes, we were victims, the museum informed its visitors through its extraordinary exhibits, but the messaging was clear on the other subject: the pursuit of peace for the sake of humankind. Fine, I thought. Postwar Japan had certainly taken the lead in anti-nuclear lobbying; but what struck me as I moved from room to room was that there was no mention whatever of the major war crimes committed by Imperial Japan itself, especially in China. The massacre of civilians in Nanjing in 1937. The medical experiments performed on Chinese prisoners of war in Manchuria that recalled Dr. Joseph Mengele's experiments on Jews at the Auschwitz camp. The museum of universal peace had neglected to complete the picture: that was how the country's history was being recast. "Peace" was an abstraction. "War" was the U.S. nuclear bombing of Japan, with not a hint of Japan's war on others.

The prospect of studying this phenomenon became even more intriguing when I learned that a war of words was waging in the country as a handful of history teachers and human rights activists tried to incorporate the full spectrum of Japan's wartime history into the national narrative. Powerful conservative factions fought back, and one of their tools consisted of controlling the way history was taught in school textbooks. In the mid-1960s, Tokyo education professor Saburo Ienaga sued the government for their censoring of textbooks, including his own, on the matter of Japanese war crimes in the 1930s. In 1982, he forced a word change in a text: the word *aggression* would henceforth replace *military advance*. And in 1997 Japan's Supreme Court decreed that the government had illegally removed a description of the medical experiments that were carried out on prisoners in Manchuria.

I was learning about how history is shaped—and the means adopted in shaping it. I was learning about the role museums play in constructing the narrative of memory. I was learning about how hard it is to suppress the truth about the past when there are survivors, their children, and their grandchildren who continue to struggle to be heard. This was learning I wished to pursue.

Back in Tokyo, I felt as though I'd returned from another planet, although I had no idea what I would do with the material I had uncovered. In any event, I didn't have to think about such things immediately, because the cultural dissonances kept on arriving. When Tom's lectures ended, for example, his colleagues decided to offer us, as a gift, a night's stay in a ryokan, a traditional Japanese inn featuring tatami-matted rooms and communal baths.

The communal baths: that got me into immediate trouble. As we were being shown around the inn, I thought I understood that we were all expected to bathe together naked, Tom, myself, *and* the philosophy professors accompanying us. Burning with embarrassment, I demurred. Our host turned on me reprovingly, "*Mrs. Robinson*, don't you and your husband bathe together?" Oh yes, of course, excuse me, I sputtered, realizing that something must have got lost in translation.

I CAN'T PINPOINT PRECISELY when I decided to pursue the larger study of how nations choose to remember, or not remember, their history. It is certain that my previous work had driven me to travel to Hiroshima, and that it lurked behind the interviewing I did there. It is also certain that without Tom's invitation to lecture in Japan I might never have made the voyage. Coincidentally, I was accepted into the Literary Non-Fiction programme at the Banff Centre in the Alberta Rockies that very summer of 1996. I had to have a writing project. And since I had just returned from my extraordinary visit, the research I did there was the obvious choice of subjects.

What a privilege it was to be in Banff that summer. Ten writers were housed, fed, and even paid to participate; what was required of us was to complete a piece of writing, hopefully of publishable quality, with the editorial assistance of two on-site professionals, one of whom happened to be my long-time friend from *Maclean's*, Don Obe.

I was assigned a writing cabin—a quiet space in the woods that surrounded the Centre with no distractions beyond the welcome sight of forest trees outside my windows and the unwelcome presence of a large elk that enjoyed lying on the path in front of my front door. We writers had private weekly meetings with our editors and with the group at large, to whom we read excerpts from our works-in-progress. On one occasion my colleagues challenged me over an important usage: the word "truth." What was "truth?" they wanted to know. There were only "truths," and they were usually relative to one another, they insisted.

This was long before Donald Trump and social media would do their own fragmenting of truth. But post-modernism was fashionable at the time, and I had long been impatient with its preciosity. Yes, biblical-style "absolute" truths were clearly out (I was an empiricist and lifelong atheist), but I would defend factual truth—after all, my writing subject that summer concerned the way facts were distorted for political ends and the bombing of Hiroshima was an indisputable fact, as was the suffering of the survivors a half-century later. I had been reading the German-Jewish-American philosopher Hannah Arendt, and I remembered the gist of what she had written about truth in *The Origins of Totalitarianism*.

That evening I went to the Banff Centre library to check her wording. She had said: "The ideal subject of totalitarian rule is not the convinced Nazi or the dedicated communist, but people for whom the distinction between fact and fiction, true and false, no longer exists." I took this to be a reference to the benchmarks, or standards, of thinking to which reasonable people adhere.

My passion that summer was not for debate, but for my daily writing, and the excitement of a whole world of moral complexities, far beyond simply Japan, towards which it might be leading me. Thinking about Japan had led me to so-called national interests. For example, in 1945 U.S. President Harry Truman had argued that the nuclear bombings were justified because they had brought Japan to its knees and ended the war. It was a logical fallacy of the sort I had studied in first-year philosophy: To end war is a good thing; nuclear bombings end war; therefore, nuclear bombings are a good thing.

With due respect to Aristotle, what was missing from this syllogism was any "ethical" flavour to the logic. Since the Allies had made a similar case for the firebombing of Dresden during two days in February 1945, I looked up that almost simultaneous event. Between 25,000 and 35,000 people had been killed in Dresden; of 28,410 houses in the inner city, 24,866 were destroyed. Among justifications was the stated strategy "to destroy communications [in order] to hinder the eastward deployment of German troops, and also to hamper evacuation, not to kill the evacuees." This latter claim was implausible. How was it possible to "hamper evacuation" without destroying the people in the evacuation vehicles? It seemed more likely, as others had suggested, that the real intent of the Dresden attack was to demoralize the Nazis by showing them what the Allies were capable of. It is a war crime to attack civilians during armed conflict, and just as the criminal nature of the bombings of Hiroshima and Nagasaki have never been adequately acknowledged, along with the criminal nature of the atrocities committed by the Japanese in the Chinese city of Nanking in December 1937, so has the firebombing of Dresden remained an open sore.

While my head was filled with the convolutions of Japanese historical memory, I began to wonder how other countries may have remembered—or chosen not to remember—an unhappy past. A decade earlier I had travelled to France with embryonically formed questions about historical memory. I had visited Israel in the same spirit, asking among other things what role the Holocaust played in the psychology of the new state and its citizens. Several things had become somewhat clearer along the way, among them the determining role of ideology—that set lens through which we view our place in the world; the difficulty of shifting gears when new circumstances require new thinking—and the apparent consequences of refusing to face the past with honesty.

Post-Banff, I found myself increasingly curious about whether there might be discernible patterns as to how national memory is shaped after a collective trauma. I began to wonder about choices, deliberate, self-serving, and otherwise. What did nations and their peoples choose to forget, and what were the implications of these choices? Yes, I had begun to explore French memory during the writing of *Unhealed Wounds*, but what about the countries on the losing side of the Second World War? Japan had lost, and I had begun to write about that crisis. But what about Germany, the perpetrator Nazi state? A shudder passed through me at the thought of travelling there—at the idea that I might willingly step back into my own Natzweiler-Struthof hallucination, now more than three decades behind me.

I ASKED MYSELF WHERE else I might pursue these questions. South Africa was on everybody's radar in the mid-1990s. In 1994 the country had held its first general elections in which citizens of all races were allowed to take part. Millions had lined up to vote under the eyes of international observers, including my friend and mentor Doris Anderson, who had represented Canada. The African National Congress had won the election, as expected, and the former prisoner, Nelson Mandela, was now president.

Would the new South African leaders be able to incorporate long-hostile populations into a national body with common interests? How would they deal with the aftermath of decades of racism and repression, since ingrained attitudes don't evaporate with a change of government? The new regime had initiated a Truth and Reconciliation Commission, something about which I knew little. If this effort succeeded, might South Africa send out a signal that it was possible to tell the truth about the past and forge something new that included healing?

Thoughts of South Africa and apartheid led me to yet another watershed moment I'd followed from afar as a young woman: the civil rights movement in the United States in the 1960s and the deep-rooted problem of American racism. The idea of exploring this issue thirty years later excited my curiosity—and, once again, my core interest was in historical memory. Why was it that, 150 years after the Civil War had ended, unresolved race relations continued to erupt into violence? Was racial hatred an ineradicable legacy of having built a free and democratic society on the backs of slaves?

Once I had boarded this train, so to speak, I thought of dozens of places where I might study the memory of past crises and their resultant effects. The Irish Troubles were a possibility; the Good Friday agreement was already in the works as I mulled the matter over (the agreement was signed in 1998). Russia, too, was an interesting candidate. The Soviet Union had imploded in 1991; Boris Yeltsin was already on his way out and Vladimir Putin was running for election. After eighty years of communism, the former world power was in serious decline and in rapid transition, its economy literally up for grabs as cunning individuals became overnight billionaires.

I decided against both Ireland and Russia for similar reasons: I didn't know enough about either at the outset, which would have made what was already looking like an unwieldly project a lot harder to manage. All the same, I was especially intrigued by Russia. Before his death in 1989, the famed dissident Andrei Sakharov had founded "Memorial," a civil rights organization that was recording and publicizing the country's despotic past. Memorial would have been a natural starting point for my research, but I thought that the convoluted strains of Russian memory called for a stand-alone work, not a book chapter. (It did feel like a lacuna, though, and when *Long Shadows* was eventually published, a British reviewer for *The Guardian* gently chided me for the omission.)

As an interesting aside, I did go to Russia—in 1999. The event was a philosophy conference in Moscow titled "A Dialogue Between Civilizations: East-West." Again, the invitation came to Tom. Again, I tagged along—and while there I constantly regretted not having included that country in my book project, even though my original reasons for not doing so still held true.

At the end of its experimental twentieth century, Russia was a poverty-stricken, still frightening, place. We few foreigners attending the conference were assigned to one floor in a residence of the People's Friendship University of Russia, where we could, I assumed, be observed. A female apparatchik squinted at us suspiciously from behind an entrance desk, and despite having absconded with our passports for the duration of our stay nevertheless examined us carefully at each coming and going.

At the conference, the perilous transition from Soviet Union to Russia was the only subject on the table. Like everyone else, these academics had seen their living standard eroded by a massive devaluation of the ruble. The villain, the conference attendees seemed to agree, was the failure of western economic liberalism: thanks to "shock therapy" recommended, it was said, by Harvard economists, five oligarchs now controlled 40 percent of the national wealth.

The Russian voices at the podium were either hopeless or strident. Most agreed that liberalization might have been a good idea in theory, just as communism was a good idea in theory, but that it had been implemented through robbery. One man shouted that the stories about Stalin's rule of terror were all lies: what Russians needed, he said, was a return to communism. A few championed the need for a western-style democracy coupled with the rule of law, but the consensus was in favour of a solution specific to Russia and divorced from western ideologies.

Among the shrillest speakers was Igor Chubais, an early democrat in the post-Soviet system and brother of the former First Deputy Prime Minister, Anatoly Chubais, the man who had invented the idea of privatizing state enterprises in the first place. Igor, a large-bodied firebrand with a mane of red hair and a red bush sprouting from his chin, spoke with thundering certainty. What was needed, he declaimed, was a return to "The Russian Idea," a concept that had first made an appearance at the end of the nineteenth century. Chubais described "The Russian Idea" as a philosophy based on "trust" rather than "contracts"—as a unifying system of moral values, ideals, and rules—a uniquely Russian expression of citizenship built upon a basis of traditional Russian culture. Afterwards, I interviewed him briefly. "In the West, lawfulness and money are the prime values. In Russia, our primary value is morality," he explained. (It is of interest that the "Russian Idea," with its mystic aura and embedded nationalism, was later adopted by Vladimir Putin.)

At a second conference in St. Petersburg, Tom and I gave a joint seminar paper titled "The Return of International Law." Tom spoke about the ancient origins of thinking on the subject. I was already beginning research for *The Sun Climbs Slow: The International Criminal Court and the Struggle for Justice*, and I spoke about more modern iterations.

It was a disaster. The interpreter couldn't keep up, or she didn't know the vocabulary. When I saw boredom, or worse, on the faces of the audience I panicked and speeded up my part of the presentation, making myself virtually incomprehensible. When it was over, a kindly professor took me aside. "Do you know why you were unpopular here?" he asked me. I didn't. "It's because we've been listening to the words "universal" and "international" for fifty years and we're sick of it."

In the fall of 1996, I made the decision to pursue those places and subjects that I knew best and were closest to my experience: the losers of the Second World War, for obvious reasons; the United States because it was familiar and close to home, and because its endemic racism had long preoccupied me; and South Africa because I wondered whether a Truth and Reconciliation Commission might hold promise for other jurisdictions. Beyond these, my longstanding interest in ethnic identity, especially Jewish identity, propelled me towards the memory of the Holocaust, the tragedy that had underpinned my life's journey. I wanted to learn more—and I wanted to learn it directly from Raul Hilberg, the author of *The Destruction of the European Jews*, a book that was, and remains, the classic work in the field. Hilberg was the first to write a work of objective scholarship, as opposed to commemoration, and he had been attacked for having done so—for not having made the survivors the centrepiece of his story. I shared his interest in the difference between commemorating a catastrophic event and studying it as verifiable history. I thought he was brave, and I wanted to meet him.

I had also been reading about the bitter controversies between competing victim groups that had obstructed the creation of the United States Holocaust Memorial Museum, which was eventually founded in 1980. Was anything more central to an understanding of historical memory than the choice over what to include, or exclude, in such an institution? My visit to the Hiroshima Peace Museum had allowed me to see something of the politics that underscore the curating of exhibits.

Finally, I was appalled and intrigued by the recent war in the former Yugoslavia. People who had lived together in reasonable comfort for fifty years had split into ethnic factions, manufactured hate propaganda against one another, and murdered one another. Within this fratricidal war I recognized social and cultural transformations I had encountered elsewhere. The shift from open tolerance to ethnic hatred in the former Yugoslavia was an eerie repeat of the process I had observed in fifteenth-century Spain, in nineteenth- and twentieth-century Germany, and to a lesser degree in modern France.

Every aspect of my book plan, every situation I wanted to research, led me back to the subject I had held at the back of my mind since university days: Justice. What was it? I had first encountered the subject in my undergraduate philosophy classes in the works of Plato, and even earlier as an (unwilling) Sunday School student at Holy Blossom Temple.

I began to think about the role of justice as an underpinning for reconciliation and a remedy for major international crimes. I had tentatively broached the issue in *Unhealed Wounds*. Klaus Barbie's trial was allowed to take place forty years after the war solely because the Nuremberg Tribunal, where the top Nazis were prosecuted, had eliminated statute-of-limitations restrictions for the sort of heinous war crimes Barbie was accused of. My study of the Spanish Inquisition had similarly aroused my interest in justice. Nasty as it was, the Inquisition had operated according to its own rules of due process, and although these seem unqualifiedly unjust to the modern mind, the ostensible goal of it all—a state living in peace and harmony—was fine enough, though not by those means, and not if underpinned by an ideology of religious homogeneity.

I had started *Long Shadows* in Japan by pure serendipity, but once I made the decision to write a book-length work, there was no question about whether I should go to the places of unassimilated Second World War history where the narrative of national memory had been shaped, and re-shaped, by the powerful. I hadn't been to Germany, the place that frightened me most, since just after my marriage to Claude. For a brief time, he had worked in the Alsatian village of Riquewihr, across the border from Freiburg in the region of the Black Forest, and during the day I'd occasionally drive into Freiburg to sightsee. I did so without much ulterior thought. As I would later acknowledge, I was young enough then to feel closer to the Brothers Grimm than to the Nazi terror.

When I eventually assembled the chapters of *Long Shadows*, I titled the section on Germany "The Stone of Sisyphus," because my exploration of that society taught me that the task of assimilating what had happened during twelve years of Nazi rule—the task of understanding and, to use an overworked but indispensable phrase, "coming to terms with" it—was a painful multi-generational undertaking with still no end in sight.

IN RETROSPECT, MY PREPARATIONS for the German trip bordered on the ghostly. Since there were, for obvious reasons, few Jews in Germany, and since much of the physical memory of the many centuries of life they had spent in that country had been destroyed, my search was for shadows and whisperings amidst emptiness.

My young guide, Lara, understood me immediately. She was a German Jew—or rather "a Jew living in Germany," as she adamantly insisted. "No one wants to be a German," she told me. "Not even the Germans."

It was fall 1997, and Tom and I had rented a small apartment in the 14th *arrondissement* of Paris—our favourite area of the city. I planned to do research in Germany, the former Yugoslavia, and in France itself, where I had a ticket to the trial of Maurice Papon in Bordeaux.

But Germany would come first. As Lara and I walked the streets of East Berlin, the empty spaces of the formerly Jewish district presented themselves. She and I peered about inquisitively, as though there was something to be seen, and talked about what used to be. In one vacant lot the artist Christian Boltanski had created a conceptual artwork called "The Missing House." Plaques engraved with the names of all those who had lived in the vanished apartment building until 1945, when it was destroyed by allied bombing, along with their dates of residence, hung on the two walls adjacent to where the original house had stood. (Jewish residencies in the house had ended in 1942.)

On the next street, next to a former school for Jewish children, was an empty space that had housed a Jewish retirement home from 1829 until it was bombed in 1945. The now-disappeared building had been taken over by the Nazis and used as a holding depot for neighbourhood Jews awaiting deportation to Auschwitz. Fifty-five thousand individuals had been dispatched from this place, but I was distracted by the presence of the still-existing apartment building adjacent to it; at least ten stories of multiple windows continued to look down on the site. It was impossible to believe that the tenants neither saw, nor heard, what was happening to their neighbours over a period of years.

That building remains imprinted in my mind's eye, and it still disturbs me. I would encounter other such signs of deliberate blindness and denial, like the elderly woman selling tickets at the Jewish Museum of Rothenberg ob der Tauber, who told me that the Jews of her town had all "gone to the country" during the war, "and were probably still living there."

I now have a better understanding of this blindness, as I have suggested, for I have encountered it in all the stricken lands I travelled to. Perhaps events that supersede our ability to rationalize, normalize, or contextualize become simply incomprehensible and are blocked by our minds. Perhaps the implications of clear-sightedness are just too painful to bear.

The largest of the disappeared places Lara and I visited was once the oldest Jewish cemetery in Berlin, in use from 1672 until 1827, but these dead had died a second time when the cemetery was razed by order of the Gestapo. Only the grave of the Enlightenment philosopher Moses Mendelssohn has been remembered and restored. What an irony. In the eighteenth-century, Mendelssohn had personified the widespread efforts of Jews to "Germanize" themselves. For this he was widely admired across society—but there were many doubters. Mendelssohn presciently rejected the demand for total assimilation as culturally impossible, and furthermore undesirable, in that it contained a wish for the erasure of Jewish identity. He promoted integration, instead. For Mendelssohn, the idea of equality that underscored the emancipation of the Jews meant the right of the minority to continue its practices within a tolerant pluralist environment.

On the flat, featureless expanse that had once been a cemetery, the single memorial stone to Moses Mendelssohn was inscribed only with his name and birthdates. It stood there as a wordless monument to the great man's failed hopes for multicultural diversity.

On the flip side of emptiness was the equally perplexing phenomenon of appropriation. Jewish chic was the latest fashion—from formal religious conversions to Judaism to klezmer bands in which German gentiles played Yiddish music for German gentiles. I learned that everything relating to the Jews was considered interesting enough for media coverage—even the hiring of a new rabbi for the tiny remnant community.

This seemed an odd transference—something that would surely have interested Freud. Not that the impulse to appropriate wasn't sincere. I personally met a fervent young convert who told me she had dreamed that it was incumbent upon her to make amends for the crimes of her family, and she had devoted her life to doing so. Several people mentioned another woman who had shot her university professor because he had mentioned the Talmud in a secular context. (The context was a university classroom, and his field was comparative religions.) She was, they told me, unrepentant, telling the police self-righteously: "No gentile should utter the name of the Talmud."

The implications seemed clear enough. Fifty years after the war, the pain of the second and third generations had barely abated.

In one way or another, all my encounters in Germany revolved around the personal and collective effort to live normally—whatever that meant—in the aftermath of Adolf Hitler. Before 1968, silence about the war had prevailed; but starting in '68, and even earlier with activists such as Beate Klarsfeld, the children of the perpetrator generation had forced a reckoning. To my mind, the most evocative story from this time dated from the late 1970s, amid questions about what should be done with the imposing Nazi edifices that still occupied the centre of Berlin. Someone proposed a plan for road construction in the area, which elicited an open letter from the International League for the Rights of Man reminding the Senator of Internal Affairs that "the brown terror once held sway on Prinz-Albrecht-Strasse," and demanding that a dignified memorial be incorporated into the plan. In 1983, the mayor announced a competition for an idea "that would reconcile the historic depth of the location" with practical functions. Someone won. Then it was decided not to proceed. But a Pandora's Box of memory had been opened, and it was not to be closed.

More time passed, then in May 1985, a small group of young people arrived on the site of the old Gestapo building, carrying signs that read, "Dig where you stand." Before a group of astonished onlookers, they began to hack at the earth, to dig into the taboo history of the place. It was a turning-point, I was told by the man who headed the Memorial Museums of the Topography of Terror project.

In some cases, anger was the route to self-preservation. Memorably, I interviewed the Hamburg journalist Niklas Frank, son of Hans Frank, Hitler's former *Gauleiter* of Poland who was convicted and executed at Nuremberg. Niklas had childhood memories of seeing Jewish infants being smashed against the outer walls of his family's Krakow "palace," as he called it, and of seeing his mother strut about in furs stolen from the dead. He hated his father with an incandescent rage, yet still loved him, or wanted to, which only exacerbated his suffering. In a scurrilous book titled "The Father," he had screamed fury at the man who had betrayed him.

I was shaken by the depth of his rage during our meeting; I thought then, and now, that his only alternative to obsessive truth-telling might have been suicide. In the intervening years since we met, Niklas Frank has persisted in his personal odyssey to inform the world about his nefarious father—in print, in film, on video, and in interviews.

Irreconcilable family betrayal also lay at the root of Gottfried Wagner's wrath. He was the great-grandson of Richard Wagner, and when we met at a conference on the Holocaust in Nuremberg (the first to be held in that city so evocative of the Nazi era), he was admonishing his cowed audience never to listen to the music of his illustrious ancestor. As a child living in Bayreuth, where his family ran the annual Wagner festival, Gottfried had happened upon love letters hidden away in the attic between Hitler and his grandmother, Winifred Wagner. That chance finding, coupled with his growing knowledge of Richard's open antisemitism (prominent in a screed he wrote called "The Jew in Music") had determined the course of

Gottfried's life, just as learning the truth about Hans Frank's life had determined the future of his son. Gottfried Wagner exposed his family's Nazi links and was ostracized by his relatives; and when his father, Wolfgang, died in 2010 at the age of ninety, Gottfried was prevented from visiting his deathbed. He was also barred from attending the funeral. None of this would interrupt his personal crusade.

On the other side of Germany's sorrow-divide was a modest man, Karl Michelsohn, who had made it his life's work to reconstitute the history of the lost Jewish community of Friedrichstadt, a small town in Schleswig-Holstein near the North Sea. I travelled to meet him there, through once-devastated, now bucolic countryside where postwar rebuilding had reconstructed bombed buildings as exact replicas of their pre-war selves, an erasure of the intervening history that disconcerted me. Karl Michelsohn was not in the tradition of forgetfulness. He showed me the space he had been provided in the small town hall to keep his records. He told me he did this because he had had Jewish school friends who never returned, and that every year the families of those who had survived and moved to other countries came to visit him. He would show them their family's history, and they would cry with gratitude.

The present was a difficult place for the children and grandchildren of the perpetrator generation. But now the government was on the side of acknowledging history. Of all the stricken places I travelled to, Germany had done the most to make amends. It had paid reparations to survivors; and every school child was taken to visit a concentration camp. I found this admirable. It is a lot easier to showcase a history of victimhood than a history of criminality. On the other hand, I asked myself if full reconciliation between Jews and Germans would ever be possible and thought it unlikely: Hitler's unprecedented exterminations would stand in the way. But that did not mean an absence of progress, nor did it mean a lack of normalized relations. It meant that the past cannot be mastered, as the writer Günther Grass once noted; it can only be acknowledged.

I still receive letters from readers of *Long Shadows*, but those from Germans living in the Canadian and American diaspora dwarf the rest in number. They write me to share long-buried secrets of Nazi parents and grandparents who committed irredeemable acts. They tell me that their lives were irrevocably altered by their discoveries.

I always thank them for having the courage to write, for I am mindful of my student self in Paris, on a sunlit autumn day, not sixteen years after the war's end, as I sat in a café with a young man about my age. He told me he was German; he had come to France to study French, just as I had. I told him I was Jewish. A wall of silence arose between us. He looked away. "It wasn't my fault," he mumbled, his voice faltering.

No, it wasn't his fault, just as it wasn't the fault of any of the post-war-born Germans I would later meet who confided their interior struggles. They had inherited a poisoned chalice of sorrow.

IN OCTOBER 1997, I returned from Germany to our rented apartment in Paris. The trial of Maurice Papon was about to open in Bordeaux, but before leaving for the southwest I spent a few days savouring the beloved city. Paris is, to me, the most sensual place in the world with its emphasis on food, art, literature, and beauty of every kind. German strudels were fine, but nothing compared with the thick hot chocolate served in cups at my favourite haunt between the Luxembourg Gardens and the *boulevard Saint-Germain*. Nothing compared with the fish market on the *rue Daguerre* near the roundabout of Denfert-Rochereau, where I once saw live sea horses offered as a holiday specialty; or the enticing aroma of corn-fed chickens from the Landes region rotating slowly on spits outside local butcher shops.

I was filled with excitement at the prospect of the Maurice Papon trial. A decade had passed since the trial of Klaus Barbie, but passions were, if anything, more violent; Barbie's return in 1983 had merely opened the floodgates. During the four years between the latter's capture and his trial in 1987, it had been impossible to open a newspaper or watch a televised news programme without being thrust into the midst of a debate between those intent on maintaining the myth that all of France had fought in the Resistance (with the exception of a few bad apples who had been duly tried for their perfidy) and those, emboldened by the evidence being brought to light by historians, who were equally intent on changing the national narrative to reflect the truth. This truth also contained emerging information about what had happened to France's Jews, and the role the French had played in their deportations.

Serge and Beate Klarsfeld and others had made sure that previously occulted memory was not going to be buried anew. For example, there had been another trial in 1994—that of Paul Touvier, a member of the *Milice,* a French paramilitary force modelled on the SS. Touvier had been protected by the Catholic Church until he was outed and arrested in 1989 (a story dramatically recounted by the Canadian Irish novelist, Brian Moore, in his book *The Statement*). He was found guilty and died in prison. Another prominent Vichy official, René Bousquet, a security official responsible for the mass deportation of Jews (like many others, he had led a successful postwar life), was also indicted, but he was murdered at his Paris doorstep before his trial began.

Then there was Maurice Papon, the very epitome of a French civil servant. Papon: former official in Bordeaux in charge of "Jewish Questions," then, after the war, a highly placed civil servant in Algeria (where he was accused of torture), chief of police in Paris (where he was accused of ordering atrocities against Algerians), and a politician under successive governments (Charles de Gaulle honoured him with the *Légion d'Honneur*). Papon now stood accused of complicity in crimes against humanity for the deportation of 1,560 Jews from southwest France

Each of these prosecutions was moving closer to the dangerous core of France's collaboration with the Nazis, a suppressed history that was relentlessly being unearthed. The inexorable progression frightened many. Klaus Barbie may have been a "monster," but he was German—a foreigner. Paul Touvier was French, but he was an indigenous Nazi of the sort that marched around in jack boots, worked with Barbie's SS, and openly murdered people. Neither resembled Maurice Papon, the personification of a high-ranking government functionary, a man with the impeccable carriage and the manners of his class. Papon was charged with being a principal *French* actor in the Final Solution. He claimed that he had only been obeying orders, but everyone now knew that this defense had been rejected at the Nuremberg Trials of 1945, and it certainly hadn't helped Klaus Barbie. Papon, too, claimed to have been a member of the Resistance, which was true in a common, murky way. Like many who went to bed as supporters of Pétain and woke up the next morning as Resistance fighters, Papon had strategically switched allegiances at the eleventh hour when the direction of the wind became clear. In 1942 he was deporting Jews. In 1943 he had metamorphosed into a member of the Resistance.

To reject the mythology of universal resistance to the Nazis was something many now longed to do, especially now that this proverbial ship had sailed, but to abandon the longstanding falsehood in favour of historical truth was to risk undermining the societal underpinnings of the last half-century. All the same, truth-telling was gaining ground. On July 16, 1995, President Jacques Chirac shocked the country by declaring that "the criminal madness of the [Nazi] occupier was seconded by the French, by the French state. Those black hours soiled our history forever…France… committed the irreparable."

I had known I wanted to be at the Papon trial since the news of his indictment was announced in the early 1990s, and strengthening my resolve was a tiny connection that felt personal. It was Papon who was responsible for the Auschwitz survivor who had sat huddled on a chair in a dark room in the city of Bayonne, near my in-laws' home, unwilling, or unable, to raise her head—a mute remnant of her murdered family.

"Are we ready to look at the true face of France, at the dark years reflected in the mirror of this trial?" In *Unhealed Wounds,* a decade earlier, I had quoted these words by the journalist Guy Baret, written in *France Soir.* Baret's reference was the upcoming trial of Klaus Barbie, but his question was even more relevant as Maurice Papon prepared to face his accusers. The legacy of the Klarsfelds' thirty-year campaign to expose the crimes and the prevarications of the past would be acted out in Bordeaux. Papon's surviving victims, and by extension all the victims of Vichy France, had waited all their lives for this moment. His innocence or guilt, as determined by this court, might indicate which of *les deux France* would carry the future.

The trial took place in the eighteenth-century, yellow-limestone Palace of Justice just up the cobblestoned way from the ancient cathedral of the city. I showed my pass, entered, and took a seat. The accused, who was seated in a box to the left of the judge, held his head high as he gazed ahead without expression; the lawyers (and there were many of them) sat to the judge's right. A palpable tension filled the room.

What became immediately clear was that the "mud" of war memory that was supposed never to be stirred was also flying about the room: the stark allegations of who did what to whom during the years of the Collaboration a half-century earlier—of who had been lying for five decades, of what myths and falsehoods about the Resistance had been taught to school children. All the divisions that had resurfaced when Klaus Barbie was arrested in Bolivia and brought back to France fifteen years earlier were as raw as ever, as though nothing had changed in the years since I first documented the chaos for *Unhealed Wounds*.

Touchstones from the past emerged. A procession of aging politicians and Resistance fighters testified for the defense. The defense? The ambiguity in their words only served to illuminate the shifting allegiances of the immediate postwar era. An elderly, former member of the Corsican parliament introduced himself as a member of a pro-Dreyfus family, thus signalling his allegiance to the republican side of *les deux France*, then described the defendant as—albeit "cold" and "firm"—a man of liberal values. "I hope this trial will be the last of a kind that can harm France," he pleaded, now signalling his second allegiance to the Gaullist mythology that had kept the country running reasonably smoothly for decades.

Other famous men stepped forward. Pierre Messmer had served with the Free French in London and as prime minister of France in the 1970s. In a booming voice he reiterated the Gaullist mythology. "From the moment the government of Vichy signed the armistice, it was *illegitimate!*" he thundered.

"An illegitimate government cannot represent France..., and that includes the functionaries who choose to obey its rules."

It was not clear to me how this was supposed to help Maurice Papon, who sat ramrod straight, his lips pursed. It seemed that Monsieur Messmer had come to Bordeaux not to defend the accused but to defend "France" against the new vision of collective responsibility articulated by President Jacques Chirac. "We need to stop hating and to forgive," he lectured the court.

"Are forgiveness and reconciliation possible before a recognition of wrong?" asked a prosecution lawyer. I thought that this was the heart of the matter for those who sought Maurice Papon's conviction, for justice demands both acknowledgement and accountability. In its aftermath, forgiveness may or may not follow.

Pierre Messmer was followed by Olivier Guichard, a man known as "the baron of Gaullism." Unlike the others, he was open about the Gaullist myth. "At the Liberation, de Gaulle had a strong desire to unite the country," he told the court. "That's why he invented the story that the Vichy regime did not exist in reality, and the other myth that we won the war. De Gaulle was trying to avoid having to try the majority of the French people. His reasoning was that you couldn't incriminate people on behalf of a state that simply didn't exist."

The courtroom fell silent, for Monsieur Guichard had uttered a truth that was known to all present, including Maurice Papon. I wondered whether Alice in Wonderland had once again dropped down the rabbit hole and resurfaced in Bordeaux. And whether any other Western country could boast a hoodwinking exercise as successful as that contrived fifty years ago in France.

In his defense, Papon rose to claim that he had always been compassionate as he carried out his legitimate orders—yes, his *legitimate* orders. He told the court that he requisitioned blankets to cover children during their deportation transit. And that one Christmas he and his wife had wept with sorrow after a wagonload of children was dispatched during a bitterly cold holy season. Murmurs of contempt arose from the rows of spectators. I shared their scorn.

Later, in his final remarks to the court, Papon, too, compared himself to the beleaguered and falsely accused Alfred Dreyfus.

Maurice Papon was found guilty on April 2, 1998, after the longest trial in French history, and repentant he was not. According to his lawyer, Papon felt only "contempt" for the process, and to prove himself he succeeded in escaping from his guards and fleeing to Switzerland, where he registered under an aristocratic name. The Swiss promptly extradited him back to France, where he was incarcerated in the formidable La Santé prison in Paris.

As I look back, one thing seems clear enough: it is impossible to move any society forward until there is a willingness to stir the mud and recognize a wrongdoing. The conviction of Maurice Papon—bureaucrat, technocrat, a man willing to compromise all in the service of his ambition—would not heal France, but his condemnation in a fair, state-run trial was a step in that direction.

For a long time after the Papon trial, the long effort to retrieve the hard truth about the crimes of Vichy France seemed to be over; the generation that lived through the Second World War was disappearing, and the Gaullist myth was losing its purchase.

Several years ago, I revisited Serge and Beate Klarsfeld in their Paris home. Then in their eighties, they told me they were content. Their life's work—to pursue the perpetrators, to confront falsified war memory, and to honour the victims—had been an unprecedented success.

One visible example of their influence can be found in the famed *Cimetière du Père Lachaise* in Paris, where many of the gravestones of deported French Jews that once were marked "*Mort pour la France*" (Died for France) have been rewritten. Today, they read: "Murdered at Auschwitz."

But current events continue to be propelled by the past in France as elsewhere, and in 2021 an unlikely figure emerged on the French political scene to revive the roiling debate. He was Eric Zemmour, a child of Jewish Algerian immigrants, and he claimed, in a blatant lie running counter to all historical evidence, that French Jews were *protected* by the Vichy state during the Second World War. He also declared that France was being "submerged" by migrants, and that parents should be forced to give their children "French names." He wanted to expel all Muslims from the country. Taking his cue from Donald Trump, he went on to dismiss the French media as "a propaganda machine that hates France."

Zemmour was an immediate sensation, his anti-Arab racism eclipsing even that of the Le Pen family. Forty years earlier, National Front leader Jean-Marie Le Pen had posted billboards around Paris that read, "Le Pen says aloud what everyone thinks to himself." Zemmour was breaking new ground on that front. That he was a Jew broadcasting lies about the tragic fate of his Jewish predecessors was both an outrage and a tragedy.

I RETURNED TO CANADA in January 1998 to learn that my father was ill. He and my mother were at their winter home in Guanajuato, Mexico—and, no, I didn't need to come, he said; he would be fine. Then the call came. He had had a heart attack during the night; he had died, ignored and comfortless, in a hospital bed while my mother returned home for his night clothes and a toothbrush.

My siblings and I watched his body being cremated in the nearby city of Irapuato; by law we had to be witnesses. There were no soothing funeral directors offering tea; there was not even a casket. He was offhandedly shovelled into the furnace on a plank.

He was gone, this powerful father who had shaped my life with childhood adventures and sharp observations about the world. He would never read *Long Shadows*, which was the culmination of his gifts to me.

I think about the experience of writing this book—about how the answered questions that had propelled me across four continents drove the five years I spent working upon it. I observe that racism, its origins, and its outcome have lived at the root of my efforts, and that while race hatred has shaped the history of many places, two countries in particular—the United States and South Africa—seem to have shared a long intimacy with it. In both countries, black populations had been either formally enslaved, or virtually so. In the former there had been periodic, and ultimately unsuccessful efforts to address this history. In the latter, the post-apartheid leadership had attempted a bold transition away from a half-century of apartheid violence by means of an election and a truth and reconciliation commission—a relatively new potential tool for peace. When I contemplated the potential structure of *Long Shadows*, I knew I would pursue how these countries had coped with their corrosive past.

I was no longer naïve about the seductions of racism: on the contrary, I was beginning to think that our disdain for "the other" might eventually be understood as a primary human characteristic that must be countered with a conscious commitment to inclusivity and tolerance.

In planning this part of *Long Shadows*, I decided to start with the United States for no other reason than that it was closest to my home in Canada and more familiar. But as I delved deeper into the preliminary research, I became aware that the America I thought I knew was nothing like the country I was about to enter. I'd been visiting the U.S. since childhood: my maternal grandparents had moved from Toronto to Phoenix, Arizona; my aunt, my uncle and their children and grandchildren lived in Los Angeles; and a cousin, Perry Nussbaum, was once a rabbi in Jackson, Mississippi. As a student at Holy Blossom Temple, I had visited the Reform Jewish community of Cincinnati and found, tellingly (for a teenager), that fifteen-year-olds there were no different from my friends at home. Between high school and university I had studied briefly at Harvard Summer School. As an adult, I'd travelled to the U.S. countless times for long and short stays.

Yet I had never encountered the other country within that geographical space: the very different abode of African Americans. I'd had indirect glimpses of the South from my youthful reading, especially the books of William Faulkner, whose portrayals of the strange, languid decline of that post-slavery world fascinated me, and those of Carson McCullers, whose mysterious, half-frightening descriptions of small southern towns stirred up images of dread. In the long ago 1960s, I'd been awakened to the contemporary abuses of human rights by the civil rights movement, which my friends and I had followed with horror and excitement. And I had developed some sense of the nature of black life under Jim Crow laws as I watched the mesmerizing pictures of U.S. cities burning with race hatred during the summer of 1967. That same year the Ku Klux Klan had bombed the home of my liberal cousin Rabbi Nussbaum and his wife Arene while they slept in their bed. They escaped unhurt, but they left Jackson forever. This near-fatal assault was bruited about by my shocked Canadian relatives, but I never quite absorbed the enormity of the event. I had not lived through any of these experiences directly; I had grown to adulthood in the sheltering country to the north.

I knew I would need to travel to the former slave states of the American South. Buried memory afflicted the entire country, but the South would be the indubitable epicentre.

The book that topped the reading stack on my desk was a ground-breaking work published in 1956, almost a century after the end of the slave era. In *The Peculiar Institution*, the historian Kenneth M. Stampp became the first to expose the true relationship between the slavers and the enslaved. In his obituary (he died in 1999), *The New York Times* wrote that Stampp "redirected the scholarly view of slavery in the antebellum South from that of a benign relationship between white plantation owners and compliant slaves to one of harsh servitude perpetuated to support the South's agrarian economy." It is not without interest that the French philosopher, historian, and political thinker, Alexis de Tocqueville, had made similar observations in his famous book, *Democracy in America,* a full century earlier.

Validating de Tocqueville's prescient observations, Stampp called slavery "America's most profound and vexatious social problem, [whose] impact upon the entire country was disastrous." The South, he added, still lay in the shadow of the tragedy brought about by slavery; the moral unease that accompanied the enslavement of human beings at the start of an egalitarian democracy continued to disturb the foundations of society.

Stampp's dispassionate scholarship allowed me to access the core of a relatively recent era in which a slaver had rights of life and death over his "property;" where tethered men, women, and children were traded like oxen, with prime prices accruing to healthy female "breeders," and where slaves were considered human only because they were believed to have a soul. No further rights flowed from this latter concession—and a concession it was, for eighteenth- and nineteenth-century Americans were as religiously minded as are their progeny today, and they scrupulously researched the Bible to justify their acts. We know that they were aware of moral hypocrisy from explicit eighteenth-century writings, such as that of Peter Fontaine, a minister from Virginia, who in 1757 claimed that even though slavery was a "sin," it was "morally impossible" to live in Virginia without slaves. In other words, the bottom line was economic: cotton and rice plantations could not survive without them.

Stampp and other authors prepared me for my extraordinary encounters with Southerners, both black and white, and helped me chart a path—for I also hoped to examine the possibilities of inter-racial reconciliation. There were, at the time, vaguely optimistic signs of this (they have since dissipated). In January 1996, President Bill Clinton came to office hoping to be "the repairer of the breach," and had subsequently established a committee called "The President's Commission on Race." That same year, Tony Hall, a Democrat senator from Ohio and a committed human rights activist, had floated the idea of a congressional apology to the descendants of the slaves. He had little support in Congress, but President Clinton had not initially rejected the idea out of hand—although he would later do so when his advisors informed him that he was embarking on a politically dangerous path.

In retrospect, the *leitmotiv* of my travels through the American South was going to be the rock-bottom subject of what it is to be human, although I didn't necessarily think of it that way at the time. That African Americans were not equal, except on paper, was as evident in the late 1990s as it is today; the legacy of discrimination is indisputable by any metric one uses to demonstrate it. The recent arrival of "Black Lives Matter," for example, has brought knowledge of systemic police discrimination to a wider swath of the population than ever before.

There were white people who argued that African Americans needed to pull up their proverbial bootstraps—an argument that has a certain merit if the playing field is an even one. But below the surface of this argument lies a shallow misunderstanding: when we brush away the impact of historic inequality on various wrongs suffered, we become agents for the continuation of those wrongs. In late 2017, for example, a study of middle class families by Prosperity Now and the Institute for Policy Studies found that white households in the United States owned nearly eight times as much wealth as middle-income black earners, and that, if current trends continued, as they were expected to do, it would take 228 years for the average black family to reach the level of wealth then enjoyed by white families. If anything had changed in twenty years, it had seemingly been for the worse.

I first thought about the perceived humanity of the slaves and of the black Americans who descended from them when I learned that only their souls had rendered slaves human in the eyes of their masters, but it was during my travels through the American South that I recognized this ancient wound as the heart of black pain. Since there were no national memorials to the slaves in the United States, I had started my journey at the mausoleum to Martin Luther King in Atlanta, Georgia. The monument was in a reputedly dangerous area of the city. And it was huge. Stately stairs climbed from the street to a white marble tomb set among fountains behind a large blue reflecting pool. Inside were shrine-like commemorations, complete with relics such as Dr. King's shirts, cufflinks, and shoes.

From the quotations preserved on the walls I absorbed the centrality of having to assert one's basic humanity. "We blacks also have a soul!" Martin Luther King cried out in his famous oration, the text of which was mounted on the museum wall. Alongside was a photograph in which four fearsome words were printed on a banner that spread across the chest of a black demonstrator: "I am a man," the wearer asserted.

"I am a man." A shock ran through me. Reading those terrible words, I wondered how many others in a nation whose very origins included a fervently defended doctrine of equality still felt the need to protest their elementary humanity.

I already knew something about dehumanization from my studies of Spain and the Holocaust. I also knew that once such propaganda has been unleashed, it becomes possible to inflict any degree of cruelty on the debased target.

I subsequently travelled to dozens of places in the American South and met dozens of people, but the experiences that etched themselves into the deepest crevices of memory involved this core reality. My interviews never started with this subject, but surprisingly often, bolstered by the chemistry of budding trust, the pained underlying words or their facsimiles would emerge: "I am a man."

I did not know before visiting an exhibition on slavery at the Avery Museum in Charleston, South Carolina, that this presentation was the first on the subject ever mounted in that old slave city. Sherman Pyatt, an archivist and the exhibition's curator, showed me around. I looked at leg irons and arm shackles, in adult and child sizes; ship manifests detailing "herbs, spices, and slaves;" and a picture of a man whose back had been lashed until no skin covered the raw, bleeding flesh. I also saw a small wooden chair that had been included in the exhibition to help visitors understand relationships: the child's chair was for adult slaves, and such chairs also needed to be lower than a white person's chair.

Pyatt was professional and reserved, but there was something about him that made me wonder if he might say more in a less formal setting, and when I asked if we might meet a second time, he agreed. Two days later, as we sat together in a private room, he told me that curating this exhibition on slavery was a personal milestone in his life. To have recovered this history, to have contextualized it with evidence, then to have introduced it to the people of Charleston as an integral part of American story was what mattered to him. It was the public acceptance of this still-radioactive history that mattered to him.

From our wide-ranging conversation, I particularly remember his unprompted comments about dehumanization. "I have yet to find a psychological study about the impact of the institution of slavery on people," he told me: "about how one who was considered a chattel and non-human had to, and still has to, constantly try to convince another group of people that 'I am human.'" I noted that he had switched to the first person. "People sometimes don't realize that when a sportscaster recently said about a black athlete, 'he runs like a horse,' then referred to the white athlete as 'intelligent'—well, that sends shock waves. I think we haven't started to look at the ramifications of dehumanization... You know there is a constant battle within the black person to... prove that he is human, and it's an ongoing battle, even today."

The first in his family to have finished high school, Sherman Pyatt had been lucky enough to attend a local college, where he studied history. He had moved out of the ghetto and into the middle class. Some among those who remained saw him as a traitor. I realized that reconciliation, should it ever happen, would have to be black-on-black as well as black-on-white and white-on-black.

He hoped he redeemed himself by mentoring elementary school children, but a ragged edge of personal guilt remained. He had a nice car, but he worried that his son would end up in the wrong community and possibly be shot; or that he would be stopped and humiliated by police who didn't think black boys legitimately drove nice cars. Like all African American parents, he had had to teach his son how to respond to racism to remain safe.

His last words also stayed with me. He was speaking about how gratified he felt to have brought together this collection on the African American experience when the expression on his face changed. "When I look at this material it saddens me terribly to see how black folk in this state and this city have been treated. On the other hand, it's uplifting to see resilience. People survived. This gives me hope I can survive, too."

"Survive?" I asked, surprised.

"Yes, we all went through it. Going to segregated schools; learning that if you went into a store you would be followed; knowing that if you tried on a hat, you had to buy it because the store wasn't going to keep a hat that had touched your skin. So, I look at the materials here and I think, 'We did not commit suicide or kill folks because of that.' It actually surprises me that we haven't had a higher suicide rate."

I haven't seen Sherman Pyatt since, but I learned that he subsequently authored a series of books on the black experience in Charleston. I am not surprised. His mission was to integrate the uneasy ghosts of the city's African American past into the mainstream history of his community. This effort would restore dignity, and it would help to underpin "survival."

President Bill Clinton's attempts at reconciliation didn't get very far. He took his political advisors' counsel and announced that the issue of an apology for slavery was essentially a press story that "was not on the minds of Americans." In this he was only partly correct: it was not on the minds of white Americans, but it *was* on the minds of black Americans. Two Gallop polls of the day indicated that 67 percent of whites were opposed to the idea of an apology and 65 percent of blacks were in favour. As for the President's "Initiative on Race," it suffered the same ignominious fate as other potentially contentious projects: knee-capped from the start, the commissioners were effectively forbidden to make policy recommendations. There was more. Towards the end of my Southern journey, I interviewed former Mississippi governor William Winter, who had sat on the commission. He argued that the Initiative had laid the basis for what would, he hoped, be a permanent effort to eliminate racism in America.

I pressed him. "Well," he said, "if some people wanted reparations for slavery, that was totally unrealistic politically."

"What about an apology?" I asked.

"Just words."

I was curious about what sort of discussions the commissioners might have had on the subject. He thought carefully, then replied, "Well, I don't recall that we had any wide-ranging discussion on that subject... We were debating what we thought were relevant subjects, not what happened a hundred years ago. I do think one of the most counterproductive things black people can do is let themselves wear a burden of victimization on their shoulders, because it reduces their ability to seize the opportunities of the present. I have heard a lot of black people say, 'Let's get on with it. Let's stop wallowing in the sloughs of the past.' And I say that to white folks too. 'Let's quit glorifying the past, let's quit refighting the civil war. Let it lie. Get on with it.'"

Senator Tony Hall had fared no better. His Congressional colleagues argued that the dead on the Civil War battlefields were apology enough, and that Abraham Lincoln had expressed the remorse of the nation in 1865. Hall had received mail on the topic of an apology, but again with a black versus white breakdown, with blacks in favour and whites opposed. We live, today, in a coarser era, thanks to the Donald Trump effect and the often-base milieu of social media, but when we met in the late 1990s, Senator Hall told me that, although he had received some supportive letters, he was "stunned" by the anger and racism that greeted his proposal, by the hate mail from people who bemoaned the end of slavery and thought that *they* should be receiving reparations.

When *Long Shadows* was published in the United States in June 2001, talk of apologies and reparations for slavery was still in the air. Bloomsbury Publishing sent me on a promotional tour, an exhausting inter-city dash from interview to interview, most of which felt rushed and *pro forma*. But not all. On the live, call-in shows one question surfaced frequently. In various guises, it was this: "Why should I worry about the legacy of slavery? My family came to America as immigrants long after the end of the Civil War. This doesn't concern me."

I suggested that, when we adopt a new country, we must also enter into and engage with its history, if the commonality of citizenship is to have a meaning. Many Americans espouse personal responsibility as an ideal—a fine conviction, but as a stand-alone belief without a related commitment to the public good, it mutates into rejection. If we are for ourselves alone, the space for empathy is reduced. An unfortunate individual becomes someone who didn't try hard enough; a group of unfortunates are just whiners. Collective responsibility—an admittedly difficult notion—is rejected, and the responsibility for slavery is left for people long dead to bear, not us.

A reluctance to visit the past also makes reconciliation even less likely. Among the responses to Senator Tony Hall's proposal for a formal apology for slavery was a striking comment from the syndicated black writer, Thomas Sowell. "Is looking backward a way to prepare for the future?" he asked.

I've thought a lot about Sowell's resonant question and the American belief in the future. The rhetoric of equal promise never subsides. Change will always come one day—even if it never does. I recall Martin Luther King's famous Washington speech in which he shared his aspirations: "I have a dream," he cried. His dream was one of equality. He believed in the power of the future as passionately as any other American, but he also faced the intractability of a history that many Americans do not want to address. To properly consider the legacy of slavery would require a collective agreement to reopen the past—to acknowledge the embarrassing fact that slavery underpinned the origins of a vaunted democracy, calling its very foundation into question.

FOLLOWING MY PROMOTION TOUR, I received a speaking invitation from a Washington D.C. synagogue. My visit was set for the weekend of September 22, 2001. The organizers did not rescind the invitation after the events of September 11.

I arrived in a dead city; virtually nothing moved except for the defiant Stars and Stripes that flew from almost every rooftop. There were few people in the streets and even fewer cars. My taxi passed by the White House. All was still, as though a thick blanket had dropped over the capital, smothering sound and life itself.

I half-expected to address an empty room, but a handful of hardy souls had turned up to hear me. I said it was a privilege to talk about *Long Shadows* in a city that had recently been a target of terror, because my book was about war and memory, about understanding the present by virtue of understanding the past. It was, I said, a book about how the narrative of history is deliberately shaped after times of crisis such as the one they had just experienced. I said that their country, and mine, was already at war with the terrorists, just days after the event, and that I wondered what national story would emerge from this shocking moment. I said that what we would eventually have to confront was not simply individuals, or groups, or even so-called rogue states that support unconscionable acts, but a complex set of ideas in the minds of other people about the way the world had evolved over the past decades. This would require us to understand "the other."

It was, I suppose, a strong message to deliver to a grieving audience, but I had done the same in an opinion piece for *The Globe and Mail* in the immediate aftermath of the attack, in which I also raised the issue of root causes—a still-taboo subject at that moment. But the Washington audience was receptive—possibly because I went on to talk about other places in the world where I had raised similar questions, or possibly because anyone who chose to leave the safety of their home that day was already primed to hear a possible alternative to rage over perceived wrongs.

Several months later, I received the following letter:

> June 14, 2002
>
> Dear Ms. Paris,
>
> I recently read your book, Long Shadows, and was inspired in an unusual way.
>
> Your analysis of the failed policies of some major countries of the world to adequately deal with their past history and the consequences of those failures moved me to create an initiative which may be of interest to you.
>
> In your book, you noted that significant progress had been made in restoring the breech between Germanic and Jewish people as a result of monuments and memorials being established throughout Germany. Recognizing the past in this way has served to bring healing. As an American, I was

> challenged to look at the slow progress that has occurred in healing the ethnic divide between black and white, a divide stemming from the institution of slavery.
>
> It came to me that possibly a monument, or memorial recognizing the contribution slaves made to the progress of our country might help further reconciliation in our nation.
>
> Subsequently, I spoke with Congressman Tony Hall from Ohio, Cliff Stearns from Florida and Eleanor Holmes Norton from the District of Columbia as well as a Presidential advisor, putting forth this idea. The outcome of my discussion has been very encouraging....

The author was Brett Fuller, president of the National Foundation for African American Heritage, pastor of Grace Covenant Church in Chantilly, Virginia, and chaplain to the Washington Redskins football team. In addition to Tony Hall (Democrat), he had already approached several members of Congress about his idea, including Cliff Stearns (Republican) and Eleanor Holmes Norton (Democrat). A Congressional resolution "proposing that a National Slave Memorial be erected in the shadow of the Lincoln Memorial" had been drafted. "This Slave Memorial would honor the sacrifice and contribution of all those who suffered under this institution. In doing so, it would serve to give some measure of dignity to these nameless people."

In his letter, Pastor Fuller invited me to a Congressional Press Conference to take place on June 19, 2002, at the Capitol Building in Washington. The purpose was to introduce the resolution to the public, and to encourage its passage through Congress. A day of lobbying, in other words.

The following Wednesday morning I was on a plane to Washington for a breakfast meeting at the Capitol. The plan, Pastor Fuller said, was to fan out across the offices of those members of Congress who were likely to be sympathetic to the initiative.

The meeting took place at the House Triangle at the north end of the Capitol Building. When I arrived, about twenty people were already seated on both sides of a long table. I was the only white person present—and thrilled that my work had inspired this project. In the room were three high-profile African American athletes: Darell Green, Mark Brunell, and Ken Harvey.

What has stayed in memory is the feel of that moment. A prayer followed breakfast, and when the large men with the famous names stood, the room fell still. The emotion was palpable. Was it possible that the longed-for national recognition of black suffering might be at hand? And might it lead to a beginning of reconciliation between the races?

We each received a list of the politicians we were to visit. Knowing I would be in Washington, I had made sure that Senator Tony Hall received a copy of *Long Shadows*.

He was waiting for me in his large, sunlit office, holding my book in his hand. He had just read my chapter on the legacy of slavery and the role he had personally attempted to play in rectifying wrongs. He talked to me about the failure of this previous effort. He talked about Pastor Fuller's initiative for a monument to the slaves on the Washington Mall. He sounded optimistic. He smiled encouragingly.

Then he waved my book in the air.

"What can we do?" he asked me.

He was asking *me*? Was this admirable man at the heart of the American political system apparently so bereft of ideas that he was asking the advice of a book author from another country? I inferred that he suspected the initiative might not go far.

The bill to create a monument on the Washington Mall was formally introduced on the same day, June 19, 2002, as the National Slave Memorial Act "to authorize the Secretary of the Interior to establish a memorial to slavery, in the District of Columbia." But any legislation intended "to acknowledge the fundamental injustice, cruelty, brutality, and inhumanity of slavery in the United States and the 13 American Colonies" was bound to be controversial, and not surprisingly, it failed. On January 7, 2003, the same wording was reintroduced into the first session of the 108th Congress as House Resolution 196. It failed again.

Brett Fuller didn't give up. In September 2002, he had written to say that the government of South Africa was seriously considering building a memorial like the one he had proposed in America. He was optimistic: the National Slave Memorial bill was still in the works, he told me, in the appropriations committee of Congress waiting for approval.

"Be encouraged," he told me. "Your thoughts can change the world."

I thanked him. I was also a realist—but happy to know that books still mattered.

Sixteen years later, in January 2018, I wrote Brett Fuller to ask what had become of his dream. To my consternation, he told me that a fundamental hindrance had been the lack of support he received from mainstream leaders in the African American community:

> Although the Congressional Black Caucus was largely in support of my initiative, and for that I am very grateful, the most prominent leaders in my community did very little to help. The National Slave Memorial was to be erected in the spirit of the Holocaust memorials you outlined in your book, that helped to heal Germany's ethnic wounds. I still hope something akin to what I have dreamed can be established soon, so that our nation can heal. Legislation can regulate conduct, but it cannot heal the heart or direct the soul. America needs to be healed...from her improper dehumanizing of an entire people....
>
> I wish I knew why I did not receive as much support from the African American community as I would've hoped. Unfortunately, I have no answers. African Americans find themselves at the greatest place of influence ever in our country. We hold more places of public office. We run more businesses. There are laws on the books protecting our rights of access. In short, this is arguably the most privileged African American generation in history. Still, things are not right. Why? Laws do not change culture, and they don't aid in the navigation of relationships. Racism (the institutional

> architecting of prejudice) can be enculturated even though it has been legislated against.

Nonetheless, he still had hope, he assured me.

At the end of my *Long Shadows* chapter on the legacy of slavery in America, I noted a speech by then-U.S. Secretary of State Madeleine Albright at a 1999 meeting in Berlin, after Germany had agreed to pay 10 billion Deutschmarks in reparations to the victims of the Second World War. Her words exposed a tragic blindness in the persistent idiom of her own country. They are worth quoting:

> ...Above all, I pay tribute to those who brought us here by insisting that hard questions be asked and answered about accountability for the terrible crimes committed more than half a century ago. This is the first serious initiative to acknowledge the debt owed to those whose labor was stolen or coerced during that time of outrage and shame. And make no mistake, that debt is huge. *For no human being should ever be treated as property, and no person can deny the dignity of another without bringing dishonor upon himself*...[italics mine, EP]
>
> Because if I have one message to convey this morning, it is this. This agreement...reflects a sense of moral responsibility that is absolutely essential to building the kind of...world in which we want our children to grow up. And it is critical to completing the unfinished moral business of the old century, before we enter the new.

MY RESEARCH ON "THE peculiar institution" and its aftermath in the United States had focused on the legacy of dehumanization, which was at the heart of slavery. The same legacy was true of my voyage to South Africa in 1996, just two years after the country voted itself into democracy.

As in the American slave era, dehumanization and oppression constituted the core of the apartheid system too, for, while never instituting a U.S-style slave system to control revolts, South Africa had enacted extreme measures to oversee every detail of black lives. Memorably, I would encounter the consequences of these policies at a meeting of the Truth and Reconciliation Commission in Lusikisiki in the Eastern Cape, a remote town in a distant corner of the former Transkei "homeland"—one of ten regions into which blacks, who had been deprived of their already second-class citizenship, were transferred, starting in 1970.

The Transkei was what Masha Gessen has called "a magical elsewhere," a place of imagined fears, and rumoured to be the real-world locus of Nadine Gordimer's 1981 novel *July's People.* In this story the dreaded apocalypse has arrived: black communists have come to destroy white civilization. A liberal white family escapes with their loyal servant, July, to his rural village. As the weeks pass, they sink into the seemingly unstructured life of the village, one slippery, irrevocable step at a time. Reading this book, I thought that Gordimer had conjured up a Conradian descent into the heart of darkness, giving shape to the primal fear of otherness from which no South African could escape.

In 1996, South Africa was still one of the world's most dangerous countries, and as a woman travelling alone I was apprehensive. Occasionally, my anxiety even amused me. In the port city of East London, strolling along the sandy shoreline of the blue-green Indian Ocean, I became suddenly aware of how alone I was. Since I was constantly travelling, no one knew my precise location at any given time, including Tom, who was lecturing somewhere in India and therefore of little potential help. I carried with me a first-generation cell phone, and on that day I entertained myself by thinking that, should I ever find myself in trouble, I needed only to politely excuse myself and dial emergency services while my assailant courteously waited.

The Transkei, as I have mentioned, had a particularly dangerous reputation. I had been informed many times about recklessly intrepid white women who had been murdered there. But I was going anyway. It would be my only chance to attend a session of the famed Truth and Reconciliation Commission.

Jabu, my driver (he was a policeman and a TRC commissioner, which was comforting), talked about the environment as we drove across stunningly beautiful terrain. Villages populated with round, mud-baked huts and thatched roofs perched on the cusps of grassy hills. The villages were not serviced, Jabu said. Women carried jugs of water from wells, and cholera was a frequent visitor. Each family tended its plot of "mealies," or maize. Children, who were obviously not in school, tended cattle, as had Nelson Mandela, who was born here.

Jabu talked about violence, before and after 1994. He told me there *was* no policing in the townships, just a war of whites against blacks, and sometimes blacks against blacks. "Life was worthless," he said. "Violence was an outlet for rage, and now the habits persist."

I was billeted in one of Lusikisiki's only middle-class homes, one owned by the town's most successful retail proprietor. In *Long Shadows* I told of the special dinner I was served at his family table—chicken, potatoes, rice, and pumpkin, followed by stewed peaches—and how I unknowingly earned the appreciation of my hosts by eating cooked "mealie-pap" with my fingers as they did. I also learned I was the first white person ever to enter their home.

But it was the TRC hearing the next day that burned grooves into my memory. It was held in a large new building that lacked electricity. A generator sputtered, constantly threatening to break down. The participants arrived hours late, by bus and on the back of trucks. They were elderly (this TRC session concerned a murderous clash that took place three decades earlier); they were poor; they wore ill-fitting clothes and shoes without socks; and their shoulders were hunched with tension.

Moments from that day flash across my mind as I write these words. One is the intimidation on the faces of the witnesses as they faced the ANC commissioners, black people like themselves but educated city people from another world. "I thought only white people could ask lawyers questions," a beaming, toothless man told me later.

One by one they were called up to the stage to take the oath. The first witness, a strong-looking individual, recounted his story of humiliation at having to wear a pass around his neck, and of the day when he and others tried to rally the government for education for their children. "The magistrate told us we were baboons, and baboons didn't go to the parliament in Cape Town."

A silence blanketed the room, broken by muffled sobs. For this man had spoken aloud about the dehumanizing heart of apartheid: the crushing mortification, the shame.

Many others spoke that day, and I have a particular memory of a woman whose boy had been arrested at age eighteen and had never returned. She begged for the return of his "bones," so she could give him a proper burial. She said she would be able to forgive the perpetrators if they would only show remorse; if they would only show her where his remains lay. Remorse. That word…which Serge Klarsfeld too had used.

Later, we all walked into the countryside to visit the site of the event under investigation. Children tending cattle stared at me in consternation. Who was I? What was I? A white presence would always be dubious in this remote place; a female white presence was unfathomable.

IF DEHUMANIZATION LIVED AT the heart of apartheid, the aftermath of the system, following the elections of 1994, created problems for many whites. In The *End of Days* I had written, regarding forcible religious conversions, that human beings cannot slough off their inner selves the way a snake sheds its skin. That same truth now disrupted the lives of South African whites, who had been indoctrinated into the ideology of apartheid since childhood. Perhaps their dismay resembled that of American slaveholders and their Confederate supporters, who had been socialized to accept slavery before the creed of universal freedom was imposed on them by the victorious army of the North.

That post-apartheid South Africa avoided civil war was a combination of luck and strategy—the latter being the signing of political accords and a timely Truth and Reconciliation Commission. The Commission had plenty of problems and plenty of enemies, but it did help to deter violence. Today, it appears evident that truth trumped reconciliation in the equation, for the latter has not happened at a level of any depth. Profound economic inequalities persist in South Africa, which could become a touchstone for future trouble. But a fragile peace has nonetheless endured in that country since the fall of apartheid, an outcome which some with a religious bent might call miraculous.

In the United States, the myth of the "Lost Cause" of Confederacy—the steadfast belief that the pro-slavery cause the Confederate States had championed was both valiant and just—continues to boast a small minority of supporters a century and a half after the end of the Civil War, the most visible example being the white supremacy members of the mob that on January 6, 2021, assailed the Washington Capitol and introduced Confederate flags into the institutional heart of America's democracy. In South Africa, the 1994 election successfully nipped much of this in the bud (at any rate visibly), as did the subsequent TRC, but what the commissioners at the TRC meeting that I attended in Lusikisiki were engaged in were obvious efforts to reconstruct a new national narrative for blacks. The body had been tasked with effecting national healing, but the story they told was one only of epic ANC heroism.

In response to the woman who begged for the "bones" of her child, one commissioner had made a stock speech: "Your children sacrificed their lives as heroes," he told the roomful of survivors. "But they would not have been willing to do so had you not brought them up to want to liberate their people. All South Africa salutes them. Their blood watered the plants of liberation."

His off-tone words were cringe-worthy, but I understood the motivation: victims and perpetrators would have to go on living together, and a dominant narrative would be useful, even if overblown or even untrue. I had already begun to grasp how powerful myths served as tools for reshaping post-conflict societies: Charles de Gaulle's longstanding falsehood about France's all-encompassing resistance to the Nazi occupiers was one blatant example. In the case before me, the mother merely looked shell-shocked. I sympathized with her, and I asked myself whether she had *really* raised her son to "liberate his people," or whether she might not in fact have begged him to stay out of politics and save his life.

In the case of the "white tribe," the national myth had been diametrically different. "We were taught to hate," said police-warrior Paul Erasmus, who had served under the brutal Eugene de Kock (also known as "Prime Evil"), an apartheid-era police colonel, torturer, and assassin. "We understood our battle was just. The blacks were satanic, godless, uncivilized, and uncontrolled in their impulses. And they were going to swamp us."

Nowhere were the myths of apartheid more visible than in the capital city of Pretoria. Museums are the locus of established cultural narratives, which is why they are so central to memory, and so often controversial. Here, in the Police Museum of Pretoria, the entire history of the apartheid state was introduced through the lens of legalized oppression, as expressed in a caption framed in the familiar language of race fear. "The aim of these enemies was the violent overthrow of the government," I read, "replacing it with a socialist African state in which whites would have no political rights." One room featured a selection of medieval-style torture instruments alongside horrifying mock-ups of actual murders of blacks and whites. These were accompanied by glass bottles of pickled intestines, hair, and bones. In yet another display, a larger-than-life black man wielded an axe over a terrified white couple cringing in a car. There was more, but the reader will get the picture.

The mythicized origin story of Afrikaners was also visible elsewhere in the city at the Voortrekker Monument, the shrine to Afrikaner nationalism that sits majestically atop a hill. If the TRC represented the "new" South Africa, this was the "old." The walls of the shrine were decorated with a sculpted wall frieze, a heroic configuration signifying the foundational story of "The Great Trek," culminating, the visitor is informed, in the creation of a "people." Other mythologized history followed. But the crowning glory of the monument, a frieze known as "The Divine Intervention," recounted the 1838 rout of several thousand Zulus by a few hundred white Christians. Attaching God to history is a perennial winner in the battle of competing war memories; all the same, the Voortrekker Monument left nothing to chance. Below one of the wall sculptures, a part of the floor had been opened to reveal a lower level, where a bronze inscription lay exposed. It read: *Ons vir jou, Suid-Afrika* (We for you, South Africa). Every December 16, on the anniversary of a critical battle, the sun penetrated an angled shaft in the ceiling and God's own light illuminated the plaque.

As the ANC took power and the TRC began its hearings, white South Africans responded in their own way to the unprecedented crumbling of certainties. There was denial, naturally, but also strong dismay over displacement. And shame in some parts, as in the case of Willy Verwoerd, the grandson of Hendrik Verwoerd, the architect of apartheid. I don't quite remember how I sleuthed Willy out, but we met one sunny afternoon in a café in Cape Town. He was a thin, frail-looking young man of thirty-two, an active member of the ANC, and a researcher for the TRC.

He had travelled a hard road. As a graduate student in Holland, Willy had written a thesis on his beloved grandfather's term as prime minister, but when the shocking truth about his personal lineage became known to him, he joined the ANC. His family immediately disowned him. They accused him of joining a black power organization of terrorists and communists. Willy knew he could never slough off his name or heritage, so he chose what he called "reconciliation." This meant acknowledging that he was "a white South African, a Christian, and a Verwoerd," but with new priorities.

Willy Verwoerd was South Africa's counterpart to Gottfried Wagner, the great-grandson of Richard. Like Willy, Gottfried too had joined "the enemy." And Willy never ended his personal struggle. In 2019 he published a powerful memoir, *Verwoerd: My Journey through Family Betrayals,* again analogously to Gottfried Wagner, who wrote *Twilight of the Wagners: The Unveiling of a Family's Legacy.*

Among the disenchanted white South Africans I encountered, the saddest, angriest, and most confused was Dirk Coetzee, a man whose personification of the sordid depths of the system took my breath away. As I travelled through the country, I had begun to think I would never understand apartheid, or the "new" South Africa, or the TRC, until I learned more about the security police, the savage law enforcement agency that was in place from 1913 to 1994, the year of the transformational elections. "Prime Evil" Eugene de Kock was in prison, but Dirk Coetzee was at home in Pretoria waiting to hear the results of his TRC amnesty application. I discovered his address easily, and somewhat to my surprise he agreed to meet me.

Several years earlier, Coetzee had exposed the existence of a state-authorized, security-police death camp called Vlakplaas, near Pretoria, where, from 1979 until 1993, captured ANC and other black activists were tortured and murdered. "I was at the heart of the whore," Coetzee publicly confessed. He subsequently fled to London, where he narrowly escaped an assassination attempt before returning to South Africa in 1997 to appeal to the TRC for amnesty.

My meeting with Dirk Coetzee stands out as one of the strangest and most startling of my career. His house was hidden behind high gates. Vicious-looking guard dogs howled as I approached. (Almost all whites had massive gates, walls, and guard dogs with bared teeth who tried to leap at the passers-by. Some also displayed a sign, featuring a shiny black revolver, that warned: "Trespassers Will Be Eaten.") Coetzee had more reason to worry than most, although his perceived threats emanated not from blacks, but from fellow whites. They thought he had betrayed them by spilling the beans on security police activities and seeking amnesty from the TRC.

He is fifty-three, fit looking, and to my consternation, already shivering with tension before our conversation even begins. He tells me he is furious with the white political establishment, whom he accuses of lying and pretending not to know what took place under their jurisdiction, and furious that the ANC did not help him after he risked all by exposing state crimes. "I told the truth because I believe we can only bury the past if we know what we're burying!" he shouts at me. Then he explains what lived at "the heart of the whore," as he had put it.

This was our verbatim conversation. It was crucial to my understanding then and it remains so now.

> **DC:** The security police were a family, an elite, and we were fighting the enemy of the family because they were supporting the right to vote and freedom of expression and all that. I mean, they were communists and terrorists, and we were the last Christian outpost on the southern tip of Africa, and we had to fight the onslaught. That's what we were taught from the beginning. If you were born into apartheid, it was everywhere, in government and the church and the family, and preached as justified and right. And if there is no independent media and everything is carefully monitored, then there is only one point of view and anyone who differs is crazy.
>
> **EP:** You [whites] were so cruel in the way you killed people.
>
> **DC:** Absolutely. It was a war. It was no big thing for me to eliminate the enemy. We abducted them and interrogated them in different ways. We gave them electric shocks or smothered them or hammered them on the head. We shot them, then we put them in a fire of tires and wood and burned them to ashes.
>
> [He pauses to peer at me closely.] You know, seven bodies will take about seventy-two hours to burn, but the hands and the feet and the head go more quickly.
>
> **EP:** Hmm.
>
> **DC:** After that we dumped the ashes into the river, but while the bodies were burning, we had a barbeque.
>
> **EP:** You what?

DC: Sure. Every Afrikaner carries a barbeque in the boot of his car at all times. It's part of the culture...It's all kind of hard to explain now...

I stared. He looked away from me.

He refused to come to the site of the Vlakplaas camp, so I hired a driver and went there alone. My black driver was frightened by my destination. A caretaker on the abandoned property showed me the places Dirk Coetzee had described: the river, an old willow tree whose branches protected a large stone burning-place flanked by a barbeque, where adjacent odours would have mingled. Killing, burning, and cooking—all in the name of "Western Civilization."

IN ADDITION TO THE names and the stories I have written about in these pages, and in much more detail in *Long Shadows*, I met South Africans at every level of society, from Desmond Tutu (who confided that he wanted to be remembered as a man who knew how to cry), to black and white academics and journalists, to ANC government officials striving to create a racially and religiously diverse country of citizenship (The Rainbow Nation, they called it), to ordinary whites and blacks of both conservative and liberal persuasions. But the last individual I want to introduce into this narrative of my experience in South African is Nkosinathi Biko, the son of the murdered founder of the anti-apartheid Black Consciousness Movement, Steve Biko, who remains a hero to millions of his compatriots and to others around the world. Biko was already a hero. He was the first to suggest that the struggle for freedom and interracial peace might be predicated upon black self-esteem. This was a radical idea in a country where blacks were called baboons and chimpanzees.

Nkosinathi wanted to meet me at the flamboyant Hyatt Hotel in the outskirts of Johannesburg, where I was staying in a local bed and breakfast. The Hyatt was as white as a bedsheet. While waiting for him in the lobby, I watched expensively dressed men and women, the latter also flashing expensive jewellery. He would be the only black in that space; I'd have no trouble identifying him.

He was twenty-six years old, slim, serious, and quiet-spoken; and our conversation took place on one of the hotel lobby couches in a room that had almost certainly never been witness to what he told me that day. His father had been killed when he was just seven, he said, but Steve Biko had influenced his life in memorable ways.

Nkosinathi was raised in the black township of King William's Town near the port city of East London. His township was, he said, separated from white South Africa by just a kilometre. That short distance incorporated a river, and "no one could have imagined on one side what was going on in the other." Violence. Charges of being a spy. Tire burnings. Daily beatings. Weekly burials of youngsters whose bodies cluttered the streets.

"So now all this is being reported, and whites think that South Africa is suddenly violent," he said in a voice that was a whisper. "That's not true. This has been the case for a long time. *We* knew about the security-police death squads and the camps they operated, because the survivors told us. There were things the people on the other side of our township could never have imagined, even in their nightmares."

He was saved, he told me, by a steadfast, loving mother, by becoming "numb" emotionally—and by the gift of education. He had a degree in economics and wanted to work in business. Normality was what he sought, in accordance with his belief that blacks would only gain real influence through economic power—until, that is, there was some redistribution of income and a measure of equality. He was also saved by knowing that his father had died for something, not for nothing. This, he said, had become his strength.

But first he would have to "wriggle away" from his famous father and become his own person. He was trying to raise money for a charitable foundation to ensure that the memory of Steve Biko would not slide into forgetfulness as the liberation struggle faded over the years. Only then would his obligation be paid.

Before we separated, I brought out my copy of T.R.H. Davenport's standard history of South Africa, and I showed him what the author had written about his father: "Steve Biko was as tragic a martyr to the cause of his people's emancipation as any person in the history of South Africa, black or white." Nkosinathi's eyes brimmed with tears as he copied down the words.

In 2021 a Google search found almost 3,000 entries on the younger Biko. He had created the Steve Biko Foundation he spoke to me about, just a year after our encounter, becoming its chief executive officer and a founding member of the board of trustees. His business career had also prospered. In 2018 he was named chairman of the board of Ogilvy South Africa, one of the largest marketing communications networks in the world. He also lectured internationally about his famous father. I watched a video of a recent interview with him on the Internet. Now middle-aged, he remained fluent, serious, and quiet-spoken. Significantly, I thought, he told his interviewer that although he was only seven when his father was murdered, the elder Biko had had time to teach him about the importance of personal agency.

Nkosinathi Biko had found the normalcy he said he craved. Both his foundation and his lecturing were a counterpoint to the persistence of violent crime in his country, where economic inequalities still divide the population.

NINETEEN NINETY-SEVEN WAS A busy research time for me. Although I was just one year into the *Long Shadows* project, the originating publisher in Germany was on my tail to finish quickly. I'd started, unexpectedly, with Japan, and had had the privilege of writing that chapter at the Banff Centre for the Arts in summer 1996, with Don Obe, one of Canada's finest editors. By early spring I had finished my preparations for South Africa, arriving there in April. In the fall, from my base in Paris I had branched out to Germany and then Bordeaux. But there was one other European region I knew I had to enter: the rump states of the former Yugoslavia, then just two years out from a genocidal civil war that had upended the region. Here was a raw land where the past bled into the present, a not-to-be-missed chance to seek out the underlying shifts in culture and politics that had led to a late twentieth-century tragedy in which 100,000 people had died and more than 2.5 million were displaced.

As I prepare to recount the story of my travels in ex-Yugoslavia, just weeks have passed since the bloodied finale to Donald Trump's U.S. presidency, when home-grown insurrectionists breached the U.S. Capitol. The event reminded me of my journey through Serbia, Croatia and Bosnia, the three countries of ex-Yugoslavia: a comparison between the world's proudest, most powerful democracy and a beleaguered ex-communist backwater that would have been unimaginable at the time.

One of the similarities between the two was public lying. For Mr. Trump, this appeared to be a lifetime habit. Part of the tragedy of the former Yugoslavia was a similar perpetration of lies, especially those that came from the mouth of a man most people outside the former Eastern Bloc state have never heard of, yet he was considered by people in the region as the individual most responsible for the Bosnian war. He was Dobrica Ćosić, the most famous writer in the Yugoslav Federation, and these were his words: "Lying is a form of our patriotism, and is evidence of our innate intelligence. We lie in a creative, imaginative, and inventive way."

I shall come back to my meeting with him, since lying is at the root of state fragmentation in both places.

Two years after the 1995 Dayton Accords ended military hostilities, my travels throughout ex-Yugoslavia still felt perilous. I was in Belgrade, and needed to get to Sarajevo, so I accepted an invitation to travel there by car—a terrifying nighttime trip in the company of Serb members of PEN, the international writers' organization, who hoped to meet with their Bosnian colleagues for the first time since the war. We spoke hardly a word all night as the driver narrowly circumnavigated known hot spots of Bosnian Serb marauders. Finally, he was foiled by a roadblock illuminated by yellow fire. Who was it? No one in the car breathed. Luckily, it was members of the NATO peacekeeping force.

Upon arrival in Sarajevo, I accepted an invitation to stay in the ruined apartment of one of the men. As we looked out his window at the destroyed city, he spoke to me about his suicidal thoughts. I asked him how it had happened that once-friendly neighbours were able to kill one another. He had replied that you need only repeat that someone is your enemy and that *they* hate *you* often enough and the contagion will spread.

My travels out of the city also included a near-death experience in a Croat village that my Sarajevan (therefore Muslim) guide had said was safe, where the two of us finished up encircled by men in pick-up trucks who pointed guns at our heads. We were, I was told, saved by my Canadian passport which they demanded to see.

My travels included interviews with many others, including a famous Belgrade dramatist who literally shrieked:

> *Anyone* can create a quarrel where there are people with different backgrounds. I can do it in my theatre in five minutes if I want to. If a Serb in a Bosnian village is angry about a cow, and if he is armed, of *course* he can kill his Muslim neighbour! You start the propaganda, and prejudice grows until people are contaminated. You ask someone why he cannot live with his neighbour, and you realize that he has *heard* he cannot live with his neighbour.... And now we have four million exiled people, and I don't know how many dead. And for what? For this crazy idea of Greater Serbia these power-mongers have killed our country! Killed our past!

I also wanted to meet Dobrica Ćosić, for people everywhere told me that his role in the tragedy of ex-Yugoslavia was pivotal. Ćosić's novels were said to dramatize the mystical Serbian "spirit," or "soul," and were taught to millions of schoolchildren. He was a powerbroker, a former political figurehead, an intellectual in the European tradition of literary figures with ideas to propagate, and an erstwhile dissident from the Tito regime who had managed to remain safe.

Ćosić had taken bold exception to Tito's decision in 1974 to reduce Serb control over the province of Kosovo by granting greater autonomy to the Muslim Albanian Kosovars who shared the territory with Kosovo Serbs. He was a nationalist—a political stance that had long preceded the advent of Communism—and in Serb mythology, Kosovo was the site of the birth of the Serb nation, which was said to have taken place in 1389, when Prince Lazar of Serbia was beheaded by the Ottoman Turks. The actual historical event was, it seems, a routine military skirmish, including the beheading (if beheading there was), but according to the story it put an end to medieval Serb independence. What it initiated was a deep sense of Serb victimhood, and the beginnings of a propaganda war between the Serb Orthodox Church and Islam that would be episodically revived over the centuries whenever some grievance triggered an outbreak of nationalism.

When Josip Broz Tito died in 1980, leaving a political void, the Association of Serbian Writers had sparked a public battle for what they called "democratic free speech" to voice their criticisms of their erstwhile leader—for without the repeal of Tito-era censorship they would be unable to promote their own new, nationalist programme. But it wasn't new; it was a revival of the older ethnic nationalism that had intermittently marked Serb history, including a drive for a "Greater Serbia" which ultimately meant gobbling up land in Bosnia and Croatia and reasserting Serb dominance in Kosovo.

The writers declared a "crisis" of identity. They held rallies, in which they emphasized the "Afro-Asian" birthrate of Albanian Kosovars, who were Muslim; and they spoke of the Serb "spirit" and "essence," which they contrasted with that of the "wild animals" (Albanian Kosovars) who were their enemies. Finally, in 1986, in the infamous "Memorandum of the Serbian Academy of Arts and Sciences," they depicted Serbs as the most oppressed group in Yugoslavia, while accusing Kosovo Albanians of raping Serb women, beating nuns, and perpetrating genocide through a policy of fast population growth. Some Academy members accused the Albanians of murdering newborn Serb children in their hospital cribs—a classic canard that recalled the medieval blood-libel against the Jews.

The blood-libel myth is resilient, because children are the symbolic future of the "race." The victimization of innocents is thus a shortcut to the purveyors' underlying message that their group is threatened with eradication. Variations have been repeated across time and cultures, including, more recently, the mad theory of "pizzagate," which falsely claimed in 2016 that prominent Democratic Party officials, including Hillary Clinton and her campaign chair, were running a child sex-trafficking ring out of a Washington, D.C. pizzeria.

The only solution to the dire situation, argued Dobrica Ćosić, along with the authors, journalists, academics, pundits, and other pontificators that he led, would be "the territorial unity of the Serbian people," which meant a takeover of the entire territory of Yugoslavia. And that, of course, meant war.

The Memorandum of the Serbian Academy of Arts and Sciences caught the eye of a communist apparatchik named Slobodan Milošević, an opportunist with an eye to the main chance. With Yugoslavia disintegrating, Titoism dying, and the fear that deep poverty might erupt into civic disorder, "the Serb nation" was an attractive hook to hang power on. As it happened, Milošević was so grateful to Ćosić for laying the groundwork that in 1992 he made him the figurehead president of the Federal Republic of Yugoslavia. Though it only lasted a year; he impeached him in 1993.

Belgrade was bone-chilling and grey in November 1997. Bosnian-Serb war veterans missing limbs begged on the sidewalks. No one bestowed a glance. Although the region had once been famed for the delicacy of its dishes, there was little available on the long menu in the restaurant of the hotel where I was staying—and few patrons, other than a group of drunken youths from Pale shouting nationalist slogans. The only visible exception to the general misery was the occasional Mercedes honking away in traffic, or a well-coiffed woman draped lavishly in furs. The black market was the way to make money, and the family of Slobodan Milošević was reputed to be the richest of the rich.

I had been told that Dobrica Ćosić didn't ordinarily give interviews, but that he was interested in my subject, which I had described through an intermediary as the making of national identity. Thus began my encounter with the man who valued lies as "evidence of our patriotism and innate intelligence." Not since my interview with Klaus Barbie's lawyer, Jacques Vergès—a man of the law who rhapsodized about the beauty of violence—had I encountered a person with such a disquieting worldview.

We met in his office in the architecturally magnificent (but now rundown) Serbian Academy of Sciences. Ćosić was then in his seventies, white-haired, solid, and pugnacious: he glared at me menacingly before we began, clearly hoping to intimidate, and I noted with interest that my young interpreter's hands were shaking. Because he is central to my story about the power of propaganda, I shall quote directly from our interview:

> **EP:** You are one of the major interpreters of this country. What do you see when you examine its history?
>
> **DC:** I see that human fate has two characteristics: first, one's family environment, and second, the larger history of the nation. In the twentieth century, historical destiny was the crucial one in determining what would happen because we live in an environment where history is alive and still happening today.... If our past history is alive and unresolved, it is because we have not developed our own national state, or a sufficient sense of nationhood to fulfil our destiny.
>
> **EP:** Why is the nation state, as you conceive of it, necessary?
>
> **DC:** I don't mean the nation state in the ethnic sense, but as a civic society.... We do not want to exclude the multi-ethnic community. In the war we have just come through, we fought for one state—one unified state of the southern Slav nations. The nation state does not have to mean an ethnic or cleansed state, the way the Croats meant it!

EP: Historians say, from the evidence, that Serbia had a very strong position in the Yugoslav Federation, but you deny this.

DC: Ha! Serbia had the most important geographical position...but we did not have the most important role.

EP: In 1987 you made speeches in which you claimed that Serbia was threatened by its neighbours in the Federation. What were your grounds?

DC: Yes, it was threatened, but indirectly. Since the 1970s, when Kosovo became a semi-autonomous region constitutionally, Serbs from inner Serbia did not have the same rights...

EP: Since you are interested in history and identity, it must concern you when the past is manipulated for political purposes. Did that happen here?

DC: Generally speaking, Serbian history is pro-liberation and pro-democratic, but some politicians and other leaders did misuse the past.

EP: Were your own writings and speeches used or misused?

DC: Certainly not! There is not a sentence or a word that is not democratic in any of my twenty books.

EP: All the same, you are certainly aware that many people draw a direct line between your public utterances in the late 1980s and the subsequent war in Bosnia. Do you acknowledge any connection between your work and the growth of a less innocent nationalism in the country?

DC: Even Christianity, a religion of love, has sometimes provoked hatred, but Jesus Christ cannot be held responsible for the Inquisition...Not that I am comparing myself to Christ!

EP: What are the consequences, now that the war in Bosnia is over?

DC: They are deep and tragic. Despite all the blood that was shed for a unified state, we are left without a Fatherland. As a nation, we are ruined.

EP: What future do you see for your country, Mr. Ćosić?

DC: Only darkness.

I have transcribed this interview for several reasons. First, as an illustration of the "patriotic, creative lie," which was widespread, as he had indicated. In her book *The Culture of Lies*, the Croatian author Dubravka Ugrešić had written: "It seems that this culture of lies is something that the small nations of Yugoslavia created long ago.... Lying, like dying, has become a normal state."

Given his many speeches and writings, which are available on the record, Dobrica Ćosić's statement that the intent of "Greater Serbia" was to create a civic society composed of happy multi-ethnic citizens didn't quite match reality.

Second, his reference to Serb victimhood (at the hands of Albanian Kosovars), a lie he had employed to unhook his compatriots from the multicultural creed of Titoism and relink them to an older thread of ethnic nationalism, confirmed what had been his central appeal to the credulous. (In reality, Albanian Kosovars, who were statistically among the poorest, most deprived people in Europe, made unlikely Goliaths.)

Third, his self-description as a democrat was strikingly at odds with the reality of what he had introduced: classic fascism—defined as a political philosophy, movement, or regime that elevates the nation, and often race, above the individual, and is characterized by centralized, autocratic rule under a dictatorial leader.

Writing these words, I see disturbing parallels in the present-day United States that would have been imaginable in 1997 when I interviewed Dobrica Ćosić. That public lies are now so readily swallowed in the rich and powerful western democracy of America is testimony, in my view, to our innate susceptibility to propaganda, whatever our political system. Although their cultural environments were very different, Donald Trump and Dobrica Ćosić employ strikingly similar rhetoric as they claim victimization by "the other," be that other "elites" or "globalists" (a well-known code word for Jews) or "Mexican rapists" (Trump) or overpopulation-threatening Albanian Kosovars (Ćosić). And each reached a very large audience.

Of all the people I met in the former Yugoslavia, one of the most interesting was Miloš Vasić, a founder of the independent Belgrade weekly, *Vreme*. It was to Vasić that the international media turned for a truthful report on the war in Bosnia. *Vreme* had people in the field, so they knew what was really happening.

He downed a hefty glass of slivovitz as we began our interview, which may explain why he said the things he did. Alcohol coupled with the fact that we were alone (he spoke excellent English) may have loosened his tongue a little. Beyond telling me about the war—including his having seen the Bosnian concentration camps, and his having publicly shown that the same faked pictures of the dead (some of them dredged up from the Second World War) were being used by all sides—he also spoke personally about his own life. He told me his wife had left him because he wouldn't follow her out of the country to safety. There was, he said, a "band-of-brothers" code that forbade him from leaving the journalistic front line. He also said this: "The most endangered 'ethnic group' in the whole of the former Yugoslavia was unarmed civilians, whatever their so-called nationality. They were the victims. And the aggressor was whoever was attacking them."

He said that the role of the Serb intelligentsia was "one of the greatest disappointments of my life," and he pointed directly to Dobrica Ćosić, whom he called "utterly despicable." "You have to understand," he added, "that what was left over from the communist state was the total obedience of the intellectuals. So, when the bugle sounded, they were there to serve—to prod people with their warmongering, their speeches, their jingoism. The same half-baked lazy scientists and journalists, the same untalented poets, the same superficial and half-literate fiction-writers joined the Serbian national cause with as little sincerity as they had joined the communist cause before that. You have a whole parasitic social class that just changed one ideology for another. Where was the "history" in their nationalism, you ask? There was none. It was just old-style propaganda."

"I am ashamed," he blurted out.

"Ashamed as a Serb?"

"No, I am ashamed as someone who has been living with all these people for decades. If you want to know, my answer is that I am ashamed as a human being."

I suppose he never imagined that anything written by a visiting Canadian author would ever see the light of day in Serbia, but it did. In 2003, *Long Shadows* was translated into the Bosnian-Serbian-Croatian language (the same language, despite nationalist denials), published by Prometej Publishers in Croatia and distributed throughout the territory. The primary launch took place in Zagreb, where I was formally presented to President Stjepan Mesić in a ceremony that flattered, amused, and perplexed me.

The president's offices were in Tito's former palace—I later learned that Tito had identical palaces built around the country so he could always feel at home—with wide outer doors leading to a royal, red-carpeted staircase. I walked up the stairs alone. Only the trumpets were missing. An aide waited at the top. Once there, I pivoted right, where, in the middle of another room with similarly wide entrance doors, I saw the man himself facing me. As instructed, I walk towards him, we shook hands, and I was invited to sit down beside him. Also present were my publisher, the interpreter, an aide scribbling notes, and the beaming Canadian ambassador to Croatia.

I had no idea why my book had occasioned this reception—until I learned that President Mesić had earlier testified as a protected witness in The Hague, at the International Tribunal for the Former Yugoslavia trial of a Serb officer charged with committing war crimes in Bosnia. It seemed that I and my book had arrived at just the right time for a photo op, which we both enjoyed.

The subsequent Belgrade book launch couldn't have been more different. Since my earlier visit in 1997, there had been a major shift in the thinking of the anti-Slobodan Milošević intelligentsia, including Miloš Vasić; the prevailing narrative now was that Serbs were victims of the war and of the West. (The NATO bombing of Belgrade in 1999 was a determining factor in this change.)

Book launches in the territory followed a certain pattern. Several people sat at a long table on a raised stage in an auditorium—the author, of course, the publisher, and others who were to speak about the work. I was seated at the centre of the table. To my right was the interpreter, whose job it was to whisper into my ear her translation of what was being said. To my left sat Miloš Vasić. To his left sat a historian, the head of the Serbian Archives.

Perhaps I should have heeded a warning about what was about to happen before the event began. "I remember you," Vasić had said with an ironic grin as we headed for the stage. "I felt desperate then. Now I don't give a shit."

After introductions, the historian-archivist began to speak. She talked and she talked, for thirty minutes, then forty, about Serb history and how I had it all wrong. Then it was Vasić's turn. He told the audience that I was "anti-Serb," and that I believed in "collective guilt." He couldn't say that I had lied, although he probably would have liked to: he knew I had taped our conversation.

People began to leave the room in conspicuous ways.

Finally, it was my turn to speak, and I had to decide on the spot whether to continue or to march off the stage. I glanced at Tom, who was seated in the front row. He looked stricken; he didn't have the benefit of an instantaneous translation, but the tone of what was taking place was unmissable. I made a quick decision to ignore my antagonists and carry on, but no sooner did I start to speak than Vasić and the archivist began to talk and laugh loudly in an attempt to drown me out. When the spectacle was mercifully over, the audience and my adversaries disappeared to drink slivovitz downstairs, leaving me alone with the embarrassed interpreter, the woman who had invited me, the Canadian ambassador to Serbia, and my loyal spouse.

Had Miloš Vasić seen the book in advance? I assume so; it was out in translation, and he was on the stage to discuss it. Ten years earlier he had risked his life to write and speak the truth. Now, in his own words, he "didn't give a shit," and he was clearly ashamed of his published remarks, since he had since then adopted the view that the West was anti-Serb.

It also occurred to me that what had taken place might not be unfamiliar here: that this was how communism had operated in the former Yugoslavia and elsewhere. By seizing control of a situation, you undermine the legitimacy of your opponent even before she expresses a view, and if she does speak, you make sure she isn't heard over the din.

I haven't been back to the former Yugoslavia since 2004, but nothing I have read suggests that reconciliation between the formerly warring entities has occurred. On the contrary, there are reports that political factionalism in Bosnia is growing worse. Much remains unchanged in the minds of many people since the wars of the 1990s. Many people still admire nationalist leaders who have been found guilty of war crimes. Until this changes, an uneasy peace will rule, until it ceases to do so.

THE TWENTIETH CENTURY WAS nearing its end, and so was my five-year-long search to uncover how history can be packaged and shaped for national consumption, and whose interests are served. It was time to return to origins, to that long-ago undergraduate class in the philosophy of history where I first learned that what I had thought of as fixed, irrefutable facts about the past could be interpreted, and not always in good faith. It was time to reconsider my inadvertent discovery of Nazi atrocities at Natzweiler-Struthof. It felt right to circle back to the Holocaust as my work for *Long Shadows* drew to a close.

I had struggled with the psychological "why" of what happened between 1933 and 1945, but also with the cultural and political trajectory whereby A led to B, and B to a fatal C. Now I wanted to explore the *postwar* history of the Holocaust, including the role it continued to play in Jewish life, and the internecine battles over whose voice should dominate the narrative. "Who Will Own the Holocaust?" is what I called the new section in the book.

Among the issues that stayed with me long after the publication of *Long Shadows* was the troubling story of the creation of the United States Holocaust Memorial Museum in Washington, D.C., possibly one of the most problematic in postwar museum-planning history. While it is true that all museums inevitably craft cultural narratives and are therefore a key item in the creation of historical memory, I had visited Holocaust exhibitions that did a much better job than others in telling a balanced story. The most successful, in my opinion, was the superb Topography of Terror Museum in Berlin, symbolically situated at the former site of the major Nazi institutions. I had seen museums that failed to present an unbiased, or even a complete narrative, such as the Hiroshima Peace Museum, which "forgot" to include Japanese Second World War crimes (it has since been modified for the better), or the Budapest History museum, where the story of the state-authorized deportations of half a million Hungarian Jews in the final hours of the Second World War sat in a distant third place, behind the narrative of the occupying Ottoman Turks in the sixteenth and seventeenth centuries and the communists in the twentieth.

The appalling Police Museum in Pretoria, which recirculated conspiratorial apartheid myths about Blacks, was in a class by itself; as was the Afrikaner Voortrekker Monument in Pretoria, which was dedicated to the purportedly heroic exploits of a blessed community of forebears. But to my knowledge there wasn't a more poignant example of quarrelling narratives than those that collided during the planning stage of the U.S. Holocaust Memorial Museum, as detailed by Edward T. Linenthal in his 1995 book, *Preserving History: The Struggle to Create America's Holocaust Museum*.

I sometimes visualize what happened there as a theatre piece with a plot and a cast of characters, each of whom was vying to be director. The setting was Washington, D.C. in November 1978, when then-president Jimmy Carter founded the President's Commission on the Holocaust. Its mandate was to create an institution that would inform and educate.

The principal cast members were U.S. President Jimmy Carter and the writer Elie Wiesel. Carter was a deeply religious Christian who believed in universality and the "lessons of the Holocaust," which meant that if the proposed museum were to find a home on the revered National Mall in Washington, as expected, the broad spectrum of Nazi crimes would need to be represented, not just Hitler's crimes against the Jews. For his part, Elie Wiesel, the chairman of the President's Commission, was a man with his own ideas. As the famed personification of the dark soul of survival and a winner of the Nobel Peace Prize (the Nobel Committee called him a "messenger to mankind"), he had long occupied centre stage in the struggle against oblivion. And, unlike other Holocaust survivors, such as the author Primo Levi and the Austrian Jewish philosopher Jean Amery, both of whom committed suicide after the war, Wiesel had survived survival.

He was also an Orthodox Jew and scholar—the first to ascribe the word "holocaust" to the mass murder of European Jews. The term derived from the Septuagint, the ancient Greek translation of the bible, where *holokaustos* was an adjective used to describe the "wholly burnt" nature of the offering, in which the entire animal is offered to God. The analogy was central to Wiesel's world view, where the capitalized word "Holocaust" became a prism through which the entire experience might be filtered: the ghettos, the deportations, the gassings, the ovens, and, for some, the terrifying years of hiding. For Wiesel, the word also represented the religious concept that the murdered Jews were "wholly sacrificed" martyrs. In his lexicon, the word Holocaust redirected memory into a metaphysical realm where Bible, pogrom, and remembrance fused into one. "The Holocaust is a sacred subject," he had said in 1973. "...One should tremble each time one pronounces the word."

It will be obvious to the reader that President Carter and Elie Wiesel were not going to agree. The commission itself was composed of Jews and gentiles, most of whom were practical-minded people, but Elie Wiesel was the voice of Jewish memory personified. Finding a common language was going to be difficult. And nowhere was the debate more charged than over the questions of the uniqueness of the Holocaust in world history—and, in tandem, how Jews and other victims of the Nazis should be represented. Wiesel and many others worried about losing Jewish specificity, and with reason, for in the aftermath of the war Jewish victims had not been identified as such in many places, but rather subsumed into the generic "war dead." Or they were declared to have died "for the sake of the country," as in France, as we have seen, or they had been absorbed into the general community of victims, as in Poland. Things had begun to change, thanks to the work of activists like Serge and Beate Klarsfeld and others, but the effort was just beginning. As recently as 2021, the Babi Yar ravine near Kiev, the site of the September 1941 massacre of Jews, still lacked a memorial to the victims, and unaware families still happily picnicked on the site.

Wiesel's powerful argument for uniqueness was built on the claim that, although there have been unspeakable massacres throughout history, no other group of people was killed because of who they were, as opposed to what they purportedly did. In other words, a profound human taboo had been transgressed. But Catholic Poles had also suffered under the Nazis, as had people in other occupied countries, and they also wanted their history portrayed in the museum.

The U.S. museum did not officially open until 1993, and during its long gestation the sometimes-bitter debates never ceased. Wiesel had many supporters, but they did not include many Holocaust scholars, who were uncomfortable with his "uniqueness" argument. Raul Hilberg, the first historian to approach the period using evidence derived from German archives, was direct when we met in his hometown of Burlington, Vermont. He said, "For me the Holocaust was a vast, single event, but I am never going to use the word *unique* because I recognize that when one starts breaking it into pieces one finds completely recognizable, ordinary ingredients that are common to other situations, such as Rwanda, or Cambodia, and possibly others I have not examined."

"In the final analysis," he continued, "it depends on whether we want to emphasize the commonality with other events, or the holistic totality—in which case the Holocaust stands by itself. I consider the latter perilous. Do we want one Rwanda after the other? Should we not look at this? The alternative is to see the Holocaust as outside history, as not part of anything. And it is impossible to learn from something that is so apart."

Elie Wiesel wasn't convinced, but he did make concessions. In his speech on April 22, 1993, at the dedication of the museum, he said, "We have learned that, though the Holocaust was principally a Jewish tragedy, its implications are universal...." First among many, he identified humanity's shared moral imperative to understand where hatred and racism come from and may lead to, and to fight against them.

The chasm between the religious view of uniqueness and the secular view of historians such as Raul Hilberg remained unresolved for decades, although today the former is beginning to fade. I ran into related problems myself in a strange encounter I related in *Long Shadows,* and will retell here. In 1996 I was invited to speak during Holocaust Remembrance Week to an audience of (I would discover) concentration camp survivors. My talk was billed as "History, Memory, and the Burden of Guilt." The immediate subject was a review of Daniel Goldhagen's book, *Hitler's Willing Executioners*, whose thesis was that ordinary Germans had zealously contributed to the killings because they had been conditioned to desire the murder of Jews.

I disliked the book. I thought Goldhagen had exaggerated his own view beyond credibility while maligning just about everyone who had ever written on the subject. I also told my audience that I thought the author had missed what Primo Levi had once called the "grey zone" of human affairs—that foggy universe of mixed motives, conflicting emotions, personal priorities, reluctant choices, opportunism, and accommodation, as the historian Christopher Browning had once described it.

I had just finished speaking when a woman in the front row jumped to her feet. "You should be ashamed of yourself!" she shouted angrily. Within a moment, others in the audience began shaking their fists at one another while arguing over my right to criticize what, unbeknownst to me, had been newly adopted as a quasi-sacred text that reflected their deepest feelings about Germans.

I apologized for having inadvertently caused hurt, and I sat down in a state of amazement. My parents and my daughter, Michelle, who were seated in the front row, looked as stunned as I was. I was further taken aback by a man who addressed me from the back of the room. He said, "Thirty years from now you can give a talk like this. When we are all dead. But while we live you have no right to talk to us like this." Another man spat out, "We don't *need* history. We were *there!* What you said is just dry linguistics!"

I learned an important lesson that night. First, that I hadn't understood my audience. I had thought, clearly mistakenly, that they would be interested in my critical thoughts on Goldhagen's book. What I also hadn't understood was that for some survivors of the Holocaust, the only acceptable response to the tragedy they endured was not unbiased history but commemoration, along with its complement: commemorative history. *Hitler's Willing Executioners* was, to many in my audience, a model of the correct approach because its indicting thesis and scholarly footnotes appeared to justify their own visceral hatred towards the nation that had inflicted unprecedented harm on them from which they would never recover. I hadn't thought about the terrible choice made by both Primo Levi and Jean Amery—and that, for some, life after the camps was simply unbearable.

In November 2019, I was once again invited to speak during Holocaust Remembrance Week—this time by the Yorkminster Park Baptist Church in Toronto. Like most people, I had changed over the course of two-and-a-half decades, and I had perhaps learnt a little more about the subject. I decided to seize the occasion to present an overview of Holocaust memory through an examination of the different phases of remembrance the world had known since 1945, and where I thought that memory might be headed.

I had just returned from a trip to Paris with my granddaughter, Julia, where we had visited sites of Holocaust remembrance, such as the Jewish tombstones in the Père Lachaise cemetery where "*Mort pour la France*" had been powerfully revised to read "Murdered at Auschwitz." We had walked together through the old Jewish immigrant quarter around the *rue des Rosiers* that had housed thousands who, during the war, were rounded up for deportation by French police. We had noted the way France's acknowledgement of its history had evolved: in recent years, plaques had appeared on schools and other neighbourhood institutions baldly stating precisely how many Jewish children and adults had been deported from each place.

As always during my visits to France, where I had spent formative years of my life and attempted to grapple with repressed national history, I experienced layered memories of my own. Julia and I had visited the Palais de Chaillot, for example, where the Third General Assembly of the United Nations had adopted the Universal Declaration of Human Rights on December 10, 1948, an event now commemorated by a stone engraved in both French and English. So it happened that I was more than primed to speak about the Holocaust on that November day, just after returning home.

I talked to my audience about the long timeline of historical trauma—about my observation that the victims of injustice will remember, even when ordered not to—and that although it may take decades before they, their children, or their grandchildren finally feel confident enough to speak out publicly, they will eventually do so, sometimes creating renewed political debate. I said that persecution, with its attendant human suffering, is always a messy business, that it burrows deep into consciousness and encompasses a range of extreme human emotions that sometimes, though apparently rarely, may even include remorse.

I pointed out what I thought were identifiable stages in the way the international community, and particular countries, have chosen to remember the Holocaust, the first being muteness: the survivors' inability either to assimilate or articulate the magnitude of their experience. This first stage was coupled with deliberate forgetfulness, or active revisionism, among both perpetrator and collaborator nations. It was also coupled with Holocaust denial, the favoured postwar tool of antisemites seeking to discredit the facts of history. Deniers have been intellectuals and others with access to public microphones; they have also been governments, such as Iran, and political leaders. And it doesn't end. As recently as 2018, Poland's ruling right-leaning Law and Justice party passed legislation criminalizing any mention of Poles "being responsible or complicit in the Nazi crimes committed by the Third German Reich."

The second stage in Holocaust remembrance was acknowledgement, a memory-era that most of the world continues to inhabit. Acknowledgement emerged in the 1960s and 1970s, thanks largely to the efforts of Elie Wiesel. Beyond speaking to governments about the centrality of recognizing Holocaust history, he loosened the mute tongues of survivors and opened the gates of silence to memoir, film, and other media. Concomitantly came the "revolt" of the second generation, especially in Germany, where the children and grandchildren of Nazis demanded an accounting of the truth.

I spoke during that lecture about Serge and Beate Klarsfeld and the long trajectory of Holocaust memory in France and Germany, including my encounters with the emotionally torn children of top Nazis; and about the ongoing debates in both countries over deflecting or managing guilt. Then I shared my personal uncertainties about a potential third stage of memory: how will the Holocaust be remembered after the remaining survivors die and its specific horrors recede from living memory?

Although they are speculative, there do seem to be visible trends—and, yes, some of it is bad news. In her recent studies of what she calls collective, or cultural memory, the reputed German scholar Aleida Assmann has argued that the duration of front-burner historical memory is seventy to eighty years. That is where we are now in regard to the Holocaust. If Assmann is correct, it will become increasingly important to keep the factual narrative of Holocaust memory alive in the face of forgetfulness, distortion, or both.

But there is also good news. For years an ongoing effort to record survivors' stories has borne fruit as filmmaker Steven Spielberg and others archive matchless testimony for future generations. Many schools around the world now teach courses on the Holocaust, just as intelligently curated museums and memorials also conserve memory. The remaining question is: what direction will Holocaust memory take?

A look at the trajectory of the fundamental argument between Jimmy Carter and Elie Wiesel over "uniqueness" may provide a clue. After the postwar hope for "Never Again" was effectively dashed during the Rwandan and Bosnian genocides of the 1990s, researchers began examining similarities among them more closely, then relating them to the Holocaust, just as the historian Raul Hilberg had been excoriated for doing in the 1960s; and by the turn of the twenty-first century multi-disciplinarian "Holocaust studies" and "genocide studies" had become part of university curricula in many parts of the world. A core hope is that by incorporating disciplines such as psychology and sociology into such studies we will learn more about the process—about the how and the why of genocide—and develop tools to recognize the danger signs. Another core hope is that future generations will learn to recognize the role played by propaganda and conspiracy theories in liberating what may be a shared, latent impulse to turn on one another.

Seen from this perspective, the Holocaust may one day be seen as a precedent-setting genocide, but one—unfortunately—among others. This may be a disturbing prospect to some, but it is, perhaps, not a bad thing. For it is possible that fifty or a hundred years from now the Holocaust might be remembered not only as tragic in itself, but also as transformative in our understanding of humankind's darkest impulses.

That evening I told my audience about an experience I'd had in Nuremberg, Germany as I listened to a Holocaust survivor tell her ghastly story to a school class of young adolescents. When she was finished, I recounted, a sensitive-looking boy raised his hand.

"What can children like us do to ease your suffering?" he asked her hopefully.

"Nothing," she replied, though not unkindly.

My heart went out to the bewildered-looking boy. I understood the survivor; it was true that there was nothing that this child could do to change her life. But I began to think that it mattered how the darker aspects of history were transmitted. I thought it crucial that children not be overly traumatized as they learn hard truths that will, one hopes, alert them to societal undercurrents and prepare them to take early action.

Teachers need to be properly trained, but not everyone is equipped to take on this task and not everyone should be asked to do so. As the early Zionist leader, Nahum Goldmann, once put it, "You need to be a poet to imagine [Dante's] Inferno."

The Globe and Mail published my lecture in its entirety. Shortly afterwards, I received a poignant letter from a senior faculty member at the University of Toronto who told me that the youngster who had tried to help the suffering survivor could well have been him. He confided despairingly that he had spent his entire adult life grappling with his tainted legacy as a descendant of Nazi Germany.

I wasn't surprised. The Germans have a word, *Vergangenheitsbewaeltigung*, meaning mastering, or overcoming, the past—an uneasy, if not impossible, endeavour. It is a Sisyphean task bequeathed to them by their perpetrator forbears.

I was fast approaching the completion deadline demanded by Propylaeen Verlag, the German publisher that was financing this expensive research, and I had to make choices. I had planned to explore the aftermath of Operation Condor, the Argentine "Dirty War" of 1976 to 1983, in which the military dictatorship unleashed death squads to hunt down political dissidents. Thousands of young people had been murdered, their horrified parents left ignorant of their fate. After the war ended, I read of cases where ordinary people crossed paths with neighbours whom they knew had abducted their disappeared children—people who now tipped their hats in macabre greeting. One story, recounted to me by the

Argentine-Canadian writer Alberto Manguel, told of a woman of his acquaintance who encountered her child's kidnapper in a supermarket just hours after President Carlos Menem's amnesty of December 29, 1990, had destroyed even the dream of justice. He was a neighbour. "Good afternoon, *Señora*," he said, pleasantly. The woman returned home and took her life.

I had long wondered how the memory of that era would be constructed, but I was running out of time, and on the advice of a friend I dropped the planned chapter.

I finished *Long Shadows: Truth, Lies and History* at the end of a spring day in June 2000, four years after I had visited Japan largely by chance. Tom took me out to dinner that night. He informed the waiter, who rushed about and brought me a single red rose.

CHAPTER ELEVEN

THE SUN CLIMBS SLOW

IT SEEMS STRANGE, EVEN to me, that it was only after I wrote the final lines of *Long Shadows* and began to think about the people and situations I had encountered throughout my career, that I became aware that an underlying subject of my work was accountability in its broadest sense. Justice, in other words—justice for the victims of atrocities and other flagrant misdeeds, justice as respect for the rule of law, justice as a balancing of a historical pendulum.

That this pendulum would often swing wildly was a given, since wars of hatred continue to intersect history. The question I had constantly wondered about was how to interrupt that wayward swing and bend it towards stability. I had come to believe that justice and its concomitant ally, peace, could be found only at the central point of this pendulum, but also that there was no such thing as complete stasis. The balancing act would always be a work-in-process.

In retrospect, I note that, without openly adverting to the slow evolution of my thinking, I had chosen to write about truth and reconciliation in South Africa, postwar trials in Germany and France, failed attempts to enable an official apology and possible restitution for slavery in the United States, and about the first United Nations *ad hoc* courts to seek accountability for war crimes and crimes against humanity, the precursors to the International Criminal Court. I had also titled a chapter in *Long Shadows*, "Is there Justice?"—an appropriately open-ended question—where I had written about the Nuremberg Tribunal and its positive influence on the second half of the twentieth century, including its creation of rule-of-law international institutions such as the United Nations. It was in that same chapter that I recounted my visit to that still-haunted courtroom in the city of Nuremberg, and to the nearby Nazi rally grounds where Adolf Hitler once stood upon a (still-extant) stage screaming toxic deceits to a rapt audience of thousands. It was in that chapter that I charted the birth, at the Nuremberg court, of legislation called "crimes against humanity"—newly codified legal language referencing what was universally known behaviour; and the equally new definition of genocide, another known, but never codified, act of mass killing.

I similarly explored the creation of Nuremberg's daughters, born in the 1990s: the United Nations International Criminal Tribunal for the Former Yugoslavia and the United Nations International Criminal Tribunal for Rwanda, both brought into being to deal with war crimes that took place during those conflicts. From 1993 until their closure in 2017, the ICTY and the ICTR expanded the scope of international humanitarian law by calling to account perpetrators who bore responsibility for atrocities and by creating a space where victims could recount their experience.

Looking back, the 1990s were an optimistic time for those who cherished the protection of human rights. They did not usher in "The End of History," as Francis Fukuyama hubristically claimed, but the dissolving of the Cold War after fifty years had led to strong commitments among democracies and those striving to be democracies. The attacks of September 11, 2001, on the Twin Towers of the World Trade Centre would fracture much of this promise, but no one knew this then.

So, it happened naturally that an exploration of the broad tableau of justice became my last book in a multi-themed series on the origins of otherness and the politics of historical memory.

Convinced as I was that the past—including influential work by long-dead thinkers—informs the present, I wanted to understand what the elusive idea of "justice" has meant across millennia. The reading transported me back to my undergraduate days, and to re-reading Plato, whose resolute protagonist, Socrates, was obsessed with teasing out multiple views on justice, especially from his "might is right" interlocutor, the sophist Thrasymachus.

At Tom's suggestion, I read Sophocles' play *Antigone*, in which the author insists that his audience confront the conflict between the interests-based rights of an earth-born ruler and what were then understood to be the universal laws of the gods—divine rules that were broken at one's peril. Further reading led me back to Thucydides' famous *History of the Peloponnesian* War and its seminal "Melian Dialogue," in which the all-powerful state of Athens offers the inhabitants of the tiny island of Melos an archetypal argument of "might makes right," while the Melians make the opposite case for what they call "the general principle of fair play and just dealing." As every student of politics knows, both these stances remain palpably present in the literary, philosophical, and real-world conduct of international relations.

If (after Plato's character Thrasymachus) Machiavelli's book *The Prince* endures as the classic literary root of the oft-repeated argument that morality has no place in interests-based politics, the eighteenth-century German philosopher Immanuel Kant continues to illuminate the Melian/Sophoclean vision of justice: that universal norms are the backbone of peace. Kant's *Critique of Pure Reason* (a dense tome I struggled with as an undergraduate) has remained the philosophical foundation of the latterly named value of cosmopolitanism, or multilateralism. Remarkably, given our own era of new tribunals whose mandate is to seek accountability for mass atrocities, Kant predicted a globalized world in which justice—a practical as well as a moral component of peace—would transcend national borders. His ideas took me back to my youthful exposure to the words of Emil Fackenheim, as he lectured his class of sleepy adolescents at Holy Blossom Temple Sunday School all those years ago.

Throughout history there have been failed attempts to find ways of confronting impunity for the most serious crimes carried out by states or large groups, but as noted earlier, before the Nuremberg Tribunal in the middle of the twentieth century there was no legal language for the very worst of these: crimes against humanity, including genocide. Aptly named, these were, and are, crimes against the whole of humanity because they attack the core of what must remain inviolate if humans are to remain human. I think it was my sense of this latter truth that inspired me to write *The Sun Climbs Slow*. I had witnessed the political, societal, and personal consequences of criminal impunity again and again while travelling through shattered lands and witnessing the aftermath of unresolved history. I'd observed what distorted national histories looked like, and their outcomes.

The birth of the International Criminal Court in 2003—the first *independent* tribunal to hold individuals accountable for the worst crimes ever written into law—was an unprecedented event. The idea of such a court had been around for a very long time, but as a dream without real prospects. Few countries, especially the most powerful, thought it in their interests to allow a tribunal they could not control to take charge of any aspect of their judicial affairs, especially if they had no real intention of bringing their own nationals to account for offenses that had sometimes been authorized by the state itself. That the ICC came into being (by means of the Rome Statute, a global treaty negotiated in 1998) was entirely the result of coincidental geopolitical events, including general desperation at the onset of renewed genocide in Rwanda and Bosnia after the world's post-Nuremberg promise of "Never Again." Without this convergence of happenstances, the ICC would almost certainly not have been born.

I detailed the dramatic (sometimes comic) story of this birth in *The Sun Climbs Slow*, and I won't repeat that narrative. The few stories I *will* retell are some of those that remain imprinted in my mind more than a decade after the book's publication—selected portraits of extraordinary people, many of whose commitments to justice and human rights I recognized as being much like my own. I'll also re-tell the story of one of the most reckless individuals I encountered: John Bolton, then Under Secretary of State in the administration of George W. Bush, a man with alarming power who carried individual responsibility for the U.S. refusal to join the International Criminal Court.

Some of these people were judges at the ICC or at the earlier *ad hoc* UN international courts. Another was an American activist lobbying for criminal accountability regarding the George Bush administration's surreptitious authorization of torture committed in Iraq and Afghanistan, and the travesty of the Guantanamo Bay prison, where suspects were held indefinitely and without charges. Others I met were individuals who had volunteered to look for the remains of missing persons in Bosnia a decade after the Dayton Accords ended overt hostilities, most memorably the Canadian forensic anthropologist from Vancouver whom I watched as she carefully pieced together the DNA-matched bones of a nineteen-year-old, murdered at Srebrenica in 1995, so his grieving parents could finally claim them. Another stand-out among my many unforgettable encounters in war-torn Bosnia was with a group of angry, morally resolute mothers and widows of the same Srebrenica genocide who had banded together to demand accountability.

Then there was my encounter with the latterly tarnished Robert McNamara, the former United States Secretary of Defense under Presidents John F. Kennedy and Lyndon B. Johnson—a man who was himself considered a war criminal by many Americans who remembered the key political role he had played during the Vietnam War. In his advanced old age, he appeared to agree with his accusers: he had become a proponent of the very International Criminal Court that might have indicted and convicted him for "command responsibility" had it existed in an earlier era.

What was it about all these people that affected me so viscerally? Sometimes, it was their intense honesty. The Canadian jurist, Louise Arbour, for example. We first met in The Hague in 1999, when she was chief prosecutor for the United Nations *ad hoc* courts for the former Yugoslavia (ICTY) and Rwanda (ICTR). Despite occupying a job of unimaginable complexity and strain, she was down-to-earth friendly, even breezy in her manner, a woman with an easy laugh whose glasses perched precariously at the end of her nose. I felt immediately at ease in her presence: two Canadian women with a passion for justice. I didn't compare myself to her; she was doing difficult field work with significant consequences—I was merely chronicling her efforts.

When I asked her if she ever compared the courts she headed to the tribunals at Nuremberg, she laughed heartily. "I think of Nuremberg *every day!*" she said. What she thought about, she went on, was how comparatively easy the prosecution at Nuremberg had been—not that she compared herself to Telford Taylor and Robert Jackson, the giants of that court, she hastened to say. No, she meant the technical things. And she didn't mind admitting she was envious. The Nuremberg prosecutors had every defendant in custody, for example, and the ones they didn't have, like Martin Bormann, they tried *in absentia.* The Nuremberg Tribunal had no appeals; and because the Nazis were obsessive record-keepers, the court had every document it needed. They also had demobilized soldiers by the thousands, including sophisticated intelligence officers. And they had "zillions" of translators, she added with a rueful laugh.

Her job was a thousand times harder, what with United Nations forces in the former Yugoslavia refusing to arrest the top indicted criminals in Bosnia, and the leaders of the political "entities" in the region refusing to recognize the jurisdiction of the court. There was also current debate about whether the ICTY and the ICTR were entitled to compliance under the founding statute of the tribunals. Louise Arbour thought they were. Others (especially the criminally indicted and their counsel) begged to differ.

One thing was certain: If Louise Arbour had one of the hardest jobs in the world, it was also one of the most critical, for the success or failure of the new UN tribunals would play a central role in determining the future of accountability for the world's worst offenses. She couldn't afford to fail.

Our conversation that day in The Hague was memorable in its entirety, but two elements remain engraved in my mind. The first was her chagrin that the tribunals under her jurisdiction were able to prosecute only the top leadership—if they were able to arrest them, that is; the terms of the Rome Statute made this difficult. This meant that thousands of victims of lesser perpetrators would never see justice done. Those victims were displaced, traumatized civilians, the people whom a psychiatrist in Sarajevo had earlier informed me would likely never heal.

They were, for example, the woman whose son or husband had been murdered by a neighbour who had once been a friend. Could a person ever properly deal with such a betrayal? "Given the impossible number of victims and perpetrators, and the limited capacity of the courts, the Bosnian woman whose husband was taken away and killed was unlikely to see her neighbour brought to account, but it was that person she cared about," Arbour said. In other words, the top leadership were abstractions to ordinary people. What they wanted was to see the individual who killed the person they loved in the prisoner's dock.

Another element of our conversation that has never left me was Arbour's willingness to talk about the nuances of collective guilt, a loaded subject I had raised with Archbishop Desmond Tutu a year earlier when I was in South Africa. Tutu had been forthright. He had said that although individuals were responsible for their actions, groups of active or passive bystanders also had to acknowledge their part.

The very idea of collective responsibility for crime is taboo in the West, where judicial systems correctly operate according to the principle that only individuals are responsible for their acts. Louise Arbour didn't deny this. On the contrary, she said: "The rejection of collective guilt is at the core of what we do here. By personalizing individual responsibility, we help diffuse the stigma on a whole nation or ethnic group."

But she also added this:

> I don't think it is as straightforward as I did before I started this work. I think that having a clear demarcation between

> the individual and the collective, or the group, works reasonably well when the perpetrators who are being tried in court are somewhat distinct from the group, and the group can distance itself from that person.
>
> Take our first case, Dusan Tadic. It was possible for the Bosnian Serb community to say he is not us; he is a war criminal. But that distance becomes more difficult when you move up the chain of command, say with Radovan Karadžić [the leader of the Bosnian Serbs]. We have become aware of this here during discussions about what would happen if there were a move to arrest him, because ultimately, when you get to the head of state, there is a fusion of the community with that individual. They may have elected that person...often with open eyes. And even if they did not know every crime by name, they heard the rhetoric of hate and supported it. So, as we move higher up the chain of command, there is more resistance, because the people we are calling war criminals are still heroes to the community.
>
> In our tribunal, we look only at personal criminal responsibility in a very tightly defined, narrow way, and we demand proof beyond a reasonable doubt about the involvement of that individual. We do not have a mandate to establish the moral responsibility of those who saw things happen and did nothing. But we have to be careful in thinking that, just because we focus on individual criminal guilt we therefore absolve the community. The old distinctions are too simplistic when we move up the chain of command and witness the merging of the collectivity into the personae of these charismatic political and military leaders.

I agreed with her, and I thought her very brave. The law may be cut and dried, but human affairs are not. My own work had more than convinced me that when we commit ourselves unreservedly to ideologies and to those who embody them, we risk becoming complicit bystanders when the admired ones behave in questionable ways. The extent to which we willingly travel along this spectrum of accommodation may depend upon individual traits, such as our susceptibility to rhetoric and propaganda. It may also depend on the personal charisma of a leader who promises to improve lives in exchange for loyalty. Whatever the case, the conventional letter of the law cannot address psychological and ethical issues such as these; it must, on the contrary, ignore them to ensure a fair trial.

The activist I spoke of earlier was Michael Ratner, a man once called "America's most important civil libertarian." He was president of the Center for Constitutional Rights (CCR) in New York City, and when we met in his office in Lower Manhattan not far from where the Twin Towers of the World Trade Center once stood, just a short time after that event, he was confronting new erosions of civil rights that had the official *imprimatur* of the George W. Bush administration.

In my mind's eye I revisit the clutter of his busy office, the empty Styrofoam coffee cups, and desks piled high with legal papers. The CCR was challenging what it characterized as violations of constitutional and international law on the part of the United States government, including Patriot Act restrictions on civil liberties and the use of the ubiquitous (but legally meaningless) tag "enemy combatant," which was coined by U.S. government lawyers to deprive of Geneva Convention protections detainees believed to be al-Qaeda members. The organization was also challenging the government over its policies of indefinite detention and imprisonment without charges, without legal representation, and almost always without evidence—all in the name of a permanent war against terrorism. Ratner and his colleagues attacked the practice of sending terror suspects to third countries where they were tortured—a deeply controversial policy that had also targeted an innocent Canadian, Maher Arar, and made possible the arrest and brutal mistreatment of Omar Khadr, a Canadian child-soldier.

But the repercussions of these Bush-era policies went further still: the torture of al-Qaeda suspects wasn't only carried out by foreign states wanting to please America, but by America itself. Years later, in 2020, the

U.S. would come under investigation by the International Criminal Court for having engaged in torture—a crime of war.

Michael Ratner's intense demeanour suggested he wasn't interested in chit chat. I asked him a conventionally open-ended question with lots of room for response: What was he hoping to accomplish long term?

"We're trying to protect the universal norms that every country has to obey in order to be accepted in the world community," he replied without hesitating. "Especially the norm prohibiting torture."

He spoke quickly, as if running out of time. "The United States ratified the UN Convention Against Torture, and we have our own criminal statutes against torture. The United States ratified the International Covenant on Civil and Political Rights that came into force in 1976, and that's a long time ago. We have bills that prohibit sending foreign aid to countries engaged in gross violations of human rights. In this country, the U.S. Constitution is our secular bible—and it was founded on the basic universalist principles coming out of the Enlightenment, on the idea that reason is better than non-reasoning, that law is better than Hobbesian thinking.... That's what we're defending; because these things have come under attack in this country."

Michael Ratner and the CCR were the first Americans to push back against the serious breaches of civil rights that followed in the wake of 9/11, and I shared his revulsion at the Bush administration's policies surrounding torture. I was similarly appalled by the linguistic pretzels the government had invented to justify human rights violations severe enough to be classified as war crimes. (At this writing almost two decades later, no senior person has been tried in the United States for commanding or inflicting torture.)

The standard rationale for inflicting torture is almost always the same: a stated desire to elicit foolproof evidence of wrongdoing. But torture ultimately fails, because most people undergoing such abuse are not heroes and will agree to say anything just to make the agony stop. This is both commonsensical and well-documented. My own first encounter with the falsity of the rationale and the inhumanity of torture had occurred in France while I was researching *Unhealed Wounds*. I wrote in that book about sitting in a Paris café with a man who had been a victim of Klaus Barbie's merciless collaborators a full forty years earlier. He had broken, he confessed, when his tormentors told him that his son had been captured and would be killed. His physical wounds had healed long ago, he said, but his psychic wounds had not. (Barbie used a bull whip to inflict pain, and he was known to play the piano when he needed a rest. *Parlez-moi d'amour* was one of his favourite songs.)

One work of literature that has attempted to penetrate the spiritual necrosis that enables extreme abuse is the astonishing novel *Waiting for the Barbarians*, by the South African writer J. M. Coetzee. At an abstract borderland of an abstract desert, located somewhere and nowhere, the administrator of a distant colonial imperium and his entourage live in relative harmony with the tribal nomads who have occupied the territory since time immemorial—until the day a sadistic police chief arrives from the imperium to put down a non-existent rebellion.

The administrator retains his humanity throughout the story, even as he is slowly reduced to servitude—a literary contrast between principled dignity and a bureaucratic war of marginalization that metamorphoses into atrocity. The psychology of what takes place is revealing. The administrator's aides side with the powerful police who have taken control, and they mock the man they once admired. They laugh as they witness the torture of captured nomads who once lived freely nearby. Brutalized by their own actions, they laughingly enlist a child to inflict physical pain. As the book draws to a close, the police, having lost their power, are routed, and these same people change sides once again. Coetzee's brilliantly told story traces the creation of "the enemy," the familiar construct of "the other," and our human propensity to mirror the most powerful actors in the room.

I have also noticed in museum photographs that torturers and those about to execute civilians frequently smile with pleasure, and I wondered whether something about holding extreme power over another, about inflicting pain or death, might liberate euphoric excitement in some people. As far back as 1961, an experiment by the American psychologist Stanley Milgram, in which people from varied backgrounds were instructed by an authority figure to inflict pain using electric shocks, found that many (though not all) of the participants were willing to do so, even when they believed that the shocks would have reached possibly fatal levels had the experiment involved real people. The Milgram study has been replicated many times with similar results, suggesting that resistance to wrongdoing commanded by an authority involves actively countering what for many feels like an instinct that is acceptable if not particularly laudable.

Michael Ratner died of cancer in 2016, the year Donald J. Trump won the American presidency. Given how exercised he was by the George W. Bush administration's breaches of universal norms, it is not hard to imagine how Ratner and his Center, which had become the first line of defense of standards that America and most other democracies had come to take for granted, would have responded to Trump's flagrant undermining of civil society norms.

I WAS ALSO CURIOUS about the first judges elected to serve on the International Criminal Court. What motivated these people? I met several of them, and I was not surprised to learn that something had marked each of them in their earlier life—a personal event or national circumstance that had eventually led them to this unique tribunal.

Judge Navanethem (Navi) Pillay of South Africa, for instance. Her presence in The Hague was something of a miracle, for she had had to learn about due process and human rights outside her national environment. As a child of Indian background, Pillay was born into an apartheid system that thwarted her every effort to become properly educated, one that had turned her into a fighter for her rights. Anger threaded through her childhood—anger at the way she was treated, anger at the way her poverty-stricken parents were treated. As we talked together in her ICC office, she startled me by confiding that she had studied law as an alternative to pursuing violence. These feelings were still present, she said quietly, for practicing law in South Africa had been a challenge: "There was so much injustice that you felt you could kill the judge in question. I became a lawyer because I thought I could fight injustice that way. I thought it would empower me to know what my rights were. My clients were accused of anti-apartheid activism or breaking apartheid rules. You had to work through the law even though the system itself was unjust."

Against all odds—she was a "coloured," female, and from an impoverished background—Navi Pillay had had a brilliant career. She was the first woman in her home province of Natal to open a law practice. In 1995, a year after apartheid formally ended, she was appointed as a High Court judge, the first woman to be so honoured. That same year she was elected to the bench of the International Criminal Tribunal for Rwanda; and in 1998 she and her judicial colleagues made history by condemning the former Rwandan prime minister, Jean Kambanda, for genocide. Kambanda (who pleaded guilty) was the first head of state ever to be convicted of the "crime of crimes."

In 1999 she was voted president of the ICTR. Now, in her fifties, she was an elected judge at the new International Criminal Court.

Her determination in the face of official attempts to prevent her from achieving her potential filled me with admiration for her, and for her parents. Despite poverty, lack of education, and social powerlessness, they had encouraged their talented daughter to reach for the impossible.

If Navi Pillay's life was shaped by her childhood in apartheid South Africa, Judge Hans-Peter Kaul's life was informed by his early years in postwar Germany. Kaul and his German colleagues had been central to the turbulent creation of the Rome Statute in 1998 that had brought the ICC into being. This was not surprising; Germans still suffer from the knowledge that the generations of their parents and grandparents were participants in the Nazi project.

Judge Kaul was born in 1943, near Dresden, in what would soon become Soviet-controlled East Germany. In 1952 his family escaped to

West Germany, where at the age of nine young Hans-Peter decided to defend the Western World against the Russians. When accomplishing this heroic feat single-handedly proved somewhat difficult, it occurred to him as a teenager that he might more usefully resist tyranny by studying law.

The Hitler era and war were never far from his mind. When the Allies firebombed Dresden in February 1945, a beloved uncle was killed along with forty thousand others; and when the Soviet army entered the city soon afterwards, his father, who had been an officer in the Wehrmacht, was taken prisoner. When his father returned home four years later, he looked like a skeleton. He died young, leaving his son, Hans-Peter, further scarred by the multiple traumas of war.

And so it was that from his earliest childhood Hans-Peter Kaul knew violence, havoc, family disruption, and loss. His favourite playgrounds, he recalled as we spoke together, were the ruins of bombed-out houses. "In our neighbourhood you had parts of cellars and balconies that were still intact. It was wonderful to play on these things... but I became politically aware very early."

One day, when he was a teenager, he inadvertently came across a newly published book that described Hitler's mass murders. It was *Der SS-Staat: Das System der deutschen Konzentrationslager* (The Theory and Practice of Hell: The German Concentration Camps and the System Behind Them) by Eugen Kogon, who was a political prisoner at Buchenwald from 1939 to 1945. Hans-Peter was terrified by what he learned, but the new knowledge further propelled him towards the study of law, then international law. As a young man, he believed that countries that were ruled by global law in their foreign affairs were less likely to commit crimes.

"In Germany, support for the International Criminal Court is universal, from the far left to the far right," he told me. "For obvious reasons, Germans understand the need for a universal court with the capacity to set legal and moral standards for the entire world."

A man of abiding principle, Hans-Peter Kaul considered his own children and was happy. He put it this way: "I think it is unhealthy when a young person accepts the exercise of power as a reality against which one can do nothing, so I am glad that my children are a little bit rebellious against the generation to which I belong and are critical. Nobody can claim that he or she will always live up to high principles, but I believe the principles must remain intact, despite constraints and occasional concessions. This is the way I have tried to live my life."

After *The Sun Climbs Slow* was published, Judge Kaul wrote to thank me for my little pen-portrait of his life and commitments. He and his wife hoped to meet Tom and me. Sadly, it never happened. He died in 2014 mere days after the onset of a severe illness. "Judge Kaul will be remembered for his multi-faceted and unrelenting support for the cause of international criminal justice," the ICC wrote on its website. Also, I thought, for his character. I, too, mourned the man, although we had met only once. As for his country, Germany remains one of the world's strongest supporters of the International Criminal Court.

Claude Jorda and I had never met before, but we might have. Judge Jorda had been at the heart of France's debate over its collaboration with Nazism. He was director of legal services at the French Ministry of Justice from 1982 until 1985, during the period when Klaus Barbie was captured in Bolivia and returned to France for trial. He was attorney general (chief prosecutor) in Bordeaux as the government prepared its case against Maurice Papon. In 1992 he was attorney general of the Appeals Court in Paris just as the René Bousquet Affair began to heat up. And in 1994 he was appointed to the newly created ICTY.

He, too, had been driven to the study of law by violence and war. Growing up in the French colony of Algeria, he had experienced the bombing of his hometown, Bône, by the Allies in 1943. His school was closed for a year; there was little to eat. But because he had played with Arab children as a child, he simply took ethnic and religious diversity for granted. That was why he was in favour of Algerian independence when the anti-colonial war began in the late 1950s, he told me. "It was very painful. I was at law school in Toulouse at the time, and the battle among students—Algerian liberationists against the extreme right—was terrible and violent. Students today cannot imagine what it was like, this terrible quarrel over decolonization."

I told him I understood, because I was in Paris then as a foreign student, and I had naively wandered close to that violence. I told him I had even tried to participate by joining a pro-independence march, but I had quickly dropped out when someone walking next to me said I'd be deported if discovered. I told him the Algerian War was my introduction to politics at its most brutal—an experience that nothing in my Canadian childhood had prepared me for.

"There is an ethical dimension to bringing justice to the victims and to fulfilling a duty to the collective memory," he had once said in a public speech. And he lived those words. In a transcript of an ICTY trial over which he was presiding, I read that he had replied to Dražen Erdemović, a Bosnian Serb defendant who claimed angrily from the prisoner's box that he was an insignificant spoke in the wheel and had had no choice when called to war, "I understand that it is painful for you. We understand that you were caught in a storm, but that is not a reason for us…to say that these many, many people who were killed will be simply written off."

Those words spoke to his priorities. Yes, one might understand the problems of the perpetrator, but they were not proportionate to the killing of thousands of civilians whose deaths could not be ignored.

Then there was the Prosecutor-in-Chief. Luis Moreno Ocampo's feet were resting comfortably on his desk. His smile was broad, and, unlike his more serious-seeming colleagues, he exuded something akin to flamboyance. First impressions aside, his credentials for the top job at the new court were impeccable. He was an expert practitioner of anti-corruption law in his native Argentina and elsewhere in Latin America. He was a founder of *Poder Ciudadano* (Citizens' Power), and an adviser to the international project "Justice in Times of Transition," which helped "recovering" states foster reconciliation, economic development, and effective governance. He lectured internationally on justice and human rights. In other words, he was a star.

Importantly, he had played a leading role in the 1984-1992 prosecutions of the top military commanders of Argentina's "Dirty War"—the first criminal cases brought against senior officers since Nuremberg. On a personal level, he had had to deal with his own mother, whose entire family was in the military. She *loved* General Jorge Rafael Videla (the president of Argentina and head of the junta), he told me.

Like the others, Moreno Ocampo began to practice criminal law as a way of mitigating the aftermath of violence.

"Where does your interest in human rights come from?" I asked him.

"From my country," he replied.

Moreno Ocampo was at pains to explain what justice meant to him—and it wasn't just the interior workings of a court room. It was an entire environment. "Courts are important, and you have to protect them, but they are technical," he said. "The analogy is this: If you have cholera, the operating room is not the solution; you need clean water, proper nutrition, and good hygiene. It's the same with justice. When basic social conditions exist, the court system may be the key to stability, but when these conditions are absent, it is not sufficient by itself."

Luis Moreno Ocampo was a man of intellectual complexity, whose youth, like those of the ICC judges I had met, had been coloured by twentieth-century violence. As a writer, I was only an observer of their world. I have loved being a writer, but in another life I like to think I would have played a more active role in balancing the pendulum of justice.

The International Criminal Court had a mortal enemy. His name was John Bolton, Under Secretary of State in the administration of George W. Bush. Bolton had called the ICC "an organization that runs contrary to fundamental American precepts and basic constitutional principles of popular sovereignty, checks and balances, and national independence." It was, in other words, undemocratic, even illegitimate. He had also claimed that American soldiers would be in the front line of ICC prosecutions, although, as a lawyer who had studied the Rome Statute, he knew that it contained layers of protective safeguards before a case could even be triggered. Importantly, the Statute included the so-called "complementary" clause, which prohibited the ICC from initiating an investigation unless the country where the suspected perpetrator held citizenship either refused to hold its own trial or was unable to hold one because of inadequate domestic infrastructure.

It was disconcerting to hear Bolton speak in these terms on behalf of the nation that had been *the* major player in advancing human rights after the Second World War. Furthermore, polls suggested that his words ran contrary to deeply rooted commitments in American society.

Why did John Bolton hate and fear the ICC? As a world superpower, the United States had sometimes behaved in dubious ways. It had intervened violently in the affairs of other countries and had never been brought to account. As Michael Ratner and others knew well, war crimes such as torture in Afghanistan, for example, were as recent as yesterday.

The real reason for Bolton's attack on behalf of his president was the fact that the International Criminal Court was not temporary, but a permanent fixture in the galaxy of global organizations. It wasn't going to disappear unless it was destroyed from the outside—a task that John Bolton had appropriated with relish.

Thanks to the efforts of the Canadian diplomat Jon Allen, who was then Director General, North America Bureau, and former Minister of Political Affairs at the Canadian Embassy in Washington, I managed to secure an interview with Mr. Bolton in the fall of 2004. He was a powerful man, and I wanted to hear his arguments in person.

John Bolton's executive assistant escorted me through security scans until we reached the inner sanctum. The wall of his outer office displayed a large, framed plaque, "JUSTICE, JUSTICE SHALT THOU PURSUE," it read, quoting Leviticus. So far, the Secretary of State and I were walking along the same path.

The executive assistant returned to usher me into a spacious corner office with a "conversation area." Bolton stood in greeting and offered me a seat.

"Have you read any of the stuff I've written on the court? Speeches I've given?" he began aggressively.

I assured him that I had. I also knew my welcome in this room was qualified and had its limits, so I followed his lead and came straight to the point.

"Why does the United States, which has been the world's strongest advocate for international criminal justice, call its opposition to the International Criminal Court 'fundamental,' and 'closed to negotiation?'" I asked him.

"The issue posed by the court has nothing to do with whether you're for or against war crimes," he countered. "The United States has a record of prosecuting war crimes and human rights abuses committed by its citizens that is, I think, unequalled in the world today. But we consider the ICC to be fundamentally illegitimate. We are aware of no other treaty in the world that anybody has ever accepted that binds a non-party to the treaty."

I knew this was a staple of the United States' position. But in the aftermath of torture at the Abu Ghraib prison in Iraq, for example, for which only a female perpetrator at the lowest level had been indicted, how many really believed that the American record in prosecuting human rights agreements was unequalled? As for binding a non-state party to the treaty, that simply wasn't the case—and he knew it: a perpetrator from a country that had not ratified the Rome Statute could only be arrested on the territory of a country that *had* ratified the Statute.

"Since the United States has such an unequalled record of home prosecutions, why would it fear the ICC? Given that record, the ICC would never need to be involved in the case of an American citizen."

"People talk about the doctrine of complementarity. That's what they call it, the *doctrine* of complementarity. Okay, so they say, take it on faith that the doctrine will protect the United States. Well, I don't take anything this serious on faith...."

"I'm sure you are familiar with Telford Taylor's dictum from Nuremberg: 'The laws of war are not a one-way street.' What is your understanding of that phrase?"

"I think Nuremberg was an example of victor's justice, and that doesn't trouble me at all."

"Why not?"

"Because we won the war over fascism. It was entirely appropriate for us to react the way we did."

"You've written that the United States must be free to conduct 'controversial missions' without fear of arrest. What kind of missions were you thinking of?"

"...Many things that are really not the subject of debate in the United States are often considered controversial abroad. That's what I was trying to say.... What has to matter to the president and the president's appointees is the protection of the American Constitution and our system, and I think that's what we're doing when we take on the court."

"You are said to be the architect and captain of this policy. Is that true?"

"I think the president is the architect and the captain."

"But you are said to be the person who initiated things."

"He [the president] raised his opposition to the ICC in the 2000 campaign."

"*You* were talking about [the subject] long before that."

"I didn't talk to him about it."

I published the entirety of this interview in *The Sun Climbs Slow*. Suffice it to note here the fact that up to this point we were clearly just sparring, and also that I knew my allotted time with him would soon be up. As with the judges whom I had interviewed, I was curious to know what had influenced the trajectory of Bolton's thinking as a young man. He seemed happy with my question. He replied that during his student years at Yale "the radical left wingers had infiltrated the university and were subverting academic freedom...." But he was a conservative long before then, he explained. When he was just fifteen, he had campaigned for Barry Goldwater. Goldwater was the first modern conservative on the American scene: a Republican from Arizona who opposed Lyndon Johnson's Civil Rights Act of 1964. He was called an extremist, a label he publicly embraced.

"Was it your family that shaped your opinions?" I asked.

"No, I read a lot of Karl Marx," he replied with a smile.

The continuous rise of conservatism in the years following the Civil Rights Act of 1964 had borne John Bolton steadily toward power. At the time of our meeting, he was near the apex of his career, from which he hoped to destroy the International Criminal Court in the name of the same country that had effectively invented international humanitarian law in the aftermath of the Holocaust. That he failed to do so is evidenced by the continued existence of the Court almost two decades after its creation.

Finally, I would meet one of the most despised men in America: Robert McNamara, described by *The New York Times* as "the most influential defense secretary of the twentieth century." McNamara had served two presidents: John F. Kennedy and Lyndon B. Johnson. He had escalated the Vietnam War out of his iron-clad certainty that the war could be won. He was wrong on that count, and he was later held responsible by many for the deaths of more than 50,000 Americans during that slaughter. McNamara had been actively reassessing his role for more than a decade before we met. He wrote books, and he made himself available to chroniclers like me. He was trying, though largely unsuccessfully, to restore his reputation by acknowledging his mistakes.

I wanted to meet him because, in extreme old age, he had become a vocal supporter of the ICC. I wanted to know why. So, I visited his Washington office, where I encountered an old man with a lined face, a laborious walk, and an intense, steady gaze.

"Why the ICC?" I asked him.

He replied that he had been interested in the ICC for a long time, because he believed that sanctions, whether military or economic, were too rough and crude in the first instance, and insufficiently effective in the other.

"I have come to believe that a third sanction would be desirable, and that is an international judicial system."

There was, in his writings, his personal appearances, and his conversation with me more than a hint that he did consider himself responsible, as his accusers held, for the deaths of thousands of young men—unquiet shades that seemed to haunt him.

His active life had ended, but he had something else to impart, insights and thoughts he had mentioned in another interview that had caught my attention. The first was an awareness born of wisdom itself, I thought, and possibly the product of reflection as he grew older. Robert McNamara now focused on one overlooked human quality: empathy, the ability to see and imagine the world through the eyes of another. During the COVID-19 pandemic of 2020 and beyond, empathy became a more talked-about personal attribute, but prior to that upheaval in the world it was usually ignored, especially in high places. Had Defense Secretary Robert McNamara talked about empathy during the Vietnam War, his subordinates might have tittered before quietly seeking the opinion of a psychiatrist.

Empathy prompts an acknowledgement that the hated enemy remains a human being—a concept that may be subversive on the battleground, which is why military recruits-in-training are frequently encouraged to call the enemy dehumanizing names. Without that psychological shield, how many men raised with civic and possibly religious values could be brought to kill another young person like themselves? Empathy can be equally subversive in other circumstances as well; for example, dehumanization is a prime tool of tyrants seeking to divide ethnically diverse populations and create hatred, whereas feeling empathy for others has the potential to sabotage such propaganda.

Whatever might be done at the level of recruit training, Robert McNamara now thought that understanding events from an opponent's point of view ought clearly to be a strategic element of military planning at the *officer* level, and he illustrated this with a story. In 1995, long after the Vietnam War had ended, he travelled to Vietnam to talk to the man who was North Vietnam's foreign minister during the war years. The meeting was a revelation. "I was shocked, because it became clear to me that we didn't understand them and they didn't understand us," he told me. "For us, the war was about keeping the security of the West from weakening by preventing the Communist Chinese and the Communist Soviets from controlling South Vietnam. We thought they wanted to use it as a base from which to extend their operations across East Asia and South Asia. But *they* thought of it as a civil war. They actually saw us as a colonial power, substituting for France."

"[The foreign minister] told me, 'You were totally wrong. We were fighting for our *independence*, and you were fighting to enslave us.' He said, 'Mr. McNamara, if you had ever read a history book you would have known that we are not the pawns of the Chinese or the Russians. We have been fighting the Chinese for a thousand years. No amount of pressure from the United States would have stopped us from fighting for our national independence.'"

I remain as surprised by his words today as I was the day he spoke them, for I too have come to believe in the (positively) subversive power of empathy in world events, as much of the present book makes clear.

But something else had become central to Robert McNamara. In his old age he had revisited his early study of ancient Greek philosophy. The moral foundations of that thinking interested him, he told me, and he had returned to that long-forgotten part of himself in his search for the foundations of a good life.

He had also been much influenced, he said, by his reading of T.S. Eliot. As part of my preparation for our meeting I had learnt that his late wife, Marg, had brought to his attention some lines from "East Coker—1940," the second of Eliot's "Four Quartets," and the work had become increasingly important to McNamara. He had quoted them in one of his earlier exculpatory works, and I repeat some of them here.

Old men ought to be explorers
Here or there does not matter
We must be still and still moving
Into another intensity…

In my end is my beginning…

We shall not cease from exploration

And the end of all our exploring
Will be to arrive where we started
And know the place for the first time...

Sadly, despite his remorse and new insights, Robert McNamara's main legacy is likely to be the so-called "McNamara Fallacy," something I was unaware of when we met. McNamara's understanding of war had previously been purely quantitative. He believed that by increasing enemy-soldier deaths and minimizing one's own, victory was assured; and he would not be dissuaded by critics who pointed out that guerrilla warfare and civilian resistance can thwart this formula. As McNamara developed a list of metrics to allow him to follow the progress of the Vietnam War in a presumably scientific manner, U.S. Air Force Brigadier General Edward Lansdale reportedly told him that he was not considering the feelings, and possible subsequent behaviour of the common people of rural Vietnam. McNamara wrote this down for possible later consideration, then immediately tore up the sheet of paper, telling Lansdale that if he could not measure it, it must not be important.

Today, the McNamara Fallacy is employed as a warning across many fields. That the qualitative—the human, the ineffable aspect that cannot be quantified—also counts is something he came to embrace as he tried to make amends before his life drew to an end. Perhaps it was his memory of having rejected the importance of what Edward Lansdale had tried to tell him that led him back to the ancient Greeks, to poetry, and to thoughts about the power of empathy.

THE DATE IS MARCH 2, 2003, and I have just arrived in Paris. I've come to Europe to witness the inauguration of the International Criminal Court in The Hague, and I have routed myself through my favourite city. Just off the plane, I breathe in a familiar scent, a passing trace of Gitanes cigarettes suffused with espresso coffee; both project a sensuous "Welcome home."

From the window of the train that shuttles passengers into the city, I observe the degradation of Paris's northern suburbs. For the entirety of my acquaintance with this metropolis, these suburbs have been poverty-stricken places where immigrants land; but now they are worse. Open garbage and gang-style graffiti spread across open spaces. At one Metro station, two youths try to snatch the purse of an Asian woman as she boards the car. She screams, and they run away. One reason these suburbs have long distressed me is that so few, even the French-born, ever manage to leave them. Discrimination against those whom the French once fought in the lost colonial war over Algeria has hampered integration. These suburbs have become explosive places populated by the angry young.

My little hotel resides on the *rue Monsieur-le-Prince* at the heart of the student Latin Quarter. I remember it well, including the next-door restaurant where I stop for lunch. Claude and I dined here a lifetime ago when I was pregnant with my first born. I stroll up the *boulevard Saint-Michel* towards the River Seine, stop for a *crêpe au sucre*, then suddenly find myself peering into the café *Le Lutèce*, where I first met Claude, looking handsome in his snazzy sunglasses and interesting because he was reading *Le Monde*. I think that without that chance meeting in this café my children would not be in the world. It is an odd thought. A failed marriage produced two lives that live at the core of my own. And now there is another generation.

I have reached the Seine. On the other side of the river, the bells of Notre Dame are pealing, calling the faithful to evening mass. The famous façade shimmers rose-pink in the fading light. Across the river and inside its great doors, I inhale a second familiar whiff: incense and tapers. I have long intuited why Paul Claudel converted to Catholicism at a mass, for its accoutrements are wholly sensual. Sometimes I wonder why I feel so at home in European cathedrals—I, a Jewish woman born in Canada of Eastern European immigrants. Is it the fact of having attended mass with Claude's family at an impressionable age whenever we visited Bayonne? Or of having had the culture and liturgy explained to me by Tom, with his inimitable grasp of art and civilization? I don't know the answer, except that the atmosphere of these religious spaces moves me—until the familiar ritual of the liturgy becomes tedious, and the feelings start to run thin.

Today, a cardinal in a red skullcap stands at the altar. His profile is refined, unmistakably Jewish, and I recognize him immediately. He is Archbishop Jean-Marie Lustiger, whom I had met at a lunch in Toronto many years earlier, both of us guests of the French consulate. We had been seated next to each other, and I had told him about *Unhealed Wounds: France and the Klaus Barbie Affaire*, which had just been published in France. I hadn't seen him since, although in the 1990s, while in France to research *Long Shadows*, I had contacted him. But he told me he was leaving the country that day, and we had failed to reconnect.

For reasons I cannot define, I have always felt "close" to Jean-Marie Lustiger, a teenage convert from Judaism who had reached the apex of the French-Catholic hierarchy. His family were Polish immigrants, like mine. His mother had been deported to Auschwitz. He himself was saved by Catholic friends who hid him.

On becoming Archbishop of Paris in 1981, Lustiger had said: "I was born Jewish and so I remain, even if that is unacceptable for many. For me, the vocation of Israel is bringing light to the gentiles. That is my hope, and I believe that Christianity is the means for achieving it." He saw Christianity as following directly from Judaism, and he believed he could incorporate both. (A former chief rabbi of Paris said he once witnessed Lustiger entering the synagogue to recite kaddish, the Jewish mourners' prayer, for his murdered mother.) Clearly a complicated man, he reminded me of the fifteenth-century Spanish *conversos*, several of whom similarly rose to the apex of the Church; and also of the Canadian priest, Gregory Baum, another convert from Judaism with humanistic commitments. On the other hand, many in the French Jewish community, including Lustiger's own father, never forgave his conversion, while many Catholic conservatives never accepted it to begin with.

I edge myself into the crowd of worshippers standing on the north side of the altar. The world is holding its collective breath today, waiting for war in Iraq to erupt—perhaps that is why so many have come here to pray. Cardinal Lustiger is speaking about the Old Testament prophet Isaiah. I watch his expressive face. His voice breaks. He speaks about the loving bond of Jesus with his people, and about moral commitments in the face of a war that now looks inevitable. He says that, although conflict may seem unavoidable, we must remember free will. We are free to favour the path of peace, free to choose the path of justice. What we can always control is the way we choose to respond to events. And my mind travels into thoughts about how some Jews were able to face death during the Holocaust by making choices about who they were as individuals. Somehow, Cardinal Lustiger is giving me courage as a war in Iraq looms. The moment feels important, because I know that I am in Europe not just to attend the ICC inauguration, but also because I am beginning to write *The Sun Climbs Slow.*

IT IS MARCH 11, and I am in The Hague, seated high in the press gallery in the "Hall of Knights," the medieval parliament of the Netherlands. Little has changed in this room over the centuries. Two regal chairs decorated with crowns and gold velvet canopies are positioned together on a raised dais. On the walls are the coats of arms of the former Dutch, Bavarian, Burgundian, and Hapsburg rulers of the country, as well as the banners of the provinces and the overseas possessions of the kingdom. Below, the guests—more than a thousand human rights activists and representatives of eighty-nine states—walk down the centre aisle to assume their velvet-covered chairs. The eighteen newly elected judges of the court take their seats in the front rows; among them are the exceptional individuals I have described above.

I remember the detail of this scene, and not only because of the pomp and (literal) majesty (Queen Beatrix of the Netherlands was present, as was Jan Peter Balkenende, the country's prime minister). I remember it for its symbolism, for the fact that it happened against all historical and political odds. The world stood just a footstep past the violence and tragedy of the twentieth century, and in the shining newness of this new millennium, already shadowed by a new war, the inauguration of the International Criminal Court mirrored a moment of hope for humanity; in particular, hope for the thousands of civilian victims in whose names it would pursue accountability and justice.

Two speakers stand out in my memory. The first was Prince Zeid Ra'ad Zeid Al-Hussein, Jordan's representative to the United Nations. His commitment to the new court was palpable and personal. He was the president of the Assembly of States Parties, made up of the eighty-nine countries that had signed the Rome Statute, the legal treaty that would underscore and inform the work of the new tribunal.

He begins by acknowledging the encroaching war. "At the very moment when our planet lives with the very grave challenges threatening international peace and security, we assemble here to confirm once again our commitment to the international rule of law...It is an occasion the root of which is to be found in the first flickerings of human common sense...yet as humanity [progressed] toward the achievement we celebrate today, people throughout the world continued to suffer horrifyingly from genocide, war crimes, and crimes against humanity—a constant reminder of what had to be done."

Such high expectations: the hope that the International Criminal Court would help to deter future genocides and related crimes; that it would be fair and transparent in all its dealings; that it would create an accurate factual record of the cases it tried for the historical record; and that it would formally acknowledge the civilian victims who had survived these crimes.

In *The Sun Climbs Slow* I wrote this:

> Those who did not survive the crimes are invisible, but conspicuously present in this room. They are the millions whose lives were shattered across the violent timescape of the twentieth century: the women, men, and countless numbers of their hapless children in whose names this concerted struggle against the age-old impunity of the venal and the powerful is being launched.

The room fell silent after Prince Zeid spoke, a stillness suffused with grief, for, the press excepted, everyone present would have understood his words at their heart's core. The choreography of the event was perfect, for slowly, from a distant corner, emerged the hesitant, poignant sounds of the Nocturne from Alexander Borodin's *String Quartet No.2*. The partnered voices of violin and cello caressed the room, speaking the language of music to us when words failed.

"Do you think this will change anything?" a *New York Times* reporter sitting beside me whispered to her colleague.

I didn't hear the answer, if indeed there was one. Had she asked me, I wouldn't have known how to reply.

It was enough for me to feel the presence of the unrequited dead as they waited for justice to be done. It was enough to know that they, like me, were watching and listening with hope.

CHAPTER TWELVE
THE CANADIAN HOMELAND

IT WOULD BE REMISS of me, in a book like this, not to examine my own country, for the collective Canadian psyche has also been disturbed by the truths of long-hidden history, such as the discovery in spring 2021, on the grounds of a former Indian Residential School, of unmarked graves containing the remains of hundreds of nameless Indigenous children—a discovery which fractured more than a century of official silence and public unawareness.

I shall come back to this transitional moment in Canada's history. Suffice it for the moment to note that, if the Canadian public was able to absorb news of this order, without the rejection that has characterized so many other nations faced with suppressed truths, it is perhaps because the distinctive trajectory of our cultural history, in combination with global attitudinal change regarding human rights, had made this possible.

Three endemic issues have historically spurred the evolution of federal government policies regarding rights and minorities, and the progression of Canada's public consensus on these matters. They are: the tensions between francophone Quebec and the anglophone "rest of Canada" that were present even before Confederation; the creation of Multiculturalism as government policy in the late twentieth century; and the perennially unresolved relations between Indigenous peoples and those who arrived in Canada as immigrants.

From the start, the victory of the English over the French on the Plains of Abraham in 1759 had a pyrrhic cast to it. The losers naturally lost influence in the territory, but they weren't going anywhere, and if the entity that became known as "Canada" in 1841 was going to survive the riots and insurrections of the era, there would need to be accommodation, for being now "the Province of Canada" didn't erase the cultural differences between French and English, or Catholic and Protestant. In the Province of Canada, both Catholic francophones and Protestant anglophones were determined to remain culturally unique, and the education of the next generation was key. Schools became a battleground, and the resolution that followed set the stage for future Canadian governance. A compromise, Article XI of the Common Schools Act of 1841, allowed for a separate school system, a duality that was later incorporated into Section 93 of the 1867 Canadian Constitution.

Nation-building of this kind has been the primary job-description of every Canadian federal leader. Their tools have been compromise and accommodation by means of civil legislation and legal precedent: case law, in other words, borrowed from the English, and based on custom and usage, which relies on the written decisions of judges in prior civil tribunals to assist judges in reaching a decision. (Reflecting the dual origins of Canada, Quebec civil law, on the other hand, mirrors the somewhat less supple French legal system of fixed statute law.)

In *Jews: An Account of their Experience in Canada,* I explored Quebec's pervasive nineteenth-century struggles with majority-minority relations, including its subsequent flirtation with overt fascism in the 1930s. I told the story of Ezekiel Hart, who, although duly elected in 1807 and again in 1808, was prevented from taking his seat in the Quebec legislature because he wished to swear allegiance on the Hebrew bible. A contemporary journal,

Le Canadien, the organ of the Parti Canadien, published a poem denouncing the prospect of allowing a Jew to take a seat as more inane than Caligula's appointment of his horse as a Roman consul and priest. Party leader Pierre-Stanislas Bédard claimed that "...no Christian nation had granted Jews the rights of citizens, not for unjust reasons, but because they themselves do not wish to be part of any country. They may make a country their residence to pursue their business dealings, but never their home. This state of affairs is a result of the Jewish tradition, which requires Jews to wait for the Messiah, their prince; while waiting, they cannot pledge allegiance to any other prince."

The Hart affair, as it was known, was followed by alternating periods of liberalism and religious or secular nationalism, and historically, the sources of nationalist anxiety in Quebec have varied. More recently, they have included the veiled "money and the ethnic vote" accusation by Jacques Parizeau following the 1995 referendum. Historic ambiguities over who is a true Québécois have persisted into the twenty-first century to settle more recently on Muslims, especially Muslim women; and in the 2020s acts of secular integralism became more prominent still as provincial politicians introduced legislation forbidding those who work in the public service to wear religious garb (Bill 21), along with a parallel bill to promote the formal recognition of French as the only official language in Quebec through a proposed revamping of the Charter of the French Language (Bill 96).

As a life-long lover of French language and culture, I am sympathetic to the desire of many Québécois to preserve their civilisation in the sea of anglophone North America, and especially to their need to turn their backs on the sombre era of the despot premier Maurice Duplessis. I was proud to record the turbulent days of the Quiet (and not-so-quiet) Revolution in the 1970s, when I interviewed several of the major players with the intention of bringing their thinking to readers in English Canada. But my own explorations over the decades have convinced me that the temptation to discriminate against "the other" is both perennial and dangerous, especially in an ethnically diverse country such as Canada, where respect for equality and human rights is not only written into the Constitution but is a cornerstone of necessary accommodation. Unless we wilfully blind ourselves to what is obvious, no amount of rationalizing on the part of Quebec politicians about "preserving our values" can obscure the fact that preventing citizens from assuming public service jobs on grounds of religious apparel is outright discrimination and a marker of inequality. Values—paradoxical as it might seem—are always subject to revision. In Canada, it was once a value, for example, to prevent so-called lesser peoples—that is to say, anyone who wasn't of British origin—from immigrating to this country. And it was a "value" to want to attempt to forcibly assimilate Indigenous children into Christian Canada.

In twenty-first century Canada, Quebec has proposed its own peculiar trade-off: assimilate to the state religion of secularism in order to gain the full benefits of citizenship. This is no simple demand. Adherents to faiths that oblige their followers to wear certain apparel in public cannot choose to behave differently without finding themselves in breach of their core religious commitments. Their only choice is to forego working in certain public places specified by a government which rejects their right to express their core identity in such places—and this makes them second-class citizens.

How did stating this obvious fact of discrimination become a reprehensible act? During the English-language federal election debate of September 2021, the moderator, Shachi Kurl, asked Bloc Québécois Leader Yves-François Blanchet why he supported discriminatory laws such as Bill 21 and Bill 96. An uproar ensued, followed by simulated outrage on the part of the competing federal leaders, who understood that the potential pay-off was votes in Quebec, and were thus willing to overlook breaches of citizenship rights. Watching this debate on television, I thought about my childhood "friend," George, whose book *Nineteen Eighty-Four* satirized similar distortions. In Orwell's dystopian society, the "Ministry of Truth" determined what was fact by citing Party doctrine. The denial of glaring evidence of prejudice in Quebec was no less nonsensical.

An Environics Institute for Survey Research poll on Canadian attitudes towards national unity and "being Canadian," coincidentally completed in

September 2021, demonstrated that, while most Canadians, *including* the Québécois, continued to feel pride in their Canadian identity, the numbers were dropping. The authors concluded that the discovery of the graves of children at former residential schools likely contributed to the decline, as did negative spill-over from the chaos of the Trump era in the United States. Feelings of support for national unity had also declined, although they remained in the majority column, suggesting that the nationalist sabre-rattling of provincial politicians did not reflect widespread anti-Canadian sentiment among their constituents, many of whom were content to reap the benefits their leaders were demanding from Ottawa while also remaining Canadian.

It is easy to understand the cultural anxiety that underpins the continuing efforts of Québécois leaders to find a comfortable place within the fabric of North America, but the failure of Canada's leadership hopefuls during the election of 2021, including the incumbent prime minister, to stand up for the equality rights under threat in Quebec was a sorry step backwards in the enduring struggle to resolve the troubled legacy of the Plains of Abraham.

The second historical marker in the evolution of Canadian national identity was the policy of Multiculturalism brought into being by Prime Minister Pierre Elliott Trudeau one hundred years after Confederation, primarily to balance out other accommodations that favoured Quebec. It was a pragmatic choice, born of smart crisis management at a time when tensions ran high. The precipitating factor was the Quebec crisis of the 1960s and early 1970s.

In response to earlier rumblings in Quebec, the government of Lester B. Pearson had created the Royal Commission on Bilingualism and Biculturalism in 1963 to recommend means of improving interprovincial relations, but Paul Yuzak, a new senator from Saskatchewan, made a critical contribution. Canada, he argued, was not simply "bicultural," but "multicultural." His message that there might be reverberations in the "rest of Canada" about being left out of the Bilingualism and Biculturalism equation struck a nervous chord in Ottawa, and the Commission was asked to take account of the contribution made by other ethnic groups to the cultural enrichment of Canada, and how to safeguard that contribution.

On October 8, 1971, Prime Minister Pierre Elliot Trudeau announced to the House of Commons that Multiculturalism would become official government policy. In addition to becoming an officially bilingual country, Canada would formally respect the diversity of its citizens' languages, religions, and cultures. He faced no opposition.

To many, the proposal felt symbolic, even cringeworthy. The 1970s were not the 1930s, when immigrants from outside Britain were rejected as "unassimilable," leaving Poles, Ukrainians, Jews, and other cultural groups already in Canada unnerved and at risk. Didn't we already respect the diversity of language, religion, and culture unofficially? And were we really supposed to don national garb and sing and dance for one another? I well remember those summer festivals. In a single afternoon you could complete a culinary world-tour eating pizza, pierogis, spring rolls, and tortillas while listening to a mariachi band and a West Indian steel band and watching Ukrainian dancing. The political strategy behind it all was transparent.

But then the unexpected happened. Over the next decades, Multiculturalism lost its hokey qualities, as well as its capital letter, and evolved into an ingrained collective value. Canadians began to define themselves as citizens of a multi-ethnic, multi-religious society.

The face of the new policy started to become became visible in the early 1980s, when Canada admitted more than 50,000 Vietnamese refugees, many of them sponsored by ordinary Canadians who remembered the St. Louis, the ship filled with Jewish escapees from Nazi Germany that was turned back by Canadian officials in 1939. (My extended family in Toronto welcomed a refugee family from what was then called Saigon.) In 1982, Multiculturalism was written into the Canadian Charter of Rights and Freedoms. In 1988, under the leadership of Prime Minister Brian Mulroney, the Canadian Multiculturalism Act came into force. And we have since seen this Canadian ethos in action more recently as Canadians welcomed refugees from Syria and Afghanistan.

But an enduring demon lurks in mixed societies, waiting for release, and in the final days before the 2015 Canadian election, then-prime minister Stephen Harper opportunistically unleashed the demon of bigotry by proposing a public snitch line to report instances of "barbaric cultural practices," a measure widely perceived as targeting Muslim communities. Mr. Harper had significant public support for his snitch line, testifying to the perennial attraction of rejection—especially when the call came from the top. There were inevitable assaults on Muslims in the immediate aftermath. It is also worth noting that Mr. Harper lost the election partly for this reason, suggesting that a strong liberal consensus still characterized the Canadian polity.

It is undeniable that the language of otherness is recurrently seductive, maybe because many of us still harbour degrees of wariness about difference, and I have sometimes thought that binary feelings of "Us versus Them" may be inborn. Our first self-conscious act as infants is to differentiate ourselves from our mothers. As neighbours, we may want to differentiate ourselves from the people who live across town. As regions, we certainly differentiate ourselves—and as countries, of course. To learn to live with difference may be less inherently "natural" than the tacit agreements we make regarding the public and private good, such as, I promise not to steal your chicken if you promise not to steal my cow—a social contract in which we adopt certain attitudes to keep the peace which then becomes ingrained. All communities must adopt this implicit contract or else fail—and in Canada, an immigrant-based society from the start, we have had to learn this truth repeatedly. We're still learning it, as we may observe every time an issue of inter-cultural misunderstanding grows hot enough to hit the news before some kind of accommodation cools things down.

Prime Minister Pierre Elliott Trudeau's single most important statement, as he introduced his new policy of Multiculturalism, was that no single culture could, or would, define Canada—in other words, there would be no single, supposedly superior culture to assimilate *to*. Canada has since become the most successful multiethnic society in the world.

When the Iron Curtain fell in 1989, delegations from eastern and western Europe descended upon Ottawa to learn how Canada integrated hundreds of thousands of new immigrants annually. At the forefront of this success was a Canadian attitude towards inclusiveness that has persisted, despite periodic hiccups.

In September 2021, the Environics Institute, in partnership with the Century Initiative, updated its research on Canadian attitudes concerning immigrants and refugees. The results indicated that Canadians continued to be positive about both, most people viewing them as making a constructive contribution to the country. A clear majority of respondents supported current high levels of immigration, viewed immigrants as good for the Canadian economy, and believed they were important for building the country's population. A plurality also rejected the idea that too many 'refugees' are illegitimate, and there was clear public support for the decision to accept 20,000 Afghan refugees fleeing the Taliban. One in four even said that number was too few. Although concerns centred around the belief that some immigrants were not adopting Canadian values, the proportion articulating this view was not on the rise, and only 2 percent of these respondents named any specific ethnic or cultural groups they believed should be kept out of the country. When asked to explain their position, the top answer among those who had a positive view of immigration was that immigration enhanced multiculturalism.

I was surprised by the positivity of this report, because elsewhere in the world nativism and populism were challenging the postwar liberal order. While it is true that our welcoming attitudes might well be contested were Canada geographically located on the Mediterranean, where boatloads of desperate migrants seeking sanctuary arrived in rickety vessels, our postwar history of growing diversity and increasing tolerance of difference has shaped us in unique ways. The Quebec model aside, Canadian multiculturalism has favoured integration, not an impossible demand for full assimilation into an overly defined national identity. We cope with flexibility by being reeds, not pokers, as the saying goes. The willingness to eschew rigid ideologies and to compromise remains the secret of Canada's success.

The Canadian experiment with multiculturalism has sometimes reminded me of the period of *convivencia* in medieval Spain, where pragmatic Muslim leaders understood that flexibility and compromise were useful tools to keep the peace in a religiously diverse environment. Christians, Jews, and Muslims lived freely under the canopy of Muslim Andalusia, and when the ethos of tolerance spread north, they lived under the broader canopy of Hispania, just as our diverse population lives freely under the canopy of Canada.

But let us not forget that *convivencia* failed. Earlier in this book I detailed how and why it fractured so spectacularly, leading to often forced conversions of Jews and Muslims to Catholicism; a Holy Inquisition to test the authenticity of these conversions; and two ethnic expulsions from the country that both groups had inhabited for a thousand years. There is no guarantee of long-term success in diverse societies—which is why the protection afforded Canadians by their own commitment to multiculturalism must be defended by responsible leaders and nurtured, generation after generation, by themselves.

The third marker-issue in Canada's cultural history has been the country's relationship with Indigenous peoples. Like most other Canadians born of immigrant backgrounds, I knew little of this occulted history. It was not on the Ontario school curriculum when I grew up, meaning that most of us knew little if anything about the Indian residential schools. Textbooks referenced the original Indian wars, but what happened to the Indigenous populations as the entity known as Canada emerged was obscured. The lives of Canada's Indigenous peoples were hidden in plain sight, viewed from afar through a disparaging racist lens. On the other hand, I think many of us may have intuited that something was amiss, and that we still may have chosen not to look too closely. The looking away included those at the top. In late 2021, former prime minister Jean Chrétien claimed in a French-language television interview that, during his time as Minister of Indian Affairs and Northern Development from 1968 to 1974, he was not aware of the abuses taking place at residential schools, and tactlessly compared the experience to that of his own childhood boarding school in Quebec. Many refused to believe he didn't "know," but they did not include me. Earlier in this work I spoke of a particular kind of blindness—that protective affect we sometimes call into play when we encounter circumstances that threaten the way we understand the world.

The long silence surrounding the history of colonial-indigenous relations in Canada began to fracture as the truth about racist policies and physical abuse in Indian residential schools climbed to the surface of public awareness. During the first decade of the new millennium, Canadians learned that 150,000 children had been forcibly removed from their homes and placed in residential schools run by often abusive religious authorities, mainly Catholic. The purpose of the schools was to assimilate the children by all possible means—language, dress, culture—and to be in breach of these rules invited punishment. Canadians learned that the children living in these 139 institutions were underfed; that many were subject to sexual assault; and that disease, neglect, and abuse had killed at least 6,000 of them.

Then in spring 2021, direct evidence of these long-buried crimes appeared literally just beneath the skin of the earth. A radar search uncovered the remains of 215 children at the Kamloops Indian Residential School, and it was widely assumed that there were thousands more elsewhere.

The discovery of the bodies of maltreated, unnamed children unleashed a cascade of grief. That this had continued for a century in the land of "peace, order, and good government" elicited outrage. In a column in *The Globe and Mail*, I mused that Canada had never been an entity of "two solitudes," as we had imagined. We had always been a nation of "three solitudes," the third being the invisible culture of the Indigenous peoples and their history.

Canadians would learn that the era during which indigenous cultures were systematically decimated while their children, called "savages," were forcibly removed from their parents to be "civilized" into the ways of Christ and the British Empire, had effectively just ended, and that this period had encompassed almost the entirety of Canada's history.

We may well ask how it happened that these truths finally penetrated the broad collective consciousness. The discovery of the graves made it hard to turn away, although "blindness" might have continued regardless in an era when the media exhibited much less interest in this sort of topic. It was a gradual evolution in social attitudes that made it possible for these buried truths to emerge, for by the turn of the millennium the Canadian federation was a far different place than it had been in the mid-twentieth century. In the 1990s, the end of the Cold War had opened a new era for global rights and international law, including the International Landmines Treaty (a Canadian initiative) in 1997; the inauguration of the International Criminal Court (another largely Canadian initiative) in 2003; and the doctrine known as "The Responsibility to Protect" (still another largely Canadian initiative) in 2005.

It was also—to put things in a broader context—a time of "democracy expansion" on the part of the U.S., now suddenly a single world power. International non-governmental organizations, including human rights groups, operated transnationally and flourished. And in many places, events had cracked open the closed doors of the past. In France, it was the return of the Nazi war criminal Klaus Barbie for trial in 1983. In Germany, it was the long-term effects of international youth revolutions of 1968, which emboldened a new generation to demand answers about their fathers' and grandfathers' wartime lives. In South Africa, it was the corrosive failure of apartheid governance, and the need to expose its workings to rebuild society under a different model.

On June 11, 2008, in a moving ceremony on behalf of the Government of Canada, Prime Minister Stephen Harper apologized to the survivors of Indian residential schools. This was immediately followed by the creation of a Truth and Reconciliation Commission, whose primary goals were to acknowledge and record the residential school experience, including its generational consequences; to provide emotional support to individuals wishing to come forward with their stories; and to educate the Canadian public about what had been done in their name. I found the broadcast sessions of the TRC affecting, but there was a major structural flaw:

unlike the South African experiment in the genre, there were no prospective consequences for the *perpetrators*—in other words, no accountability. The Harper government had carefully excluded legal culpability from the commission's formal mandate. The TRC would "not hold formal hearings, nor conduct a formal legal process...." the document read.

With the Commission thus hobbled, the perpetrators—primarily, though not exclusively, priests and nuns of the Catholic Church—were paradoxically allowed to behave like social workers to the very community they had harmed. (Their limited role was to comfort the survivors as they completed their testimony.) It was true that individual bishops had issued apologies, to be joined (in late 2021) by an apology from the Canadian Conference of Catholic Bishops. There were also signs that the Vatican might soon do the same, an important step forward. But at the Truth and Reconciliation Commission, no person or entity would be held legally accountable for decades of abuse.

How much more compelling it would have been, I said publicly at the time, had Canadians been allowed to watch the upper echelons of the clergy testify to what they knew about gross breaches of human rights and possible criminal behaviour, even if the original perpetrators were dead. Ottawa may well have feared the emergence of evidence that successive Canadian governments had known about the abuse and did nothing. It is worth noting that *as early as 1907*, a lawyer who conducted a review of the schools told Duncan Campbell Scott, then deputy superintendent-general of Indian Affairs, that *"doing nothing to obviate the preventable causes of death brings the Department within unpleasant nearness to the charge of manslaughter."* [my italics, EP]

I also uncovered a personal connection between my own work and Canada's emerging acknowledgement of its past. *Long Shadows* may have directly inspired the formal apology by the Government of Canada in 2008. I can't remember who alerted me to this, but I looked up Hansard and saw that, on May 1, 2007, Gary Merasty, a Liberal member of parliament from Saskatchewan, had moved the following:

> That this House apologize to the survivors of Indian Residential Schools for the trauma they suffered as a result of policies intended to assimilate First Nations, Inuit and Metis children, causing the loss of aboriginal culture, heritage and language, while also leaving a sad legacy of emotional, physical and sexual abuse.

Merasty then cited my work:

> In her book, *Long Shadows: Truth, Lies and History*, Canadian author Erna Paris examines the manipulation of history, using examples from all over the world, and how countries shape historical events in the aftermath of tragic events. She argues that decisions made by those in power cast long shadows into the future, and that countries must confront these painful episodes in order to resolve them and heal as a nation....
>
> It appears as though there is a disconnect between the version of history put forth by a prime minister...to a foreign audience that British approaches to the aboriginal populations were some of the fairest and most generous of the period. This greatly diverges from the version of history put forward by the testimonials of the survivors, federal government department officials from the time, and the extensive work of the Royal Commission on Aboriginal Peoples. Among others.
>
> This disconnect is precisely what Erna Paris wrote about. That is how the past is managed by those in power today to suit present day needs. I have to ask whose perception and whose needs the prime minister's...statements suit. I can say that they are not tailored to suit the truth....

The motion passed unanimously.

THE INADVERTENT DISCOVERY THAT my book had inspired a historical event of this order was an unparalleled moment in my life. It is true that publishing is currently in decline, and that many authors ask themselves why they bother to indulge in the solitary labour-intensive activity known as book writing when the current shelf life of new works may be just a few weeks. The role that *Long Shadows* played in symbolically helping to right a grievous historical wrong mitigated that reality for me, as did the role the same book played in the United States, when it was the inspiration for a Congressional motion to build a monument to the slaves on the Washington Mall. Both these outcomes suggested to me that books can still matter, even in a fractured Internet age.

Canada is the only country I have studied whose ignominious past was so well hidden that its own citizens were almost entirely unaware of the human rights crisis taking place under their noses. There are several possible explanations for this. The first is that public ignorance, in part a consequence of the fact that school textbooks omitted any version of this history, obviated the need for governments to construct an alternative, more truthful narrative about what had occurred. The second explanation may be the sheer physical size of Canada, meaning that residential schools were often located in remote, unvisited areas. A third possible reason was the widespread prevalence of assimilationist ideology: a few non-Indigenous Canadians may have known something about the residential schools, but their existence was deemed acceptable because they were believed to be helping First Nations children become, well, more like us. And if you believed that this was in the best interests of everyone, there *was* no human rights crisis to be concerned about....

The author who best retells the story of the aftermath of residential school trauma is, in my view, the Ojibwe journalist Tanya Talaga. Her 2017 book *Seven Fallen Feathers: Racism, Death, and Hard Truths in a Northern City* connects the dots between contemporary miseries and past abuses through profiles of several high-school age children

who left their northern reserves for schooling in the Ontario city of Thunder Bay, where the police force has been accused of ignoring their subsequent deaths through inadequate investigations. The wretched lives of these damaged students disturbed me in the reading. They arrived in the "big city" without orientation and with little personal resilience; their families of origin were frequently dysfunctional; alcoholism was rife throughout the generations; drinking until they fell unconscious was these children's sole leisure activity, with predictably deadly results. Talaga's book is a primer for the uneducated, which included me.

In late 2021, reconciliation between Indigenous and non-Indigenous Canadians was only beginning. The Canadian Conference of Catholic Bishops may have offered an apology, but little in the way of badly needed reparations. (Documents revealed that the Church had tried to secure a release from the millions of dollars it owed to the survivors of residential schools). There had been some, but not enough, concrete repair. For example, many Indigenous communities still lacked clean drinking water in a land that held one of the largest renewable supplies of freshwater in the world, and where supply and sanitation are otherwise universal. The Federal Court found that Ottawa wilfully and recklessly discriminated against Indigenous children on reserves by failing to provide funding for child and family services, a ruling that could cost billions at a time when the Canadian government was over-extended because of the COVID-19 pandemic. However, the moral pressure to act in the name of reconciliation had also increased exponentially.

While realistic financial reparations remained in dispute, symbolic gestures abounded. These included the lowering of the Canadian flag to half-mast on Parliament Hill to mourn the still-unknown numbers of dead children, and the inauguration of a National Indigenous Peoples Day and a National Day of Truth and Reconciliation, during which many Canadians wore orange in memory of the lost children. However, while it is good to be moved by symbols of goodwill, in the long term it is the commitment of money for the repair of damage done that will matter.

Most Canadians seem eager for such repair, and to date the most important of these is that school curricula at every grade are being emended to teach young people about Canada's historic third solitude in the hope of rectifying collective ignorance. School texts are key, which is why they are battlefields in the struggle to bring truth to national memory in places where a falsified historical narrative has taken hold. As noted earlier, Saburo Ienaga, a professor of education in Tokyo, Japan, sued his government for censoring textbooks, including his own. In France, Serge and Beate Klarsfeld were eventually successful in having school history texts teach the truth about the Vichy government's collaboration with the Nazis in deporting Jews to Auschwitz, almost a half century after the events. Only Germany, in its attempts at national recovery, adopted the educational tool early.

There is, however, a caveat to this good will, for, even with the best intentions, the transition from ignorance to knowledge to hoped-for reconciliation will likely take decades or longer, just as it has in other places, for entrenched ways of viewing the world have a way of sinking deep roots, and the money required to effect substantive change is often in short supply. This timeline may be hard to tolerate in the age of Internet and social media, where the expectation of split-second responses, including pat solutions, is customary.

We may reasonably hope that the current presence of goodwill and supportiveness will sustain the present trajectory towards acknowledgement, and that reconciliation will follow. What is undeniable is that Canada sought to silence the vibrant voices of those who originated not elsewhere, but here. And that these voices are now returning to our land.

CODA

THIS BOOK GESTATED FOR a very long time before it was written; and even after I began, it trailed over an entire decade. I needed to chart my writing life as a path I came to recognize only as I re-travelled it. I needed to make sense of the decades of exploring I had felt compelled to undertake—decades of "hunting history" without always knowing what I was looking for. The way forward was not always obvious.

The world has become a different place since I began my writing career in the 1970s. When I started out, the postwar economy was still booming. The Holocaust had inspired the Nuremberg Tribunal, where major criminals were prosecuted according to evolving international law rather than summarily executed. Global institutions had been created, and more were envisioned. The promise of my Sunday School days at Holy Blossom Temple, where I was taught that the world was becoming a better place, did not seem too naïve. And it seemed that the postwar mindset would continue, for by the 1990s there were few alive who, based on their own experience, might have contested such optimism.

Then the American tragedy of 9/11 redirected the world back to war, and to mass migrations of civilian refugees that, in their turn, triggered the re-emergence of solipsistic nationalism (epitomized in the person of Donald Trump) and the slamming of once-welcoming doors.

At the end of this long journey, several thoughts emerge. First, I am convinced that social peace in democracies can only be sustained through strategic policy-making and constant vigilance, especially in ethnically mixed societies, and that this necessary vigilance demands an educated population with the capacity to pay attention to the stories they are being told by their leaders (in other words, a learned capacity to recognize propaganda). This will almost certainly become more difficult, for the digital world of social media is today as anchored and permanent as was the printing press after its invention by Johannes Gutenberg.

The second thought that preoccupies me is the importance of justice and the rule of law: the acknowledgement of wrongdoing, accountability for criminal acts, recognition of and recompense to those who have been harmed, and the imperative to mount an attack on the criminal impunity of some who continue to commit the worst crimes humankind has known. The social balancing that I spoke of earlier is entirely dependent upon this: without a hope for justice, victims of crimes against humanity, including genocide, are never free from suffering down through the generations, a situation which is not only personally destructive, but potentially socially destructive too.

Finally, I have learnt that history cannot hide its hidden truths forever, regardless of fabricated narratives meant to conceal and mislead. Those most affected—the children of unacknowledged victims, for example—will eventually start digging into the past until its taboo secrets are revealed, forcing the societies in question to take heed and to take stock, sometimes at great cost.

In the final chapter of *The End of Days* I once again returned to my companion, George Orwell. I recalled that in an essay about Arthur Koestler, written during the dark days of 1944, Orwell wrote despairingly, "It is possible that man's major problems will never be resolved." But as a democratic-socialist utopian, he could not tolerate the implications of his own words. "It's unthinkable!" he added immediately. "Who is there who dares to look at the world today and to say to himself, 'It will always be like this, even in a million years...?'"

I imagine that he might have thought for a while before he added this: "Perhaps the choice before man is always a choice of evils.... Perhaps even the aim of Socialism is not to make the world perfect, but to make it better."

Since childhood, Orwell's thinking has helped shape my own emerging views. I have "hunted history," but caught only glimpses of its power to shape the present and the future. As for the past, it "can only be managed," I once wrote, "with remembrance, with accountability, and with justice—however frail, however inadequate, however imperfect."

As for myself, my quest, if I can call it such, has often reminded me of a phrase sometimes attributed to Hannah Arendt:

"The luckiest writers are those who find a subject that is worth a life."

# ACKNOWLEDGEMENTS

WRITING ACKNOWLEDGEMENTS FOR SOMEONE else's book is not a straightforward task—least of all your mother's posthumous memoir—but some people clearly deserve thanks: Matt Joudrey of At Bay Press, for bringing the book to publication; Michael Levine, Erna's agent and a longtime friend of the family, for indefatigably supporting her project; and Karen Clavelle, for her editorial guidance and care. Erna also benefited from advice and encouragement from numerous others during the long development of this project and we know she was grateful for their support, too.

It will come as no surprise to readers that family was central to Erna's life. In these pages she writes candidly about a complex relationship with her mother and, even more so, with her father, yet her love for them was unmistakeable and powerful. No one she loved could have doubted the sincerity of her affection, for she expressed it freely in both words and acts of care.

It is fitting, then, that she dedicated her first book—*Jews: An Account of Their Experience in Canada*—to four generations of her own Jewish family: her grandparents, Anne and Isaac Lipkin, and Ethel and Benjamin Newman; her parents, Christine and Jules Newman; her siblings, Peter R. Newman and Jill Solnicki; and us, her two children. Her second book, *Step-Families: Making Them Work* (which she did not mention in this volume), was written shortly after her marriage to Tom Robinson. It explored the delicate art of weaving new bonds in reconstituted families; and its dedication, simple yet telling, was to Tom and her children. All of her subsequent books were likewise dedicated to various combinations of Tom, her parents, her children, and her beloved grandchildren—Julia, Simon, and Jackie Paris—and to one close friend, the late writer David Lewis Stein, whom she mentions several times in this memoir.

We hesitate to speak for her, but we are certain Erna's deepest thanks would go to Tom, her life partner and greatest supporter. After her death, publishing this book became his overriding priority—a final act of devotion. She would have been heartbroken to know that he, too, would die soon afterwards, the victim of a tragic accident. But he, like her, continued to pursue his life's work and passions until the very end; and she might have seen a certain poetry, however tragic, in the fact that he passed away in Paris, a city that meant so much to them both. We also believe that our mother, ever fascinated by families and the legacies they pass through generations, would have been deeply moved to know that, in Tom's absence, her own children would see this book through to publication.

Finally, as this memoir revisits her earlier books, we wish to honour the many people who played a part in those publications. A complete list of individuals she thanked in those seven works appears below, assembled with care by Erna's youngest grandchild, Jackie.

Roland and Michelle Paris

People acknowledged by Erna Paris in her previous books

(*listed alphabetically*)

Irving Abella • Nidžara Ahmetašević • Jon Allen • Ewen Allison • Marc Aron • Katherine Ashenberg • David Assouline • Lucie Aubrac • Raymond Aubrac • Jennifer Barclay • Nikki Barrett • Marcia Basman • Cherif Bassiouni • Janice Bearg • Catherine Bergman • Haskel Besser • Shira Herzog • Michael Bouteiller • Renée Bouthot • Jean-Claude Buhrer • Henry Bulawko • Mossie Van Der Burg • Avraham Burg • Brian Burke-Gaffney • Mary Burton • June Callwood • Doris Cowan • Frank Cunningham • Lynn Cunningham • Louise Dennys • Jacques Derogy • Richard Dicker • Paul Druckman • Claudio Durán • Marcella Durán • Isolda Dyson • Annegret Ehmann • Bernice Eisenstein • Beverley Beetham Endersby • Aliza Factor • Bernie Farber • Charles Favre • Sead Fetahagić • Ronald Finegold • Thomas Frankl • Gerda Freberg • Stephen Friedman • Carole Garber • Jane Gelfman • Hermann Giliomee • Richard Goldstone • Gena Gorrell • Louis Greenspan • Penny Gross • Phyllis Grosskurth • Nelly Gutman • Mark G. Hall • Brandon Hamber • Günter Harig • Ruth and Berry Hayward • Samantha Haywood • Marion Hebb • Dorothy Hershfield • Alvin Holmes • Sam Hutamo • Yves Jouffa • Lila and Bob Julius • Raphael de Kadt • Hans-Peter Kaul • Ben Kayfetz • Thomas Keenan • Robert Kellerman • Aggrey Klaaste • Beate and Serge Klarsfeld • Charles Korman • Jacques Kornberg • Myrna Kostash • Nemanja Krajčinović • Robert S. Kriger • Kemal Kurspahić • Bora Kuzmanović • Michelle Lapautre • Malcolm Lester • Michael Levine • Jean-Pierre Lévy • Joel J. Levy • Sam Lipshitz • Tanya Long • Thomas Lutz • Minouche Mangnus • Alberto Manguel • Michael Marrus • Patrick Martin • Yoshiyuki Masaki • Yukiko Matsuda • Lillian Messinger • Anne Michaels • Ruth and Eric Miller • Tony Miller • Stephen L. Mitchell • Daniel Mogües • Ian Montagnes • Luis Moreno-Ocampo • Ed Morgan • Michael Mouland • Bandi Mvovo • Gilles Najman • Walter Neutel • Adam Newman • Chris Newman • Jules Newman • Peter R. Newman • Esther Nisenholt • Don Obe • Yossi and Devora Oreg • Pascal Ory • Maurus Pacher • Mladen Pandurević • Katie Paris • Michelle Paris • Roland Paris •

Gunther Plaut • Léon Poliakov • Julie Popkin • Richard H. Popkin • Mark Potoc • R. John Pritchard • David Refson • Alison Reid • Scott Richardson • András Riedlmayer • Heather Robertson • Tom Robinson • David Rome • Thom Rose • Danny Rubenstein • Pat Russo • Hanoch Smith • Geneviève-Dominique de Salins • Slavo Šantić; William Schabas • Michael Schellenberg • Klaus Schütz • Patricia Sellers • Vernon Seymour • Allan Shapiro • Maxine Sidran • Amela Simić • Dan Simon • Gail Singer • Catherine Sissé • Jill Solnicki • Victor Solnicki • Robert Spencer • Hilary Stanley • Alison Stein • David Lewis Stein • Janice Stein • Paul Steinhauer • Masamichi Sugihara • Akitsugo and Saori Taki • Katsukuni Tanaka • Kazuo Tanaka • Noboru Tasaki • Jean-Marc Théolleyre • André du Toit • Harold Troper • Mike Usiskin • Kathy Vanderlinden • Lucinda Vardey • Jacques Vergès • Duško Vidak • Marq de Villiers • Linda Walter • Joshua Washington • Penny Weaver • Gail Weber • Bruce Westwood • Margaret Woollard • Joseph Wong • Noelle Zitzer •

Her publications were also supported, in part, by the Canada Council for the Arts, Ontario Arts Council, Toronto Arts Council, Japan Foundation, and Banff Centre for the Arts.

Photo credit: Helen Tansey

Erna Paris, a frequent contributor to opinion pages of *The Globe and Mail,* was the author of seven acclaimed works of literary non-fiction and the winner of twelve national and international writing awards for her books, feature writing, and radio documentaries. Her works were published in fourteen countries and translated into eight languages. They included *The End of Days: A Story of Tolerance, Tyranny, and The Expulsion of the Jews from Spain* (1995); *Long Shadows: Truth, Lies,* and *History* (2000), which won the Pearson Writers Trust Non-Fiction Prize and the inaugural Shaughnessy Cohen Prize for Political Writing; *The Sun Climbs Slow: The International Criminal Court and the Struggle for Justice* (2008); and *From Tolerance to Tyranny: A Cautionary Tale From Fifteenth-Century Spain* (2015). Appointed to the Order of Canada in 2015, she was also a member of the Canada Committee of Human Rights Watch; a vice-president of the Canadian Civil Liberties Association; and a past chair of the Writers' Union of Canada. She completed the manuscript of this book shortly before she died of cancer in February 2022.

OUR AT BAY PRESS
ARTISTIC COMMUNITY

Publisher – Matt Joudrey

Managing Editor – Alana Brooker

Substantive and Copy Editor – Karen Clavelle

Consulting Editors – Roland and Michelle Paris

Graphic Designer – Lucas c Pauls

Layout – Lucas c Pauls and Matt Joudrey

Publicity and Marketing – Dani Arieli

Thanks for purchasing this book
and for supporting authors
and artists. As a token of gratitude,
please scan the QR code
for exclusive content from this title.